Popular Music in the Class

ALSO EDITED BY DAVID WHITT
AND JOHN PERLICH

*Millennial Mythmaking: Essays on the Power
of Science Fiction and Fantasy Literature,
Films and Games* (2010)

*Myth in the Modern World: Essays on Intersections
with Ideology and Culture* (2014)

LIBRARY OF CONGRESS CATALOGUING-IN-PUBLICATION DATA

Names: Whitt, David, editor
Title: Popular music in the classroom : essays for instructors / edited by David Whitt.
Description: Jefferson, North Carolina : McFarland & Company, Inc., Publishers, 2020. | Includes bibliographical references and index.
Identifiers: LCCN 2020018843 | ISBN 9781476671574 (paperback : acid free paper ∞) | ISBN 9781476638898 (ebook)
Subjects: LCSH: Popular music—Instruction and study—Outlines, syllabi, etc. | Popular music—History and criticism.
Classification: LCC MT10 .P79 2020 | DDC 781.64071—dc23
LC record available at https://lccn.loc.gov/2020018843

BRITISH LIBRARY CATALOGUING DATA ARE AVAILABLE

ISBN 978-1-4766-7157-4 (print)
ISBN 978-1-4766-3889-8 (ebook)

© 2020 David Whitt. All rights reserved

No part of this book may be reproduced or transmitted in any form or by any means, electronic or mechanical, including photocopying or recording, or by any information storage and retrieval system, without permission in writing from the publisher.

Front cover: (on screen) Bono of U2 on the Zoo TV tour in Cleveland on March 26, 1992 (photograph by Steve Kalinsky); classroom photograph by Syda Productions/Shutterstock

Printed in the United States of America

McFarland & Company, Inc., Publishers
Box 611, Jefferson, North Carolina 28640
www.mcfarlandpub.com

Popular Music in the Classroom

Essays for Instructors

Edited by DAVID WHITT

McFarland & Company, Inc., Publishers
Jefferson, North Carolina

For my mom, dad, and sisters Jennifer and Robin,
with whom I associate my earliest music memories

Acknowledgments

Some of my most vivid and cherished memories center around music. For example, I remember being around eight years old and playing my mom's *Elton John's Greatest Hits I* record on our stereo, being in high school and listening to Police, Donnie Iris, and English Beat albums with my friend Gordon Jones, driving from Michigan to Nebraska with my dad and sisters listening to Neil Diamond, Kris Kristofferson and Billy Joel cassettes, and seeing five U2 tours over 20 years around the San Francisco Bay Area with my friend Byron Bonsall. So, to all of my family, friends, concert buddies, and road trip companions, thank you. Those music moments made me who I am, and without you I doubt this book would have ever been created.

Next, I would like to thank my communication studies colleagues at Nebraska Wesleyan University for their constant support and enthusiasm. You inspire and motivate me each day to be a better teacher, and most importantly, a better person.

Sincere thanks to Layla Milholen and McFarland for, once again, giving me the opportunity to create another book. A fist bump and high five also to Brian Robison who reviewed the Introduction, and John Perlich who provided feedback on my U2 essay.

Finally, I would like to thank each of the authors who contributed their time and effort to this project. I appreciate your patience, willingness to collaborate and good humor throughout the writing and editing process.

Table of Contents

Acknowledgments — vi

Introduction
  DAVID WHITT — 1

Part 1: Popular Music History and Genres

Highway 61: Alan Lomax and the Mythology of the Road in American Folk Music
  RAYMOND BLANTON — 7

"There is no revolution without songs": Teaching Latin American Resistance Music in the Spanish Curriculum
  EUNICE ROJAS — 23

Teaching the Music of Sunshine and Noir California: From "California Dreamin'" to "Straight Outta Compton"
  SHAWN SCHWALLER — 38

Remembering Tomorrow: Exploring the Deeper Transatlantic Story of the Birth of the Psychedelic Sixties
  TOM ZLABINGER — 53

Globalizing Jamaican Music: From Reggae to New Wave
  WILLIAM M. KNOBLAUCH — 72

Teaching Black Music as a Living Tradition: Pedagogically Connecting the Past to the Present
  JUSTIN PATCH — 85

Part 2: Artists and Icons

Good Rockin' in the Classroom: Teaching Elvis Presley and Popular Music
    JAY SCOTT CHIPMAN   103

Teaching the Beatles!
    JEFF MOHR   116

People, Hell and Angels: The Sociocultural Contributions to the Rise and Demise of Jimi Hendrix
    IGNATIUS CALABRIA   129

Songs of Ascent: Teaching the History, Music and Activism of U2
    DAVID WHITT   146

Part 3: Popular Music Analysis and Other Instructional Tools

Musical Identities: Teaching Race, Class and Gender Through Popular Music
    JAMES L. DEYS *and* JACOB A. DICKERSON   163

Patriarchy, Cross-Dressing, Agency and Violence: Women and the Pedagogical Opportunities in Heavy Metal
    DANIEL GUBERMAN   178

Music and Protest: Dissecting and Creating Social and Political Music
    MICHAEL W. MCFARLAND   194

Can Bro-Country Kill Your Parents? Using Shifting Musical Taste to Explore the Relationship of Youth and Parent Cultures
    CHARLES R. WARNER   207

Game-Based Learning in the Popular Music Classroom
    BRIAN ROBISON   222

About the Contributors   243

Index   245

Introduction

DAVID WHITT

Despite being a communication studies professor, and teaching courses in mass media and persuasion, I am not a particularly active user of social media. I quit Facebook in 2012, have no idea how to use Instagram or Snapchat, and use Twitter primarily as my news feed. When I do tweet the message typically leans toward the humorous rather than the political, commenting on popular culture, sports, or my dog. However, on January 7, 2017, I posted the following message:

> First, it was @TIME reporting about a class on Beyoncé and now @EW one on OutKast. I'll be expecting a call about my U2 class any day now.

My comment, half-joking and half-serious, was in response to *Time* and *Entertainment Weekly* posting articles on Twitter about college classes focusing on popular music artists. Given that I was teaching, for the third time, a college course on the Irish rock group U2 (discussed in my essay here), it seemed perfectly reasonable that my class should also receive recognition in these publications. I am still waiting for *Time* and *Entertainment Weekly* to contact me.

That tweet became the impetus for *Popular Music in the Classroom*. Classes on Beyoncé, OutKast and U2 are unique in higher education, and I wondered if there were others who developed courses on musical artists, genres, criticism or used popular music as a method of instruction. After essay proposals began to arrive in my inbox I was excited, and relieved, to see that there were. Moreover, the topic areas submitted quickly began to expand my idea of "popular music." Originally, my vision for this book was to include essays about musical artists and genres that were more mainstream such as country, rock, and rap. However, after reading several proposals it became apparent that popular music can also be more narrow in scope, reflecting geographic regions (folk in the American South) and political ideology (Latin

American protest music). Realizing that popular does not have to mean ubiquitous or trendy expanded the possibilities of what this book could be, and eventually, what it would become.

Music, Culture and Education

The origins of popular music, at least in the modern sense, followed technological innovations which triggered a gradual, but dramatic transformation in the recording, mass production and distribution of music. Inventions such as Thomas Edison's phonograph (1877) and Emile Berliner's gramophone (1887) were some of the earliest music playback devices, while the work of Nikola Tesla, Guglielmo Marconi and Lee de Forest in the late 19th and early 20th centuries built the foundation for radio. These mediums not only provided entertainment to millions, but also transformed American culture. For example, popular music in the 1930s and 1940s was dominated by the dance and big band swing of Glenn Miller and Benny Goodman, and crooners like Frank Sinatra and Bing Crosby.

However, in the 1950s this music was quickly overshadowed by rock and roll, with the more rhythm and blues and rockabilly stylings of Chuck Berry, Little Richard, and Elvis Presley. Consequently, a generational divide was created as kids no longer wanted to listen to what they perceived as their "parents' music," embracing rock and roll's sound, rebellious attitude, and fashion. Rock and roll at this time also broke down racial barriers as white teenagers would buy music by black artists, and segregated audiences would interact during concerts. Not surprisingly, many in the older generation, and even the press, were critical of rock and roll and its perceived negative effects on '50s youth. Over the next several decades the social and political influence of popular music would continue to be debated and discussed in relation to different artists (e.g., Bob Dylan in the 1960s), forms (e.g., MTV in the 1980s) and genres (e.g., rap and hip-hop in the 1990s).

Because of its widespread and transformational impact upon culture, popular music has been the subject of numerous books (histories, biographies, memoirs), television comedies and dramas (*The Monkees* [1966–1968], *The Partridge Family* [1970–1974], *Nashville* [2012–2018]), reality shows (*American Idol* [2002–2016, 2018–present], *The Voice* [2011–present]), television documentaries (*Time Life*'s ten-part series *The History of Rock 'n' Roll* [1995]), and even Academy Award–winning films (*Woodstock* [1970], *Ray* [2004], *Walk the Line* [2005], *Bohemian Rhapsody* [2018]). While these books, programs and movies line individual bookshelves and DVD collections, they have also been used by educators in the classroom to highlight a specific musical artist, genre, or event. However, the educational value of popular music is not limited to television and film clips. Not surprisingly, popular music is recognized as a subject of study in many higher education music departments. According to Walker (2007):

> Popular music is to be found now in practically all school music curricula across the western world. Most, if not all, university music departments include popular music as part of their academic and performance offerings, and a not insignificant number of university music departments across the world specialise in popular music studies [p. 103].

While university music departments are a natural fit for studying popular music, other disciplines have also embraced this rich area of study. Partridge (2014) explains:

> Not only is music per se now understood to convey meaning, but the social and cultural significance of popular music has been recognized and, consequently, the analysis of it has emerged as an established field of research, informed by a range of disciplines [pp. 13–14].

Indeed, popular music has been studied in English, history, modern languages, art, psychology, sociology, and religion courses, to name a few. Additionally, there are numerous academic journals that publish articles on popular music (*The Journal of Popular Music* has been around since 1988), and the Popular Culture Association and American Culture Association hold regional, national and international conferences with music falling under a number of different subject areas. Such diversity of scholarly inquiry reflects Middleton's (1990) contention that "[p]opular music is everywhere. It is at the centre of several crucial arguments concerning the nature of music, of culture and modern society" (p. v). Middleton's statement is something of an appropriate thesis for this book, but with the center of popular music, culture and modern society explored in the classroom. To that end, the authors in this book examine the history, musical catalog and sociocultural influence of a specific music artist or genre, and discuss readings, assignments, activities, audio-visual materials, as well as the successes and challenges teaching their respective popular music subject.

Overview

Popular Music in the Classroom is divided into three different sections. The first, "Popular Music History and Genres," takes a relatively loose, chronological journey through various genres of popular music including: American folk, Latin American protest music, music produced in and about California, psychedelic music, Jamaican reggae and new wave, and the roots of Black music through the concept albums of singer/songwriter Janelle

4   Introduction

Monae. The second section, "Artists and Icons," focuses on individuals and groups—Elvis Presley, the Beatles, Jimi Hendrix, and U2—who have left an indelible mark upon culture not only through their groundbreaking music, but also their style, concerts and activism. The last section, "Popular Music Analysis and Other Instructional Tools," is a mixture of criticism and methodology. The essays on identity, heavy metal and bro-country examine how popular music can convey messages about personal development, social groups and culture. Finally, the protest music and game-based learning essays provide artistic, analytical and entertaining teaching methods that encourage student creativity and critical thinking. The variety of topics and instructional strategies will be of interest to educators at all levels, musicians, and even the average music fan looking to learn more about music history, genres and influential artists.

Conclusion

At this point it appears neither *Time*, *Entertainment Weekly*, nor any other major news outlet will interview me about my U2 class, a journalistic oversight I have reluctantly come to accept. Instead, I hope this volume serves as a valuable resource for educators that has more influence and longevity than fleeting social media recognition. Perhaps this book will even inspire a teacher to develop a class or unit on popular music. Regardless, the study of popular music is worthy of our attention as music has been, and will always be, an important part of our history, culture and personal identity. As Bono, lead singer of U2, once said, "Music can change the world because it can change people." And, given my own experience teaching a class on U2, who am I to disagree with Bono?

References

Middleton, R. (1990). *Studying popular music*. Milton Keyes, UK: Open University Press.
Partridge, C. (2014). *The lyre of Orpheus: Popular music, the sacred and the profane*. New York: Oxford University Press.
Walker, R. (2007). *Music education: Cultural values, social change and innovation*. Springfield, IL: Charles C. Thomas.

PART 1

Popular Music History and Genres

Highway 61

Alan Lomax and the Mythology of the Road in American Folk Music

Raymond Blanton

> The stuff of folklore—the orally transmitted wisdom, art and music of the people can provide ten thousand bridges across which men of all nations may stride to say, "You are my brother."
> —Alan Lomax, "America Sings the Saga of America"

Ten Thousand Bridges

This book considers how teachers explore musical eras, innovators, artists, genres, events, and technological developments for what they reveal about our collective and individual identity and our cultural history. In particular, this essay explores the mythology of the road in American folk music (AFM) through the fieldwork of Alan Lomax—an ethnomusicologist (one who studies the social and cultural dimensions of music from the perspective of the people) with more than six decades of fieldwork as a folklorist. Specifically, I argue his work offers us an advantaged access point for apprehending meaning in AFM in twentieth-century American culture through the intonation of triumph and tragedy in the sounds and sentiments of everyday people. As we traverse these roads, I hope to help you see how AFM functions as an archetypal mythology that privileges encounters with the *other*.

To begin, I want you to imagine the history of music as a collection of roads that meander through various cultural regions and times. Along these rutted routes, as we get acquainted with specific times and places, we also encounter various artists. As students and teachers, what regions, times, and people have you encountered? What do these mythical poets and cultural stories indicate about who we are as a nation, as communities, or as individuals? As this essay is concerned, I argue that some of the most storied roads in contemporary music derive from the back roads of American hymns and ballads, cowboy songs, spirituals, field hollers, prison and work songs, protest songs, freedom songs, and the blues. More than historical relics, these people and their stories have and continue to animate contemporary music.

This is the music of the people—folk music. It is the music that Alan Lomax spent essentially all of his life encountering and collecting. Its indelible mark led him to declare that folklore is common to all mankind. In its purest form, it calls us to, as Alan Lomax (2003a) noted, "recognize the cultural rights of weaker peoples" (p. 91), demonstrating how music provides "ten thousand bridges across which men of all nations" stride to say, "You are my brother" (p. 91). As such, having incorporated the teaching of AFM into a broad range of courses, including *Communication in Popular Culture*, *Communication and Theology*, and *Public Advocacy and Civic Engagement*, I account for how the fieldwork of Alan Lomax animates our appreciation and understanding of the mythology of the road in AFM and conclude with four considerations—assignments, benefits, challenges, and recommendations—related to designing a course on AFM. In sum, on "Highway 61," otherwise known as the blues highway in the Mississippi Delta, we encounter more than bucolic sounds, but more so, brothers and sisters. In all, I hope this essay (and volume) contributes to your affinity for music and serves as a valuable resource for instructors looking to teach popular music in the classroom.

American Folk Music

Music plays a prominent role in the formation of both our individual and national identity, with people cohering around the underlying principles of individuality and nationhood promoted in the images, sounds, and stories propagated in our songs. This particular journey will acquaint us with the mythology of the road in AFM, leading us in spirit through the fields, porches, and prison farms of the Mississippi Delta, onto the streets and marches of the American civil rights movement (spirituals and freedom songs), over the airwaves of a contentious postwar America (protest music and classic rock), and into the clubs and streaming services (dance and electronic) of today.

Myth

Much of our national identity derives from the mythological stories found in our music. Our anthems and hymns exert a powerful influence on our collective consciousness as Americans, influencing attitudes, shaping values, and building beliefs. When we stand and sing the national anthem, "The Star Spangled Banner," at public sporting events, for instance, we are performing the mythic ritual of remembering and honoring America. In "Revolutionary Symbolism in America," civic and rhetorical theorist Kenneth Burke outlines his philosophy of myth as a social tool and psychological bridge for working together with others to promote social justice. In short, Burke contends that myths are not illusions, but rather, in the organization of the mind, perform very real and necessary social functions. Burke wrote:

> Myths may be wrong, or they may be used to bad ends, but they cannot be dispensed with [...] they are our basic psychological tools for working together. A hammer is a carpenter's tool; a wrench is a mechanic's tool; and a "myth" is the social tool for welding the sense of interrelationships by which the carpenter and the mechanic, though differently occupied, can work together for common social ends. In this sense a myth that works well is as real as food, tools, and shelter are [1989, pp. 267–8].

Comparably, I argue that music is one of our foremost social tools for working together with others for common social ends. Pedagogically, there is much we can learn from studying and listening to the fieldwork of Alan Lomax in the Mississippi Delta. Moreover, as it pertains to music as a mythic tool, the road plays prominently in the very essence of fieldwork (i.e., collecting music in travels, as well as in the themes and lyrics of AFM). More than a contemporary trend, the mythology of the road spans human history. We find it prevalent in the ancient Hebrew Exodus and their pilgrimages to Zion in the Songs of Ascent (Psalms 120–134). We also find it in the canons of secular history in both Homer's *The Odyssey* and Plato's *Phaedrus*. In sum, culturally and historically, musical stories oriented around journeys and roads animate human history. As such, I consider three aspects of Alan Lomax's fieldwork to explore how the mythology of the road develops in and through AFM.

Alan Lomax

The collected works of Alan Lomax provide a valuable resource for exploring the mythic dimensions of the road in American culture. For instance, Piazza (2013) has noted:

> His career was a tug-of-war between a profound respect for the indigenous expressions of culture and a relentless desire both to make those expressions available to as broad an audience as possible and to evolve some system, some narrative that could lend them all a common mythos [p. 54].

Of note in his work, is an affinity for the music of the people. Piazza has reminded us, Lomax was able to "record some of the last of a breed, musicians and singers who had been influenced only minimally by the commercialization not just of the music but of the music's context" (p. 53). To this end, Lomax's field recordings were filled with the intrusions of everyday life, the sound of a passing train or the chatter of friends and neighbors listening to a live recording. Indeed, when one grasps the full scope of his work, it is hard to imagine what our musical landscape might sound like without his and others' fieldwork. To be clear, though, I want Lomax's fieldwork to function as a bridge to accessing AFM. Alan Lomax is mere guide. The mythical and musical stories of the people are the focus. For distinction, I focus briefly on three song-collecting trips in the Mississippi Delta in 1933, 1941, and 1959, respectively, to demonstrate the breadth of his work on the road and how the road plays so significantly in the sentiments and songs of the people he encountered.

Myth and the Art of Recorder Maintenance: 1933

More than 35 years before Robert Pirsig embarked on a motorcycle odyssey through Minnesota and the Dakotas with his son Chris, leading to the renowned *Zen and the Art of Motorcycle Maintenance* (1974), John Lomax and his son Alan set out on the road in 1933 with their sound recorder in search of the folk songs of America. Alan Lomax wrote, "This past summer I spent traveling through the South with my father collecting secular songs of the Negroes, work songs, 'barrelhouse' ditties, bad-man ballads, and corn songs" (Cohen, 2003, p. 9). For months, they traveled 16,000 miles throughout the South, across Texas, Louisiana, Mississippi, Tennessee, and Kentucky to record and collect African American folk songs, including chants, work songs, hollers, spirituals, blues, and ballads (Gioia, 2008). They journeyed in a Model A Ford, traveling with only a few changes of clothes, two army cots and some camping gear, with the back seat removed to store all of their recording equipment. John and Alan Lomax were ballad hunters, driving all across America preserving the past before it disappeared forever (Scorsese, 2003). For days upon days, mile upon mile, father and son sped down "rutted highways, by night camping on beaches, washed over by birdsong and the cool Gulf breezes" (Hamilton, 2008, p. 98).

Along the way, they faced many moving individual singers and an abundance of overwhelming music. Interestingly, it was one of his first encounters on the road in the summer of 1933 that sparked a lifetime of collecting AFM. They were just outside of Dallas, in Terrell, Texas, when Lomax observed a young black woman passionately expressing herself in song while washing clothes:

> She started slow and sweet ... she sang faster and with more and more drive ... and as the song ended, she was weeping and saying over and over, "O Lord have mercy, O Lord have mercy" ... I was seventeen [and] embarrassed. But beneath ... I wondered

what made her voice soar so beautifully ... what sorrow lay behind her tears [Szwed, 2010, p. 36].

This moment, I argue, exemplifies what the moving mythical stories of the people can (perhaps should) do *to* and *for* us—move us, emotionally, bodily, and otherwise. Music, so often a leisurely backstory to our elevator rides or coffeehouse encounters, in this context, is something more substantial and essential. It reminds us, if not awakens us to the civic dimensions of music that should be explored in our coursework on musical history. And as one reads and listens to Lomax's work, it becomes clear that moments like this, at every stop along the road, convinced Lomax that collecting folk music must be done, at any cost.

Specifically, as Lomax and other folklorists collected AFM, moving through remote communities, plantations, lumber camps, and city streets, it would be the oldest prison system in Mississippi, Parchman Farm, where they encountered the source of some of the their most important and interesting work. Lomax considered the southern penitentiaries invaluable for African American folk songs, from which those who might never experience the men firsthand would encounter them through their poetry. Alan Lomax recalls the significance of these moments:

> The people who sang for us were in stripes and there were guards there with shotguns. They were singing there under the red-hot sun [...] but when they opened their mouths, out came this flame of beauty. This sound, which matched anything I'd ever heard from Beethoven, Brahms, or Dvorak. They sang with beautiful harmony, with enormous volume, with total affection. And this was the second stage of my conversion to my profession. I had to face that here were the people that everyone else regarded as the dregs of society, dangerous human beings, brutalized, and from them came the music, which I thought was the finest thing I'd ever hear come out of my country. They made Walt Whitman look like a child [Szwed, 2010, p. 49].

Ferris (2013) contends that Alan Lomax's passion for folk music is part of an ongoing American tradition with the likes of Walt Whitman, who in *Leaves of Grass* (1855) also celebrated the road as when he wrote (or sang) about gathering "the minds of men ... to know the universe itself as a road, as many roads, as roads for traveling souls" (Whitman, 1980, p. 142). At the end of the summer of 1933, John and Alan Lomax returned to Washington, D.C., with a collection of more than 100 songs. And in the winter of 1934, Lomax published his account of the trip in the *Southwest Review*, titled, "Sinful Songs of the Southern Negro."

Indeed, toward the end of his life, Lomax indicated that this particular trip was the occasion when he heard the music that first allied him with the people and made him "forget Beethoven and all that ... where black men ... under the shotgun had the glorious humanity to make great music" (Piazza, 2013, p. 30). Each of these encounters, by Lomax's own admission, were encounters that transformed him, possessing the same revelation of spiritual sight that the Apostle Paul received on Straight Street after his encounter on the Damascus Road (i.e., Acts 9: 1–19). More than a collection of recordings, Lomax's fieldwork attempted to preserve both the culture of song and the context of style and performance, believing that a collector with a pen and notebook could only capture an outline. In the people, and within their music, there was a mythic dignity, passed from generation to generation—lore that possessed a degree of artfulness that made living more possible. For the remainder of his life, Lomax would be concerned with that mythic image, as when he wrote in a letter to the Carnegie Foundation, "These songs are, more often than not, epic summaries of the attitudes, mores, institutions, and situations of the great proletarian population who have helped to make the South culturally and economically" (Szwed, 2010, p. 38).

Muddy in Mississippi: 1941

In late August 1941, Alan and his wife Elizabeth went on the road for a three-week trip to Mississippi to record revival sessions in collaboration with Fisk University in Nashville, Tennessee, and the Archive of American Folk Song with the Library of Congress. However, when they reached Mississippi on August 29, they learned the revival season was winding down and had missed their chance to record. Undeterred, they traveled to Coahoma County for a week to look over the area, where Alan Lomax and John Work had aspirations of finding the legendary blues guitarist Robert Johnson. In both their fieldwork, and most especially in the music of the people they encountered, the mythic character of the road becomes more distinct. Gioia (2006) provides an eloquent summary of mobility in AFM:

> Whatever truth there might be to these generalizations, the growing mobility of the African American workforce in the final decades of the nineteenth-century ensured that a tremendous cross-fertilization of songs and singing styles would take place. Black farm laborers would follow the ripening crops, migrating from place to place to find communities where pickers were in demand. Delta bluesman Muddy Waters recalled moving from the cotton fields to the berry harvest and the sugar beet harvest, then to the pea and bean harvest. His song "Rolling Stone" was written to describe these travels, which were often made by hopping onto passing trains. And where workers traveled, music came as well, thereby providing a constant exchange of work songs throughout the South and even beyond [p. 45].

Leaving behind the paved blacktop, Lomax and Work followed the dusty uneven roads into the country, driving mile after mile on the rutted roads that separated the cotton fields. As they drove, Lomax and Work could see black sharecroppers at work, hoeing and weeding in preparation for the harvest. They found their way to the Stovall Plantation, three or four miles outside of Clarksdale, where they drove up a narrow dirt road to a cabin, where they encountered McKinley Morganfield—the man who would become known internationally as Muddy Waters. Born in Rolling Fork, Mississippi, in April 1915, Waters spent his years picking cotton, usually for 50 cents a day, and humming on his harmonica or strumming a guitar. Looking out the back door of his home, he saw miles of cotton fields; out the front, across the dirt road, stretched the cypress swamps. According to Lomax, "Waters was bare-footed in raggedy overalls. He was very shy and his house was in the middle of one of those endless cotton fields" (Szwed, 2010, pp. 181–182). Waters, then just a 26-year-old tractor driver on the Stovall plantation, worked in the fields during the week and played for county dances on Saturday nights. Waters earned about $250 a year farming 16 acres of land, earning 21.5 cents per hour in addition to the income he acquired from his homemade moonshine whiskey at his home, which doubled as a juke joint on weekends. While Waters was more interested in having his music play on the jukebox than for a library, he played two songs on that day for Lomax, both steeped in the mythology of the road: "Country Blues" and "I Be's Troubled."

When Lomax later played back the music for Waters, it was then and there, on a Saturday afternoon, that he came to believe that he could inspire others with his music. In a sense, Waters inspired himself, but it was Lomax's willingness to return to the region, with the vision from his 1933 odyssey, that helped introduce us to Waters. For Waters, that August afternoon recording session was a first step toward his musical discovery and self-discovery. Gioia (2008) noted:

> Waters himself has remarked how hearing his own music played back that day radically changed his conception of himself, gave him an unprecedented sense of confidence as an artist and performer, and perhaps even an awareness of how he might reach others through his playing [p. 204].

What this encounter further demonstrates is how the road continues to play prominently in AFM through fieldwork, and that the essence of the stories Lomax recorded focuses on the plights of the people and the theme of the road at its center. Put differently, these encounters stress the importance of the road as an active mythology in the blues, possessing a "fascination with travel for its own sake, rooted in years of black captivity" (Palmer, 1981, p. 18). Passed down from generation to generation, these songs hold mythic meaning both for the people and our nation. More than just a prominent lyrical theme, the road in the blues possesses both archetypal and cultural myths. According to Mark Humphrey in Gioia's (2006) *Delta Blues,* the Delta tradition has the "weight of myth" in the music (p. 95). In part, this travel motif reflects the state of African American society in the first part of the twentieth century. According to Taft (2006):

> From the turn of the century to World War I, traveling was on the minds of African Americans, and this is reflected in the high frequency of "traveling" formulas in the blues. If a theme of a particular song was love or love troubles, there was a good chance that its underlying theme was movement: leaving town, going to some place, not having a place to go, going back home [p. 194].

The importance of movement in the blues is such that the formula *go to some place* is the most frequently recurring formula in the corpus.

James Carter and the Southern Journey: 1959

It was during Alan Lomax's first summer recording odyssey, as a teenager, that he experienced a firsthand look at the pain of the people through their songs. The prison work song, in particular, produced a deeply personal and active confrontation with real conditions. Lomax was "powerfully affected by what he heard and saw, and it would be a reference point for the world's music for the rest of his life" (Szwed, 2010, p. 49). So after returning home from a self-imposed exile in the British Isles, Spain, and Italy, it is not surprising, then, that Alan Lomax returned to the place and the people he encountered during his trips in the summers of 1933 and 1941.

It was during this period that Alan Lomax undertook his Southern Journey from August 24, 1959, to October 12, 1959, spanning more than seven weeks across eight states, producing 85 reel-to-reel tapes and more than 500 photographs. Discontent with simply recording the music, Lomax's notes spilled over onto the insides and backs of tape boxes, where he recorded details about the prisoners and what they talked about that day. Lomax was concerned with capturing the entirety of the moment, the "embodiment of the people and culture that produced the music, rather than just sounds" (Piazza, 2013, p. 44). During his Southern Journey, Lomax recorded 80 hours of music and conversation. Of note, within those 80 hours of recorded music, is a four-and-a-half-minute song titled "Po' Lazarus." Lomax considered "Po' Lazarus" one of the finest African American ballads he had ever heard or recorded, and "concerns the doomed attempt of an exploited and underpaid black laborer to even up the score by stealing the payroll from his bosses [...] set forth in stark and unforgettable language" (Kaye, 1997). Recorded at Camp B, Mississippi State Penitentiary at Lambert, "Po' Lazarus" features 33-year-old James Carter leading a group of male prisoners in song. In this rendition, Parchman prisoners perform in the "compact, bluesy call-and-response style of work-camp singing" that Lomax found permeated the Mississippi penitentiary system (Kaye, 1997).

At the time of Lomax's visit, Parchman had more than 2,000 inmates in segregated camps. Over the course of five days, Lomax recorded music in Camps 7, 11, and Camp B in Lambert. These recordings produced nine reel recordings and more than 100 photographs. In a retrospective book by Lomax titled *The Land Where the Blues Began* (1993) he wrote, "The faces of the prisoners, so shadowy and fawning in repose, so fiery and powerful in song, their touching and powerful melodies, their graceful, golden voices all conspired to win our allegiance" (Piazza, 2013, p. 78). One of the voices that inspired Lomax's loyalty was James Carter. On that day in 1959, unbeknownst to any of them, Carter, through the microphone of Alan Lomax, would leave his mark on American culture. That mark would come more than 40 years later when his song "Po' Lazarus" was featured in the opening of Joel and Ethan Coen's *O Brother, Where Art Thou* (2000), a Depression era film and its plot of singing convicts on the run. In the script, it is noted:

> In black, we hear a chain-gang chant, many voices together, spaced around the unison strike of picks against rock [....] They are black men in bleached and faded stripes, chained together, working under a brutal midday sun. It is a flat delta countryside, the straight-ruled road stretches to infinity [Coen, 2000].

In between hammered clanks, we hear a man call out, "Po' Lazarus," with each man down the line resounding the name, like an echo in a canyon. With rich cinematic detail and cultural cohesion, the Coen Brothers bring together the singing voices of mid-century convicts with cinematic images of convicts building a road, singing about a convict on the run. Moreover, given the film is a retelling of Homer's *The Odyssey*, and given the folklore and mythic dimensions of the Delta Blues, the film contributes one of the great mythological moments of the early twenty-first century, a true representative anecdote and portrait of twentieth-century America.

What is most unique about Lomax's encounter with James Carter is that it mediated, quite literally, millions of encounters with Carter and his chain gang singers while also connecting twenty-first century Americans to both their own national history and a rich mythological history about the road as an encounter with the other. With the success of the Coen Brothers' film, and perhaps more so the soundtrack, which sold millions of copies and won the 2001 Grammy for Album of the Year, James Carter was driven, like the axe handle he swung that autumn day, into a newfound world of recognition. And at the center of this popular American tune, is the mythology of the road—in the fieldwork of Lomax, in themes of the songs sung by the men he encountered, and eventually, as the thematic backdrop to a cinematic story about roads.

Just think—"Po' Lazarus," first heard on that recording trip in 1933 was now embedded in the contemporary cultural mindset through the medium of film. As a case study for teaching a course on AFM, at the crossroads of a new century and millennium, *O Brother* provides an ideal framework for a deeper understanding and appreciation for AFM in twentieth-century

America through an extensive examination of race using the mythology of the road through the mediums of film, radio, political and public discourse, and AFM.

Course Reflections

Given the significant cultural reach of AFM, I now turn my attention to how to design and incorporate its varied themes into a coherent and productive course on popular musical. Specifically, I focus on four dimensions—assignments, benefits, challenges, and recommendations.

Assignments

In all of the courses I teach, my aim is to have students account for their learning in three distinct but interrelated ways: written, spoken, and creative. Indeed, much of our learning in the classroom demands we write and speak. But these alone miss many of the valuable ways we express our sensibilities about the human experience. We find these in dance and cuisine, engineering and architecture. In essence, there is a craftsmanship dimension to learning I aim to capture in my assignments.

As it relates to oral communication, I design my courses to incorporate both instructor and self-guided conversations and questions related to reading and learning outcomes. For instance, in an assignment I refer to as "Front and Center," I begin each class by calling students (usually at random) to the front and center of the room to account for a personal perspective on a subject of interest, which does not have to explicitly relate to AFM. To be clear, this is more about teaching students the art of preparedness and developing confidence through competence than some veiled (authoritarian) pedagogical power play. Collectively, over the course of an entire semester, the students get genuinely and deeply connected to their fellow students because they have conversed with them on various occasions—they learn nuanced aspects about a range of subjects along with the affinities and concerns of their classmates. In short, I use these conversational oriented experiences to build toward a final individual and group presentation related to our subject(s). This way, each student has a variety of public speaking experiences that range from casual discourse to formal presentations. For instance, one student who grew up in Nantucket, Massachusetts, with pop musician Meghan Trainor arranged for a private interview to be included with their group presentation on celebrity music culture and social media.

Second, as it relates to written communication, I have all of my students write short critical reflections related to our course readings and discussions.

While some students prefer to focus almost exclusively on contemporary artists, many students use the opportunity to uncover historical influences. For instance, some students explore the history of sampled songs and hooks from their favorite artists while other students delve deeper into the roots of their favorite genres of music. Specifically, though, most of my undergraduate courses are not primarily designed with writing as the main objective. Regardless, I work with students to account for their reading, listening, and watching through an assessment that considers: (1) *what* is important about the subject, (2) *why* this is significant culturally (beyond the individual's interest), and (3) *how* they intend to address or confront the issue through a specific action plan. If the course is more oriented to writing, as my graduate classes usually are, then I coalesce the reflections with a larger research project and have students read their final projects aloud to the class.

Third and finally, I try to have students account beyond the traditional means of speech and writing. That is, I ask them to identify an area of ability or interest (e.g., photography or filmmaking), and challenge them to design, develop, and deliver a class project or presentation, such as the student projects that have focused on the relationship between music and social movements (e.g., freedom songs of the American civil rights movement or the rediscovery and resurgence of lost blues artists like Son House in the 1960s). Additionally, some student projects have chosen to demonstrate how music embodies symbolic meaning, as when one student explored the use of music in political campaigns (e.g., Barack Obama's use of Stevie Wonder's "Signed, Sealed, Delivered" or Aerosmith insisting that Donald Trump *not* play their music at rallies). Altogether, student projects have explored a range of social issues related to domestic violence, sexuality, gender, racial equality, social class, and justice spanning nineteenth-, twentieth-, and twenty-first-century America. Though this element can be abstract, I have found that it enlivens the learning experience for many, and develops confidence in those students who tend to struggle with the more privileged and recognized aspects of learning found in reading, writing and speech.

Benefits

In my experience, there are two particular benefits to a course related to AFM: (1) scope and (2) intercultural dimensions. First, when we consider the scope of AFM, which spans the late nineteenth and much of the twentieth century, one can creatively and selectively custom courses that move in and through an array of eras, regions, technological developments, innovators, and artists. Put differently, teachers could design a course that considers the relationship between music and historical moments and movements. For instance, by coordinating a focus on mythology or essential stories in twentieth-century American folk music, I have been able to establish a cultural connection between seemingly unrelated eras and movements through the aforementioned archetypal mythology of the road—moving from the fieldwork of Alan Lomax to the preeminent road themes in work and prison songs and the blues, to the marches of the American civil rights movement on city streets all over the nation, and even to a particular ethic in the sermonic discourse of Martin Luther King, Jr., from the parable of the Good Samaritan, which is a road parable.

Second, with this last point in mind, the intercultural dimensions also serve to make a course on AFM ideal. As the James Carter example illustrates, the mythology of the road in American culture brings us to a cultural crossroads where music, film, religion, and politics collide. One can teach a course, for instance, on AFM with attention given to the religious themes of the spirituals and their relation to the freedom songs of the American civil rights movement, or to the political themes associated with race and social justice prevalent in prison and work songs, blues, protest music, and classic rock, among others. Collectively, these two benefits bring further credibility and possibility to how a prevalent public issue like racial equality could be explored through music—making volatile subjects more accessible through music. As an additional example, I have utilized the film *O Brother, Where Art Thou* as a platform for considering the theme of incarceration in cinema history through related films like *I Am a Fugitive from a Chain Gang* (1932), *Sullivan's Travels* (1941), *Cool Hand Luke* (1967), and *The 25th Hour* (2002).

Challenges

Though there are many beneficial aspects to teaching a course on AFM, there are also some challenges. There are three in particular: (1) scope, (2) visceral/volatile subjects, and (3) generational gaps. First, though the scope of AFM is a significant benefit it also presents interesting challenges. That is, because AFM spans more than a century of musical eras, artists, genres, and technological developments, it can make course design complex. For instance, because there are so many eras, developments, artists, and genres, coordinating specific learning outcomes, where to devote time to achieve them, and what assignments to use to measure are challenging. To counter this challenge, teachers should be decisive as it pertains to their particular learning outcomes.

Second, and further complicating the scope, is the potentially visceral/volatile nature of the subjects inherent to AFM (e.g., civil rights issues associated with protest music, work and prison songs, field hollers, blues, and other forms). For example, listening to protest music from Woody Guthrie, Joan Baez, or Bob Dylan will naturally bring various social issues related to injustice and inequality to the forefront of discussion. Though this is of particular importance for learning and civic engagement, it seems especially challenging given our current political climate. Though I see this as ideal to learning, it also presents pedagogical challenges that should be pondered in course design and implementation.

Third, and finally, both the scope and visceral/volatile nature of the subjects associated with AFM also have to contend with generational gaps. For instance, I recall a moment recently when my oldest daughter, apparently troubled by the reality of having to listen to music from another era, asked if we could listen to "real" music (insert traditional fatherly eye roll). Put differently, in my experience, students, if they do not already have a vested interest in related genres and styles of music related to AFM, often have trouble determining the value and importance of the music, at least initially. I have observed gleefully the light turning on for many students as they begin to see points of musical connection and meaning, as when students learn that the hook from Notorious B.I.G.'s "Hypnotize" (1997) actually comes from an instrumental jazz song released in 1979, titled "Rise," featuring Herb Alpert. In other words, the more experiences like these, the more students seem to enjoy and broaden their music interests.

Reconsiderations

Given the benefits and challenges of teaching a course on AFM, I want to acknowledge one potential shortcoming in the course design that could be reconsidered. Specifically, redesigning the chronology of the course to flow from present to past might be better for establishing rapport and demonstrating the significance of AFM. In other words, rather than beginning with the early twentieth century and progressing chronologically forward, one might begin with more culturally viable and contemporary musical examples and then work chronologically backward. For instance, one could explore the cultural salience of American folk music—the blues in particular, in relation to contemporary remix culture. For example, musical artist Moby's "Play the B Sides" album, released in 2000, features an array of songs sampled or remixed from recordings by Alan Lomax, including "Find My Baby," a sample of Joe Lee's "Rock" by Boy Blue, "Flower," a sample of Mattie and Mary Gardner's "Bring Sally Up," "Honey," a sample of Bessie Jones' "Sometimes," and "Natural Blues," a sample of Vera Ward Hall's "Trouble So Hard." Alan Lomax recorded this last example, for reference, on October 10, 1959, at her home in Livingston, Alabama; John Lomax had recorded her in 1937 (Piazza, 2013).

Moreover, musical groups such as C2C, the Black Keys, Jack White, the White Stripes, ZZ Ward, and others draw much of their inspiration by either explicitly covering older folk artists or integrating their musical style and intonation. Likewise, if instructors were to begin with contemporary forms of protest music and work back to artists like Joan Baez and Bob Dylan, rapport may be more readily established. By beginning with music that is culturally viable and moving chronologically backwards, the course might generate more sustained interest. In sum, any appreciation of contemporary music, from rock and roll to rhythm and blues to soul, funk, rap, hip-hop, and remix, among others, should account for the relationship between early AFM and its relationship with contemporary music. In this essay, I have argued for consideration of the fieldwork and recordings of Alan Lomax, which help mediate these realms. Whether one wants to focus on Lomax's vast fieldwork, or his recordings in the Mississippi Delta, or specific genres such as Delta blues, classic rock, contemporary rock, electronic, or remix culture, among others, Lomax provides a broad range of musical history to consider.

Conclusion

Having incorporated various dimensions of AFM into courses such as *Communication and Popular Culture*, *Public Speaking*, *Communication and Theology*, and *Public Advocacy and Civic Engagement*, among others, much of the course content derives from a versatile collection of music, documentaries, film, and popular and scholarly research. One of the preeminent learning outcomes I have observed in my courses related to AFM is a more refined critical consciousness. That is, an ability to critically perceive the themes of our time and intervene actively in reality with an "especially flexible, critical spirit" (Freire, 2013, p. 6). As to critical consciousness, Paulo Freire (2005) declared:

> If [we] are unable to perceive critically the themes of [our] time, and thus to intervene actively in reality, [we] are carried along in the wake of change. [We] see that the times are changing, but [we] are submerged in that change and so cannot discern its dramatic significance. And a society beginning to move from one epoch to another requires the development of an especially flexible, critical spirit. Lacking such a spirit, [we] cannot perceive the marked contradictions which occur in society as emerging values in search of affirmation and fulfillment clash with earlier values seeking self-preservation [p. 6].

A critical consciousness, then, is an ability to both recognize and respond to prevalent cultural themes. Ideally, those students most impacted by such courses have been able to identify and broach discussion of issues related to racial equality, domestic violence, and social justice, for instance. Put differently, students become more mindful that, culturally and historically, music is so much more than a leisurely affinity or activity. Music is a means of civic, not merely commercial, expression. For instance, I often ask students to consider the socio-political context embedded in Lynyrd Skynyrd's "Sweet Home Alabama" (1974), which is a musical discourse with Neil Young's "Southern Man" (1970) about racial in/equality in the South in the 1960s. Using contemporary artists like Kendrick Lamar and others, teachers can animate the multidimensional nature of music as a mythic storytelling device that confronts vital issues of human nature and experience.

With this in mind, students often remark that one of the preeminent takeaways from an exploration of AFM is the recognition that the roots of music are grounded in storytelling that is driven by passion and activism rather than solely for the purposes of consumerism or leisure. To this end, throughout his career, Lomax maintained a disdain for "chair-bound scholars," and chose instead to journey in search of truth in the beauty of folk songs (Ferris, 2013, p. 11). Lomax wrote, "There is an impulsive and romantic streak in my nature that I find difficult to control when I go song hunting" (Ferris, 2013, p. 11). More specifically, Lomax's work went beyond documenting African American music, extending his critical work to the "harsh social conditions and racial divisions of midcentury American life" (Gioia, 2006, p. 215).

Lomax once asked, "What path shall my feet follow? All the paths that have opened up before me so far have been the paths of *other* people" (Piazza, 2013, p. 38). Lomax's work, then, reminds us that we belong to the human race, that the ultimate benefit of music is neither "self-expression" nor "personal vision," but rather, "ligature with the community and with our history" (Piazza, 2013, p. 38). Through all his road encounters, Lomax learned to see the self in the plights of others, and in so doing, allows us to comprehend something of the history of AFM. As the epigraph featured at the onset of this essay has indicated, for Lomax, the mythic songs of the people "can provide ten thousand bridges across which men of all nations may stride to say, 'You are my brother'" (Cohen, 2003, p. 91).

REFERENCES

Burke, K. (1989). Revolutionary symbolism in America. In H.W. Simons & T. Melia (Eds.), *The legacy of Kenneth Burke* (pp. 267–281). Madison, WI: University of Wisconsin Press.
Charters, S. (2004). *Walking a blues road: A blues reader, 1956–2004*. London: Marion Boyars.
Cohen, R. (2003). (Ed.) *Alan Lomax: Selected writings 1934–1997*. New York: Routledge.
Ferris, W. (2013). Alan Lomax: The long journey. In T. Piazza (Ed.), *The southern journey of Alan Lomax: Words, photographs, and music* (pp. 10–21). New York: W.W. Norton & Company.
Freire, P. (2005). *Education for critical consciousness*. New York: Continuum.
Gioia, T. (2006). *Work songs*. Durham, NC: Duke University Press.
Gioia, T. (2008). *Delta blues: The life and times of the Mississippi masters who revolutionized American music*. New York: W.W. Norton & Company.

Kaye, A.L. (1997). Liner notes. In *Southern journey 5: Bad man ballads, songs of outlaws and desperadoes.* Prestige International.

Lomax, A. (1968). *Folk song style and culture.* New Brunswick, NJ: Transaction Books.

_____. (1975). *The folk songs of north America.* Garden City, NY: Dolphin Books.

_____. (1993). *The land where the blues began.* New York: Pantheon Books.

_____. (2002). Look down that long lonesome road. In *Deep river of song: South Carolina, got the keys to the kingdom,* recorded by Alan Lomax, CD.

_____. (2003a). America sings the saga of America. In R. Cohen (Ed.), *Alan Lomax: Selected writings, 1934-199* (pp. 86-91). New York: Routledge.

_____. (2003b). Saga of a folksong hunter. In R. Cohen (Ed.), *Alan Lomax: Selected writings, 1934-1997* (pp. 173-86). New York: Routledge.

_____. (2003c). Sinful songs of the southern negro. In R. Cohen (Ed.), *Alan Lomax: Selected writings, 1934-1997* (pp. 9-31). New York: Routledge.

Palmer, R. (1981). *Deep blues: A musical and cultural history, from the Mississippi Delta to Chicago's south side to the world.* New York: Penguin.

Piazza, T. (2013). *The southern journey of Alan Lomax: Words, photographs, and music.* New York: W.W. Norton & Company.

Scorsese, M. (Director). (2003). *The blues: Feel like going home.* [DVD]. Los Angeles: Cappa Productions.

Taft, M. (2006). *The blues lyric formula.* New York: Routledge.

"There is no revolution without songs"
Teaching Latin American Resistance Music in the Spanish Curriculum

Eunice Rojas

In teaching several different courses on contemporary Latin American literature and culture one of my main goals has always been for students to understand the twentieth-century political history of some Latin American countries and how that history intersects with cultural production. Achieving this goal has been challenging at times because I have found many students, despite majoring or minoring in Spanish, struggle with literary texts in Spanish and are often reluctant to read anything they might consider lengthy. Adding to the difficulties students have in connecting linguistically to the class material, the political events that I cover are relatively recent, mostly from the mid-twentieth century to today. But for many of today's students even the 1970s seem hopelessly long ago. In addition, despite the internet's power to globalize, students frequently find the countries that we study geographically and ideologically remote, and consequently the material that we study can also often be problematic. Having grown up hearing at every turn a narrative of American exceptionalism and a demonization of socialism, it is often difficult for U.S. students to grapple with the history of U.S. military and intelligence involvement in Latin American politics. Because of this, they have trouble understanding the negative attitude of many left-leaning Latin Americans towards the United States. My students often tell me that they only first heard of U.S.-backed military dictatorships in Latin America within their college foreign language courses, and are sometimes shocked that their high school and even college-level history books have glossed over or completely ignored this aspect of U.S. history.

Perhaps these challenges are merely partially a product of the time in which we live. British neuroscientist Susan Greenfield, in her work on the effect of digital technologies on the brain, posits that widespread use of the internet, texting, and video gaming may have us living in an era in which many young people have a mindset that is characterized by "a short attention span and a reckless obsession with the here and now" (Greenfield, 2015, p. 199). In addition, despite the internet's power to offer us a wealth of information literally at our fingertips, in my experience most students rarely come into my courses having already harnessed the internet to access information regarding Latin American news, history, literature, or music. With this profile of my average student in mind, I have taught a course designed to examine a few aspects of Latin American culture and history through the study of popular music from several different Latin American countries. Through music we study political and historical topics by examining brief and engaging musical texts. In addition to being short and entertaining, these songs have the advantage of serving as historical primary sources that are also literary in nature.

The Effectiveness of Music in Teaching Culture and Literature

Like most Spanish professors, I use music in the classroom for linguistic purposes on a regular basis. Multiple studies examine the effectiveness of music as a pedagogical tool in the language classroom, confirming what may seem obvious that music can: help improve students' listening skills and cultural appreciation (Lacorte & Thurston-Griswold, 2001), teach certain grammar concepts (Anton, 1990), aid in students' acquisition of vocabulary (Adkins, 1997), lower anxiety and increase enjoyment in the language classroom (Dolean & Dolean, 2016), and be of great benefit in teaching culture (Failoni, 1993; Griffin, 1977). While many instructors also employ music occasionally in upper-level Spanish or Latin American literature and culture courses there are fewer scholarly accounts of this practice. One such study is Catherine Bellver's description of how she incorporates music into her course on *Medieval and Golden Age Spanish* literature by playing music to introduce each new literary period studied in the course. According to Bellver (2008) music is "a universally known idiom that can be channeled to introduce students to literary expressions unknown or intimidating to them" (p. 894). My course goes a step further and introduces musical texts *as* literary expressions (with important cultural components) that are less intimidating to students than traditional literary or historical texts. Similarly, Benjamin Leff (2012), who uses popular film and music as historical texts to teach high school American history, finds that songs allow students to do "the complex work of identifying the ideological content of a mass media text and grappling with the difficult question of what popular culture tells us about the historical context in which it is produced and consumed" (p. 228).

With regard to the use of music in the literature classroom, Pichaske (1999) argues that to restrict poetry courses to printed texts is to fail to acknowledge the reality of our changing world, since "just as film and television fill the need of most Americans for narrative, popular music fills the need of most Americans for poetry" (p. 90). Rather than struggle against this reality, Pichaske advocates for bridging the gap between literary and popular culture by studying the songs of certain musical artists as literary texts. The appropriateness of the inclusion of musical texts within the literary canon was confirmed for many of us in 2016 when the Swedish Academy, somewhat controversially, awarded the Nobel Prize in Literature to singer-songwriter Bob Dylan. This happened during the semester in which I taught a Latin American resistance music course for the second time, and we used the news as an opportunity to discuss the debate surrounding the Nobel committee's acceptance of popular music as literature, and to ask ourselves about the requirements should be for a text to be considered literary. Furthermore, I would agree with Pichaske that in the classroom "[music] can be used with, in lieu of, or as a vehicle into printed poetry" (p. 96). By introducing elements of literary analysis in texts that simply by virtue of being set to music are more appealing and inviting to students, I have found these same students to be more receptive to traditional printed literary texts studied later in other courses.

Teaching Conversation and Culture Through Latin American Resistance Music

With this in mind I have begun not only to incorporate musical texts into my Latin American literature courses, but also to teach an upper-level Spanish course wholly through the lens of music. The new course I designed and added to the Spanish curriculum is saddled with the somewhat cumbersome title of *Spanish 441: Advanced Conversation and Culture Through Spanish Language Resistance Music*. The clumsy title reflects the multiple diverse objectives of the course, which include gaining an understanding of historical and contemporary issues in Latin America as well as the music associated with them, studying literary analysis in the context of the poetry of song lyrics, and developing critical thinking skills, including the ability to view issues from a cultural perspective different from one's own. In addition, the course also aims to help students improve their aural comprehension and speaking fluency in Spanish.

Born from an effort to present Latin American history and culture with authentic texts that students would find accessible, engaging, and stimulating, this course draws from my own research on imperialism, anti–Americanism, and anti-capitalism in Latin American music. It focuses on a handful of Latin American countries (Cuba, Chile, and Argentina) in order to examine their political and social history since the mid-twentieth-century through music that espouses social justice causes or expresses resistance to systemic or imperialist oppression. The idea is for my students to study the perspectives of some Latin American citizens towards the political and social realities in their own countries, and understand how those perspectives have informed often negative attitudes towards the United States. Music has proven itself to be the ideal vehicle for the course objectives as many of the songs studied simplify and summarize complex historical and political issues and deliver them with the passion and intensity of musical expression.

One of my priorities for this course is to trace the transnational processes that inform both the musical and the political movements present in different parts of Latin America during the last half century. The 1960s, for example, saw a proliferation of left wing ideologies and a wave of anti–Americanism in the wake of the Cuban Revolution. The music of the transnational Latin American New Song Movement, tightly aligned with the left, reflects these political ideologies and the social causes related to them. In the 1970s and 1980s, with U.S.–backed military dictatorships installed in the Southern Cone countries of Chile and Argentina, the musical focus of the course turns to punk inspired rock as resistance to the oppressive regimes. In this section of the course we discuss the effect of governmental censorship and persecution on musical production, as well as artists' strategies to surmount these challenges. Finally, in the 1990s and 2000s, we look at the ways in which Latin American hip-hop and contemporary folk music challenge U.S. imperialist practices, as well as the Castro regime in Cuba, and critique the effects of neoliberal policies after the return to democracy in the Southern Cone.

The first time that I taught the course as an experimental *Special Topics in Spanish* class, I included units covering six different Spanish-speaking nations: Spain, Chile, Argentina, Mexico, Cuba, and Puerto Rico. Nevertheless, from the final exam and informal conversations with students I came to the conclusion that including so many countries actually resulted in the students confusing and conflating both the music and the historical processes of the different countries studied. For this reason, the second time I taught the course I reduced the countries to just three: Cuba, Chile, and Argentina. With this format I found students understand better how the specific political and social situation in each country informed its music. In the next section I will describe in detail how I teach the Cuba section of the course, and then give a broad outline of the Chile and Argentina unit.

Cuba: From Revolution to Rap

I begin the course by giving students some background of the Cuban Revolution, using a short video produced by the Ministry of Education in Argentina (Canal Encuentro, 2015). The video summarizes the causes and timeline of the conflict, and how Fidel Castro's successful struggle against the capitalist, imperialist, and oppressive forces of the U.S.-backed dictatorship of Fulgencio Batista inspired many others in Latin America to want to follow suit against their own governments. Having grown up with a narrative of Castro leading a dictatorial and authoritarian Communist regime with no redeeming qualities, students often find it difficult to understand the reasons why the Cuban Revolution would have received so much popular support. The music of Carlos Puebla, who composed songs criticizing the Batista regime during the 1950s and praising Castro's Revolution in the 1960s, is a useful tool in helping students view the issue from a different perspective.

Just a few days after the triumph of the Cuban Revolution in 1959, Puebla composed his first song celebrating Castro's accomplishment, "Y en eso llegó Fidel" (And That's When Fidel Arrived) (Moore, 2006, p. 60). Over the next several years Puebla followed with songs lauding and explaining different aspects of the Cuban Revolution which "received widespread airplay, converting them into revolutionary anthems" (Moore, p. 60). In 1969 a number of these songs were collected in an album entitled *Cronología Musical De La Revolución Cubana*. In "Y en eso llegó Fidel" (And That's When Fidel Arrived) we discuss how Castro is portrayed as a hero/savior who awakens the Cuban people to the exploitation of those who are enriching themselves and claiming to do so in the name of democracy. The song "Todo por la reforma agraria" (All for the Agrarian Reform) explains that the Cuban Revolution's controversial land reform project will go forward despite the protests of those whose property is to be expropriated by the government. In class we discuss how this song criticizes some of the opponents of land reform as favoring sugarcane crops over the poverty of the Cuban people.

An important aspect of the Cuban Revolution that generally surprises my students is the massive year-long literacy campaign of 1961. According to Supko (1998) hundreds of thousands of literate Cubans, some as young as ten years old, volunteered to teach other Cubans how to read and write. The results were rather spectacular, as over seven hundred thousand Cubans achieved literacy, bringing the overall illiteracy rate in the country down to 3.9 percent. Carlos Puebla's song "El son de la alfabetización" (Literacy Son) helps students to understand the connections between the literacy campaign and the ideological position of the Castro regime as the song implies a direct correlation between freedom and access to literacy. Along with Carlos Puebla's song, we study Eduardo Saborit's "Himno de las Brigadas Conrado Benítez" (Anthem of the Conrado Benítez Brigade), which was written specifically to be sung by a volunteer literacy brigade that was named after a teenage Cuban literacy volunteer who was killed by CIA-backed counter revolutionary forces in the early days of the literacy campaign (Pérez Cabrera, p. 71). Finally, we end the Carlos Puebla section of the course with a pair of songs that emphasize the anti-imperialist and anti–American attitudes of many pro–Castro Cubans in order for students to grapple with the negative way in which their own country is often seen by others and understand the reasons for this. "Mira yanqui cómo nos reímos" (Look, Yankee, at How We Laugh) and "Yanqui go home" (Yankee Go Home) both invite the listener to look at the U.S. government from the perspective of a supporter of the Cuban Revolution.

From Carlos Puebla our course turns to Pablo Milanés and Silvio Rodríguez, two of the main representatives of Cuba's *nueva trova* movement, a musical movement that began in the second half of the 1960s, and infused Cuba's traditional folk-style singing with elements from contemporary and international musical trends and often highly politicized lyrics. With the help of Haydée Santamaría, who fought for the Revolution alongside Fidel Castro, the *nueva trova* movement became part of a national cultural institution. In class we study two songs released by Pablo Milanés in 1980 that deal with the ways in which Cubans loyal to the Revolution respond to dissidents. "Yo me quedo" (I'm Staying) is structured as a series of questions that the poetic voice poses to someone who appears to be contemplating fleeing the island in exile. The questions highlight the unknown future of those who chose to leave Cuba, while the poetic voice appears confident in his decision to stay, alluding to reasons that are described as both worthy and beautiful. In "No vivo en una sociedad perfecta" (I Do Not Live in a Perfect Society), as its title suggests, the poetic voice concedes the faults of his society, and yet criticizes detractors, who are described as extremist and cowardly.

With Silvio Rodríguez's prolific output of songs over the course of several decades it is difficult to choose which ones to study in class, but the ones I have found most useful have been "Fusil contra fusil" (Rifle Against Rifle), which is dedicated to the memory of Ernesto "Che" Guevara, "El unicornio" (The Unicorn), in which the poetic voice describes his search for a beloved missing blue unicorn, and "El necio" (The Fool), in which the poetic voice appears to be defending himself against criticisms for having remained loyal to the Revolution. "Fusil contra fusil" offers us the opportunity to discuss the importance and idolatry of the figure of "Che" Guevara, the Argentine guerrilla leader who fought for Marxist ideals alongside Castro in Cuba, as well as in several other locations in the developing world. With "El unicornio" we discuss the many possible symbolic interpretations of Rodríguez's missing blue unicorn, including political readings in which the unicorn represents a Cuban government that has fallen from its original political ideals. We compare these readings with the author's stated explanations of the song in order to engage in the debate on how much weight to give authorial intent. "El necio" is a challenging text that offers an abundance of poetic devices to analyze, the most interesting of which is an inversion of religious symbolism in which the poetic voice rejects a divine conceptualization of the Revolution in favor of a more human one. He does so by confirming his decision to die in the same manner in which he has lived his life, while leaving God to the far-away realm of the heavens. The implication is that the poetic voice recognizes that even if the Revolution is indeed foolish, as many critics claim, he will continue working for its ideals.

While both Milanés and Rodríguez include in their music some light critical commentary of society functioning under the Cuban Revolution, Manuel, Bilby and Largey (1995) argue that most *nueva trova* songs "implicitly endorse the ideals of the Revolution" (p. 57). The first half of the 1990s, following the collapse of the Soviet Union, Cuba's main trade partner, provoked an economic crisis on the island known as Cuba's "Special Period." Silverstein (2013) explains that during this period of disillusionment with the policies of the Revolution, Milanés and Rodríguez were criticized for receiving from the government economic advantages not afforded to the members of the general public who were suffering from great scarcity. Pedro Luis Ferrer, another Cuban singer-songwriter who had briefly aligned himself with the *nueva trova* tradition, broke from the movement because of its close relationship with the dogma and power of Cuba's government (Shaw, 2013). For this reason, in examining some of Ferrer's songs students are able to detect a more heightened level of criticism of Cuban bureaucracy than what is present in the songs of Milanés and Rodríguez.

Ferrer's "Yo no tanto como él" (I, Not as Much as Him) is an important text to help discuss the diverse and nuanced attitudes of many Cubans towards their government. The poetic voice distances himself somewhat from his own father, whom he describes as fiercely loyal to the Castro regime. Nevertheless, the political distance between father and son is merely one of degree, as the song implies that the son believes in the same ideals as the father, just not to the same extent. Furthermore, the poetic voice clarifies that even if he lacks his father's strong allegiance toward Fidel, he maintains a deep devotion to his father. Another song by Ferrer, "100 por ciento cubano" (100 percent Cuban) also offers a critique of Cuban society, and additionally it gives our class the opportunity to discuss the author's use of irony. In the song the poetic voice lists all the touristy things he plans to do since Cuba is one hundred percent Cuban. The irony lies in that since the Cuban currency in which citizens are paid by the government is practically worthless compared to the tourist currency, an ordinary Cuban would be able to do none of the things mentioned in the song, such as rent a beach house, stay at a fancy hotel, or buy an airline ticket. According to Shaw (2013) "the critical commentary [of the song] would evade the foreigner, which in fact, shows how much Ferrer's songs require more than the ear of the tourist" (p. 161). In order for my students to better pick up on the irony of the song with the ear of an informed listener rather than of a relatively ignorant tourist, we listen to a recording of a live performance in which the audience can be heard laughing loudly at each outrageous claim by the poetic voice regarding the lofty plans he has for the meager earnings he has garnered from working in the sugarcane fields. Written in a decidedly different tone, another song by Ferrer also takes up the topic of Cuban currency. In the somberly nostalgic "La Habana está poblada de consignas" (Havana is Populated with Slogans) the poetic voice laments that Havana is a city divided because of its multiple systems of money.

Ferrer's mention of the national currency, and the ways in which it interacts with the tourist currency, requires that we have a broader class discussion regarding the history of Cuba's dual currency system and its social implications. In Cuba the *moneda nacional* (national currency) operates alongside the convertible Cuban peso (CUC) which is worth 24 times the national peso. CUCs are solely for the use of tourists and Cubans who profit off of the tourist industry, while the availability of products priced in *moneda nacional* has continuously dwindled over the years. Ferrer's mention of how currency issues have divided the city of Havana allows us to discuss how the dual currency has provoked increasing social stratification in a society that was founded on the idea of classlessness.

Besides Ferrer, the Cuban musicians who have taken up the topic of the dual currency in their music have generally been hip-hop artists. The first Cuban hip-hop group to gain international notoriety was Orishas, formed in 1999 by a trio of Cuban expats living in Europe. The group generally shied away from overtly political commentary in their lyrics and famously developed a friendly relationship with Castro, convincing him that hip-hop needed institutional support in Cuba. Despite having been somewhat happily folded into the Revolution, in 2005 Orishas released a song that appears to be critical of the government's dual currency. The name of the song, "El kilo" (The Kilo), refers to a term generally used for one cent of a Cuban peso in the national currency. A *kilo*, which originally received its name because it had once been enough to purchase a kilogram of rice, had seen its value drastically reduced with the introduction of the U.S. dollar during the height of the "Special Period" in 1993. With a clever play on words the song emphasizes the worthlessness of the *kilo* while implying that the problem has no solution. In class we discuss how the song, within the context of the reality of the dual currency, appears to be asserting the hopelessness of trying to remedy the social issues that have arisen from it.

The Cuban hip-hop group that has most openly and provocatively attacked the Castro regime for failing to live up to its Revolutionary ideals is Los Aldeanos, a duo that famously and unwittingly found itself on the receiving end of money provided by the U.S. Agency for International Development to foment dissidence against the Castro government (Weaver, para. 3). "Tiranosaurio" (Tyrannosaurus), a song recorded in 2005, whose title appears to refer to Fidel Castro as an ancient and monstrous tyrant, laments that the fruits of Cuban labor have gone to entertain foreigners with their tourist currency. In two other songs Los Aldeanos criticize the government for paying its citizens in the practically valueless national currency, while effectively forcing them to pay for even the most basic of household goods in the tourist currency. Similarly, "Viva Cuba Libre" (Long Live Free Cuba) complains about how Cubans are paid in the national currency, but charged for everything in the tourist currency. Furthermore, the song describes as hypocritical the way in which the Cuban government attributes their citizens' complicated access to money to the forces of imperialism and yet continues to claim that all Cubans are treated equally. Similarly, the song "Mi hermosa Habana" (My Beautiful Havana) from 2009 exposes the double standard of the Cuban government in denouncing imperialism and exploitation on the part of the U.S. while allowing the dual currency to keep a significant portion of its citizens lacking any sort of appreciable purchase power.

In addition to matters of social stratification, we study how the complicated currency situation has led to issues of sexual exploitation, as many people, particularly women, have turned to sex work in order to access the purchase power of tourist currency. A number of songs help illustrate both this issue, as well as the different attitudes towards Cuban sex workers on and off the island. Willy Chirino, a Cuban dissident musician who left Cuba for Miami in 1960 as a teenager, released in 1995 a song entitled "La jinetera" (The Prostitute) which tells the story of a 17-year-old prostitute named Eve who sells her literal and metaphorical apple for a few dollars. In class we discuss how the song then goes on to implicitly compare Eve's sadness about not being able to be with Adam, to the desire expressed by the exiled poetic voice to return to Cuba.

One of the first hip-hop groups to take up the topic of prostitution was Primera Base, which formed in the mid–1990s, and by 1997 released an album with a song entitled "Jinetera" (Prostitute). The Primera Base song offers a negative portrayal of the figure of the prostitute, accusing her of selling her body to foreigners in the name of materialism and becoming worthless in the process. A 2002 song by the husband and wife hip-hop duo Obsesión takes a more sympathetic view of prostitution. Sung entirely by the female voice of Magia López, "La llaman puta" (They Call Her Whore) focuses on the economic conditions that force women into prostitution, and the fear and disgust that many women experience during sex work. Similarly, Pedro Luís Ferrer's "Marucha la jinetera" (Marucha, the Prostitute), which has not been recorded on an album, but which dates from the decade of the 1990s (Padrón, 2016, para. 8), explicitly absolves the figure of the prostitute of any sort of blame, and describes her as having suffered through a childhood of rape and abuse. Through an examination of all of these songs, our class discusses the both the reasons why prostitution has been so widespread in Cuba, particularly in the 1990s and early 2000s, and what the different attitudes towards sex workers are in Cuban society.

Chile and Argentina: Social Justice and Resistance

Having completed our unit on Cuba, our class turns its attention towards Chile, returning to the 1960s to examine the Chilean *nueva canción* (New Song) movement, which predated and influenced the Cuban *nueva trova* movement already studied. Specifically, we look at how the *nueva canción* movement engaged with, reacted to, and influenced political processes in Chile. Members of the *nueva canción* movement such as Víctor Jara, Ángel and Isabel Parra, Patricio Manns, Rolando Alarcón, and the groups Quilapayún and Inti-Illimani in Chile actively supported Salvador Allende's left wing Popular Unity political alliance for the 1970 Presidential elections, and frequently distributed their music on a record label created and financed by the Communist Party. These artists and others famously gathered together in support of Allende during his election campaign under a banner that read, "There is no revolution without songs" (García, 2013, p. 125). In addition to fairly well-known songs by Violeta Parra, such as "Al centro de la injusticia" (At the Center of Injustice), I find in this unit that an examination of Patricio Mann's cantata *El sueño americano* (The American Dream) helps students to see the history of the entire Latin American continent in the context of imperialist exploitation, first by Spain and Portugal, and later by the United States. The twelve songs endeavor to relate chronologically the history of Latin America's struggles against oppression from colonial times to the then present day.

Chilean *nueva canción* music also at times compares the oppression of the rural and working class in Chile to the struggles of African Americans during the U.S. Civil Rights Movement of the 1960s. We study a series of songs sung by 1960s Chilean *nueva canción* artists that reference the issues faced by African-Americans during the U.S. Civil Rights Movement. For example, Chilean *nueva canción* artist Víctor Jara sings a song written originally by Nobel Prize winning poet Pablo Neruda entitled "Así como hoy matan negros" (Just Like Today They Kill Blacks), which compares the antagonism towards African Americans during the Civil Rights era to the imperialist tendencies of the U.S. towards Latin Americans. Similarly, Rolando Alarcón's "La balada de Abraham Lincoln" (The Ballad of Abraham Lincoln) and his "La balada de Luther King" (The Ballad of Luther King) both take up the topic of the treatment of blacks in the United States in order to imply a correlation between the U.S. government's imperialist treatment of Latin Americans abroad, and its violations of the civil rights of African Americans at home. In general, I find that by relating U.S. racial tensions to Chilean music, students are better able to understand both the culture and history of Chile as well as that of their own country.

Another album I find particularly useful for the Chile unit of our course is Ángel Parra's 1969 *Canciones funcionales* (Functional Songs), which provides a bitter satire of the negative cultural and economic influence of the United States on Chile as seen by the Chilean left in the lead up to Salvador Allende's election in 1970. Distributed by the Discoteca del Canto Popular (DICAP), the record label financed by the Communist Party in Chile, the album highlights the hypocrisy of wealthy people who claim loyalty to Chilean nationalism, and yet allow U.S. culture to invade practically every aspect of their lives. With biting sarcasm Parra's *Canciones funcionales* admonish the Chilean public for allowing a cultural and economic dependence on the United States.

Another area in which I have found it useful for students to make connections between the United States and Latin America is related to each country's treatment of indigenous people. In Argentina folk singer Atahualpa Yupanqui became a model for music espousing social justice causes related to Latin America's indigenous cultures beginning in the 1940s and 1950s, and Chilean music has engaged with the topic of the oppression of the Mapuche people from the 1960s to the present day, so we study indigenous issues in both the Chile and Argentina units of the course. One of the assignments that I gave to the students in the most recent iteration of the course was to compare the indigenous rights issues reflected in the contemporary Chilean music of artists such as the hip-hopper Subverso and singer-songwriter Joaquín Figueroa to the Standing Rock controversy that occurred in North Dakota in 2016. After studying issues of oppression, environmental concerns, and land disputes in songs such as Subverso's "Resistencia Mapuche" (Mapuche Resistance) and "Newen peñi" (Force, Brother) as well as Figueroa's "La cruz del sur" (The Southern Cross), I encourage students to find similarities in the concerns held by the different indigenous groups as well as in their recent treatment by the U.S. and the Chilean governments.

Another topic that comes up frequently in Latin American resistance music and is relatable to issues that students see covered in our own national news is that of police brutality. In both Chile and Argentina we study songs from before, during, and after the dictatorships that condemn oppressive police practices. For example, there is a series of songs from different genres of Chilean music that criticize the use of the water cannon truck to repress street demonstrations, and we use these songs to compare the use of high pressure water on protesters in the U.S. to its use in parts of Latin America. Víctor Jara's "Móvil Oil Special" (Mobile Oil Special) and the group Amerindios' "Juan Verdejo," (Juan Verdejo) both written and released during the lead-up to Chile's 1970 presidential elections, satirize the government's use of the *guanaco* (water cannon truck) to quell popular protests. More recently, hip-hop artists have taken up the topic of the Chilean police's use of the *guanaco* on student protesters demanding education reform in songs such as Subverso's "El jarrazo" (The Jug Attack) and Ana Tijoux's "Shock." A discussion of these songs allows students to discover the parallels between Chilean popular protests in the late 1960s and the heated student protests of 2006 and 2011, comparing attitudes towards issues of police brutality in Chile to current controversies in the United States.

Teaching Strategies and Challenges

All of the songs that I use in this course are available on YouTube, and most of their lyrics can be easily accessed online as well. For the few songs whose lyrics I have not been able to locate, I assign students to write out the lyrics themselves, which serves as an intense listening activity. In order to maximize our class time, I assign students to listen to and read the lyrics of the songs to be discussed in the next class period and answer comprehension questions for homework. The first time I taught the course I found that we spent too much class time listening to music and too little time discussing it. We still listen to a portion of every song that we discuss, but I generally limit it to a 30-second snippet as the students have listened to it on their own and have the lyrics printed out in front of them. One of the challenges teaching the course is that I have trouble limiting myself to a manageable number of songs discussed in each class period. We generally only have time to discuss a maximum of four or five songs in a 50-minute class period, so I am never able to include all of the music that I would like to study. I have found that it is helpful, though, to slightly over-assign songs for homework in order to see where the discussions take us.

Finally, I have incorporated blogging into my *Chilean Culture* and *Latin American Literature* courses, both of which contain significant units on music, and the next time I teach a course on Latin American resistance music I plan to have the students blog as well. In the two courses in which I already use blogging I have created assignments and supplementary materials, and each student is required to create a blog, which is then linked to our course blog site. The students' blogs are public spaces in which they engage with and reflect on the music prior to class, answering homework questions as well as asking and responding other students' questions in order to pave the way for class discussion. As most of the course materials for my music course are publicly available online, a course blog including links to YouTube videos, lyrics, musicians' biographies, and articles explaining historical information and other relevant course material would be a centralized way of organizing course content.

Conclusion

Overall, I have found music to be an extremely useful vehicle through which to teach Latin American history and culture in an upper-level Spanish language course. Over the course of the semester students' familiarity with Latin American music increases exponentially as most non–Hispanic U.S. university students have a very limited repertoire of Spanish language music with which they are familiar. Luis Fonsi and Daddy Yankee's catchy and sensual 2017 summer hit "Despacito" is one of only three Spanish language songs that have made it to number one on the U.S. Billboard Hot 100 chart since it began keeping records in the 1950s, and it only made it into the top ten of that ranking after a remix was released featuring Justin Bieber singing in both in English and in Spanish (Schiller, 2017). Prior to "Despacito" the last Spanish-language song to make it to number one on the U.S. charts was also an English-tinted remix, as in 1996 it was a Bayside Boys version of the original hit by the Spanish group Los Del Rio that catapulted "La Macarena" to the top of the charts (McIntyre 2017). On the other hand, crossover artists such as Shakira, Ricky Martin, and Enrique Iglesias have achieved success in the U.S. primarily by releasing entire albums in English. Therefore, through a music-based course such as the one I have outlined here, students are exposed to different genres of authentic Latin American music that challenge their stereotypes regarding what music from south of our border can sound like. Furthermore, the social, historical, and political issues that can be discussed in a course such as this are fairly limitless, considering the overwhelming amount of material that is already out there and that continues to be produced on a daily basis.

Appendix of Songs

Cuba

"100 por ciento cubano" (2008) Pedro Luís Ferrer
"Fusil contra fusil" (1968) Silvio Rodríguez
"La Habana está poblada de consignas" (2010) Pedro Luís Ferrer
"Himno de las Brigadas Conrado Benítez" (1961) Eduardo Saborit
"La jinetera" (1995) Willy Chirino
"Jinetera" (1997) Primera Base
"El kilo" (2005) Orishas
"La llaman puta" (2011) Obsesión
"Marucha la jinetera" (2010) Pedro Luís Ferrer
"Mi hermosa Habana" (2009) Los Aldeanos
"Mira yanqui cómo nos reímos" (1997) Carlos Puebla
"El necio" (1992) Silvio Rodríguez
"No vivo en una sociedad perfecta" (1980) Pablo Milanés
"El son de la alfabetización" (1961) Carlos Puebla
"Tiranosaurio" (2005) Los Aldeanos
"Todo por la reforma agraria" (1965) Carlos Puebla
"El unicornio" (1982) Silvio Rodríguez
"Viva Cuba Libre" (2009) Los Aldeanos
"Y en eso llegó Fidel" (1959) Carlos Puebla
"Yankee, Go Home" (1975) Carlos Puebla
"Yo me quedo" (1980) Pablo Milanés
"Yo no tanto como él" (2014) Pedro Luís Ferrer

Chile

"Al centro de la injusticia" (1968) Violeta Parra (recorded by Isabel Parra)
"Así como hoy matan negros" (1967) Víctor Jara
"La balada de Abraham Lincoln" (1967) Rolando Alarcón
"La balada de Luther King" (1968) Rolando Alarcón
Canciones funcionales (1969) Ángel Parra
"La cruz del sur" (2017) Joaquín Figueroa
"El jarrazo" (2008) Subverso
"Juan Verdejo" (1970) Amerindios
"Móvil Oil Special" (1969) Víctor Jara
"Newen peñi" (2001) Subverso
"Resistencia Mapuche" (2014) Subverso feat. Wenu Mapu
"Shock" (2011) Ana Tijoux
El sueño americano (1967) Patricio Manns

REFERENCES

Adkins, S. (1997). Connecting the powers of music to the learning of languages. *The Journal of the Imagination in Language Learning and Teaching, 4*, 40–48.

Anton, R.J. (1990). Combining singing and psychology. *Hispania, 73*(4), 1166–70.

Bellver, C.G. (2008). Music as hook in the literature classroom. *Hispania, 91*(4), 887–96.

Canal Encuentro [ProyectoBux]. (2015, November 17). Revolución Cubana—Canal Encuentro [Video File]. Retrieved from https://www.youtube.com/watch?v=2WtdDNXSeSI.

Chandler, M.A. (2017, April 18). Feeling stuck in your social media bubble? Here's the latest in a growing class of apps designed to help. *The Washington Post.* Retrieved from https://www.washingtonpost.com/news/inspired-life/wp/2017/04/18/feeling-stuck-in-your-social-media-bubble-heres-the-newest-of-in-a-growing-class-of-apps-designed-to-help/?utm_term=.bb2ca7cc5e74.

Dolean, D.D., & Dolean, I. (2016). The effects of teaching songs during foreign language classes on students' foreign language anxiety. *Language Teaching Research, 20*(5), 638–53.

Failoni, J.W. (1993, Spring). Music as means to enhance cultural awareness and literacy in the foreign language classroom. *Mid-Atlantic Journal of Foreign Language Pedagogy, 1*, 97–108.

García, M. (2013). *Canción valiente 1960–89: Tres décadas de canto social y político en Chile.* Santiago, Chile: Ediciones B.

Greenfield, S. (2015). *Mind change: How digital technologies are leaving their mark on our brains.* New York: Random House.

Griffin, R.J. (1977). Hispanic culture through folk music. *Hispania, 60*(4), 942–45.

Lacorte, M., & Thurston-Griswold, H. (2001). Music in the foreign language classroom: Developing linguistic and cultural proficiency. *NECTFL Review 49,* 40–53.

Leff, B.J.J. (2017). Popular culture as historical text: Using mass media to teach American history. *The History Teacher, 50*(2), 227–53.

Manuel, P., Bilby, K.M., & Largey, M.D. (1995). *Caribbean currents: Caribbean music from rumba to reggae.* Philadelphia: Temple University Press.

Moore, R.D. (2006). *Music and revolution: Cultural change in socialist Cuba.* Berkeley, CA: University of California Press.

Padrón, J.A. (2016, February 12). Pedro Luis Ferrer and the double meaning in the Cuban song. *Havana Music.* Retrieved from https://havanamusicschool.com/pedro-luis-ferrer-and-the-double-meaning-in-the-cuban-song/?lang=en.

Pérez Cabrera, R. (2013). *Pilares del socialismo en Cuba: El poder revolucionario 1959–2012.* Havana, Cuba: Juan Carlos Pérez Hernánd.

Pichaske, D.R. (1999, Winter). Poetry, pedagogy, and popular music: Renegade reflections. *Popular Music and Society, 23,* 83–103.

Shaw, L. (2013). *Song and social change in Latin America.* Lanham, MD: Lexington Books.

Silverstein, S. (2013). The Cuban protest song from Pablo Milanés to Los Aldeanos. In E. Rojas E. & L. Michie (Eds.), *Songs of resistance: The role of music in multicultural activism* (pp. 397–421). Santa Barbara, CA: ABC-CLIO.

Supko, R. (1998). Perspectives on the Cuban national literacy campaign. Paper prepared for delivery at the 1998 meeting of the Latin American Studies Association, Palmer House Hilton Hotel, Chicago, Illinois, September 24–26, 1998. Retrieved from http://lasa.international.pitt.edu/LASA98/Supko.pdf.

Weaver, M. (2014, December 10). US agency infiltrated Cuban hip-hop scene to spark youth unrest. *The Guardian.* Retrieved from https://www.theguardian.com/world/2014/dec/11/cuban-hip-hop-scene-infiltrated-us-information-youth.

Teaching the Music of Sunshine and Noir California

From "California Dreamin'" to "Straight Outta Compton"

Shawn Schwaller

Teaching about music and music festivals in American studies and history courses provides a path for understanding a wide range of social and cultural experiences. Popular music teaches lessons about race and privilege, gender and sexuality, different regional experiences, identity formation, and a wide host of other topics. The incorporation of popular music in course curriculums encourages students to enjoy history because it helps them contemplate and understand the popular culture they consume in a media dominated society. Most importantly, understanding the societal and cultural significance of popular music helps students have more nuanced perspectives about the society around them. As explained by Lauri Väkevä in *The Politics of and in Teaching Popular Music* (2017), popular music education helps students move "toward more critically informed ways to participate in social-cultural life" (Väkevä, p. 23). In other words, popular music education can help students ultimately become more informed citizens.

As described by American studies scholar George Lipsitz, explorations of popular music in the classroom provides a space for the examination of the myriad of voices, struggles for power, cultural ideologies and different realities that exist outside of traditional academic paradigms (Lipsitz, 1990a). I have used popular music to teach about the state of California for over a decade in U.S. history and American studies courses. Students often express they enjoy the exploration of popular music out of all the material covered in a given class. They also learn a great deal of social and cultural history, and hold more informed perspectives about music in the contemporary era. While I do not teach courses focused specifically on popular music, I do weave it into the broader curriculum I cover to explore social and cultural issues. To encourage lyrical analysis among students during class, I provide them with a copy of lyrics to read while we listen to various songs. In terms of course assignments, many former students have opted to write short essays on topics like the image of California promoted by groups such as the Beach Boys and the Mamas and the Papas. Moreover, students have also juxtaposed lyrical content with music groups like the Beach Boys and N.W.A. in essays, as both call out specific California locations that are rooted in different historical and social contexts.

When a classroom of millennial students is asked if they have heard the 1964 hit single by the Mamas and the Papas, "California Dreamin'," a significant portion of the class will likely not raise their hand. However, once they hear the song played in the classroom, most students recognize the song, while some might even comment they regularly listen to it on their digital devices, or it was one of their parents' or grandparents' favorites. If students fail to know they have listened to a song until they actually hear it, chances are they have never explored its lyrical content or the social and cultural context of when that music was produced. A wide range of different primary and secondary sources assist with this teaching and learning process.

Music with lyrical content about California produced during the late twentieth century adds greatly to understanding different realities and experiences. While California was home to the first pop and rock music festival in U.S. history, the Monterey Pop Festival in June 1967, there was also a seemingly endless number of songs that referenced life and experiences in the state during this period. In addition, California's status as a major producer of popular music, especially from the 1960s onward, as well as its multiethnic population and long-standing attention garnishing image in popular culture, solidify the importance of exploring music produced in the region. California-based music and music festivals in the second half of the twentieth century can be incorporated into curricula in a variety of different U.S. history and American studies courses. Moreover, there is a broad historiography of academic books and journal articles, documentaries, and Hollywood films that focus on music in California in the late twentieth century—from the 1988 film '68 to the 2015 film *Straight Outta Compton*.

Popular music produced in California and music festivals in the late twentieth century pull on two main threads in the state's history, "sunshine" and "noir." Both of these threads in popular music relate to broader social and cultural histories in the state. The sunshine image depicts California as a sunshine-laden, beach, and palm tree filled pastoral Eden, with endless happiness for its inhabitants. The noir image, on the other hand, pulls on themes of death, destruction, urban decay, racial segregation, oppression, and the myth that everything is perfect in the Golden State.

The Hippies and the Sixties: Sunshiny Freedoms and Conservative Nightmares

Importantly, the "sunshine" image and the "noir" image reside on two opposing ends of a continuum that are not necessarily mutually exclusive, and depend upon socially constructed notions of morality, progress, and a host of other potential variables. Different realities and systems of cultural belief, for that matter, work to give popular music and the world that surrounds it different meanings. As explained by George Lipsitz (1990b), "images and icons compete for dominance within a multiplicity of discourses," as "consumers of popular culture move in and out of subject positions in a way that allows the same message to have widely varying meanings at the point of reception" (p. 13). In other words, music, as well as the way it is viewed and consumed by different peoples, helps to uncover the "multiplicity of discourses" Lipsitz is referring to. Combined with the fact that there is an abundance of examples to choose from, the multivocal nature of popular music in California makes for a rich discussion about different realities, experiences, and identity.

While the San Francisco Bay Area "hippie" counterculture movement of the 1960s, driven by Baby Boomers and inspired by the 1950s Beat Generation poets, writers, and folk, only lasted between the late 1960s and early 1970s, it was highly representative of the youthful revolt against the middle class consumer culture of their parents' generation. Jefferson Airplane, the Grateful Dead, Santana, the Steve Miller Band, and Janis Joplin and Big Brother and the Holding Company epitomized the music of this movement. The scene pushed the boundaries of style as the fashion centered around frayed leather jackets, bell bottoms, and tie-dyed shirts pulled the youth look away from the conservative clean-cut middle-class suburbs. Popular songs showed the way in which musical artists were experimenting with distorted sounds, new instruments, and lyrics which centered on social alienation and the use of psychedelic drugs. The "hippie movement" began with the Human Be-In staged in San Francisco's Golden Gate Park in January of 1967. The event drew in 20,000–30,000 attendees and acted as a prelude to the "Summer of Love." It was driven by the anti–Vietnam War movement and the 1966 California law that banned the use of the popular drug LSD. Primary video footage of this event, as well as interviews from attendees, can be found in the DVD documentary *Berkeley in the Sixties* (2002), and on various online video-sharing websites.

In the summer of 1967, the Monterey Pop Festival took place June 16–18 at the fairgrounds in Monterey, California. Organizers expected 50,000 attendees, but over 200,000 showed up. The event popularized Janis Joplin as well as Jimi Hendrix, the Who, and Buffalo Springfield. Released on DVD as a three-disc set, the 1968 documentary film *The Complete Monterey Pop Festival* (2002) contains numerous live performances from the event and excellent footage of attendees. The DVD version of the documentary is organized in a manner that makes different sections of the film and individual performances easy to navigate and present in the classroom. Especially noteworthy is Jimi Hendrix's legendary performance of "Wild Thing" and the Who's performance of "My Generation."

Illustrative of the limitations of the movement, Otis Redding, half of the members of the band that backed him, Booker T. and the M.G.'s, and Jimi Hendrix were the only nonwhite performers at the event. The lack of a multiracial scene in the so-called liberal Bay Area counterculture scene served as the cultural baggage carried from their formerly racially segregated suburban lives. Additionally, a wave of migrants in their parents' generation moved into post–World War II suburban subdivisions that restricted the sale or rental of property to people of color. The continuation of this lack of racial diversity in the hippie scene showed that there were racial barriers even among the most liberal rebellious white youth. A segment of this youth supported the anti-Vietnam and Free Speech Movement at University of California, Berkeley, but questions of race relations and how to embrace the civil rights movement left them stumped, especially as the Black Panthers became the vanguard of the movement after it was created in Oakland, California, in 1966. Covering the hippie counterculture in this context, helps students understand the movement with a more critical perspective, and provides a gateway to the exploration of broader racial faultiness in the late twentieth-century U.S.

The hippie counterculture that started in the Bay Area went from "sunshine" to "noir" in a few short years. When Ronald Reagan was running for governor of California in 1966, he used the Free Speech Movement at University of California, Berkeley and the broader counterculture movement in the Bay Area as a major campaign issue. Reagan catered to the older conservative population in California when he addressed music concerts held at Berkeley and elsewhere. In a speech at the Cow Palace in San Francisco, he stirred conservative fears about the Baby Boom youth by describing the multicolored psychedelic films projected onto the walls which included images of nude torsos of young men and women moving in "suggestive positions" as rock and roll bands performed. The chapter entitled "Reagan's Conservative Wave" in Kirse Granat May's *Golden State, Golden Youth: The California Image in Popular Culture, 1955–1966* (2002) provides an excellent backdrop for the study of Ronald Reagan's relationship with the Baby Boom counterculture.

Reagan posited that there was a "morality gap" between his supporters and the counterculture, free speech, and anti-war politics more popular among the younger generation. Music and concerts played a central role in his public attacks on the movement. The 2002 film *Berkeley in the Sixties* includes scenes from Reagan's "morality gap" speech, Joan Baez performances at pro–Free Speech protests, and Country Joe and the Fish appearances at anti-war events, among other things. When Reagan ran for a second term as governor in 1970, he found support among the likes of Frank Sinatra, a musical favorite among the older conservative generation in California and elsewhere. Fresh into the Republican Party like so many early neoconservatives, Sinatra was not a fan of rock and roll, stating in a 1957 interview that it was for "cretinous [sic] goons" and was "the most brutal, ugly, desperate, vicious form of expression it has been my misfortune to hear" (Szatmary, 2014, p. 24). Sinatra continued, claiming that rock and rollers attracted teens with "almost imbecilic reiterations and sly lewd—in plain fact dirty—lyrics" (Szatmary, 2014, p. 24).

The more conservative listeners who enjoyed Sinatra and agreed with Reagan's take on leftist politics in the 1960s also consumed the country music which emanated from California's Central Valley and greater Los Angeles. The chapters titled "The San Francisco Sound" in *Rock and Roll: A Social History* (Friedlander, 2006) and "Acid Rock" in *Rockin' in Time: A Social History of Rock-and-Roll* (Szatmary, 2014) are excellent resources for the music of the 1960s youth counterculture, while *Proud to Be an Okie: Culture, Politics, Country Music, and Migration* (La Chapelle, 2007) and *American Exodus: The Dust Bowl Migration and Okie Culture in California* (Gregory, 1991), trace popular music in conservative late-twentieth-century spaces. The rise of the "Bakersfield Sound" from artists such as Buck Owens and Merle Haggard is also chronicled in part three, "Beyond the Nashville Sound" in the 2003 British Broadcasting Company (BBC) documentary series entitled *Lost Highway: The Story of Popular Music.*

By the end of the 1960s, young people from across the U.S. had converged on the epicenter of the hippie counterculture movement, the Haight-Ashbury District in San Francisco. By the early 1970s, however, the movement burned out. Janis Joplin, Jimi Hendrix and many other popular music artists died from drug and alcohol overdoses. In summer 1969, the Woodstock Music & Art Fair in New York, held August 15–18, was portrayed in popular media as a garbage-filled, muddy, drug-induced disaster for the 400,000 people that attended. Later that year, on December 6, the Rolling Stones hosted the Altamont Speedway Free Festival on a racetrack outside of San Francisco in the hopes of making a live concert documentary with other groups such as the

Grateful Dead. The Rolling Stones selected the Altamont location after city officials in San Francisco denied them access to Golden Gate Park. The event was billed as "Woodstock West," and attracted around 300,000 attendees. However, Altamont turned disastrous as the Hells Angels motorcycle gang, who had been hired to work as security guards and paid, in part, with alcoholic beverages, attacked attendees, leading to one death and numerous injuries. Additionally, several cars were stolen and there was a great deal of property damage.

Several musicians were also violently beaten by members of the Hells Angels at Altamont. The Grateful Dead showed up and promptly left because it had turned into such a disaster. Footage of the concert at Altamont, the Hells Angels attacks on the crowd, and performances by the Rolling Stones with Mick Jagger's plea with the hired security guards to stop attacking the crowd, are included in the 1970 documentary film *Gimme Shelter*. The chaotic events at Altamont signified the beginning of the end of the counterculture movement which had swept through mainstream U.S. popular culture. In addition to the full-length documentaries on the hippie counterculture Bay Area–based movement, YouTube and other video-sharing websites provide a wealth of primary and secondary source video clips.

One example of the incredibly large amount of video content online is the 1967 CBS News Special Report "The Hippie Temptation." Filmed mostly in San Francisco's Haight-Ashbury district, the report depicts the hippie movement in cautionary terms for the show's older generation audience showing footage of the Grateful Dead in the living room of a house shared by the group in the neighborhood. The interview with the Grateful Dead in the CBS special is also included in the 1995 *Time-Life* multipart documentary series *The History of Rock 'n' Roll* in the episode entitled "My Generation."

California Dreaming: From the Monterey Pop Festival to Wattstax

As illustrated by the counterculture hippie movement, as well as the more conservative world of post–World War II suburbia, the "California dream" took different forms in the second half of the twentieth century. White middle class and aspiring middle class peoples fled to segregated suburban spaces, as urban centers faced deindustrialization. Additionally, the buildup of the prison industrial complex, and other economic issues, related to disinvestment in "inner city" neighborhoods. The juxtaposition of urban and suburban spaces through the medium of music highlighted diverse realities in California.

In 1965, the sunshine pop group the Mamas and the Papas, a Los

Angeles-based group composed of middle and upper-class white Baby Boom youth, released their signature hit "California Dreamin'." Peaking at #4 on the Billboard Pop Chart, and gaining gold certification for the sale of 500,000 copies by the summer of 1966, the song was a major success. The song's lyrics came from the perspective of someone who had left Los Angeles for a place that was dark and cold, and wanted to return because it was safe and warm. By evoking the sunshine, and presumably, outdoor recreation, the song played on the suburban version of the teenage "good life" in California experienced by so many Baby Boomers.

While groups like the Mamas and the Papas, the Beach Boys, Jan and Dean, and the Sun Rays sang about teenage romance, social mobility, the middle class suburban economy, and the enjoyment of safe spaces in the Golden State, the black residents of greater Los Angeles had experienced a long history of racial profiling conducted by law enforcement officials, high poverty and unemployment, and residential racial segregation. In response to the 1960s and groups like the Beach Boys, May (2002) explains, "never before in the short history of rock and roll was the focus so exclusively on particular lifestyles, marked by mobility and the beach, in such a specific location" (p. 98). To the young black population in places like the Los Angeles neighborhood of Watts, the society to which groups like the Mamas and the Papas and the Beach Boys sung about must have seemed like it was on another planet.

From World War II into the 1970s, African Americans were channeled into South Los Angeles due to the widespread usage of racially restrictive covenants, and places like Compton were recognized as being an "all American" suburb as it transitioned from a majority white to a majority African American community. Yet, by the middle of the 1960s, it was wracked with poverty that stemmed from the loss of industrial jobs in the region, as well as a shrinking tax base and plummeting property values. Likewise, the African American population in Watts increased by eight times between 1940 and 1960, and accounted for 87 percent of the population by 1965. Around the same period, the median black family income in Watts was $4,669, considerably less than that earned in predominantly white racially segregated suburban communities (Wyatt, 1997).

In stark comparison to Watts, Orange County in Los Angeles was 90 percent white with a median family income of $7,219 and home to new post–World War II suburban subdivisions that were all but off limits to African Americans and other people of color (McGirr, 2001). The county was the embodiment of economic prosperity in the post–World War II U.S., while Watts was distinctly not. Orange County, moreover, was representative of the ideal and romanticized imagery of postwar society found in the pages of *Sunset* magazine and in the music of the Beach Boys and others, while Watts was the home of the worst urban rebellion in U.S. history at the time. On the evening of August 11, 1965, a 21-year-old African American motorist was pulled over near his home by law enforcement officials after being suspected of reckless driving. After a crowd gathered to confront the law enforcement officials, a skirmish took place, which then tuned into a five-day revolt in the greater Watts area. The arrest of the young African American motorist was essentially the last straw as the region's black population had faced a long history of residential segregation and systemic racism. While editions of the popular *Sunset* magazine touted the backyard party's centered around swimming pools and barbeques and other aspects of life in the suburbs, covers of *Life*, *Time*, and *Newsweek* magazine contained images of destruction in the aftermath of the rebellion.

Popular music and festivals followed the "sunshine" and "noir" threads in the world around them. The Mamas and the Papas' "California Dreamin'" was released a mere three months before the Watts Rebellion, with the latter commemorated seven years later during the Wattstax benefit concert held at the Los Angeles Coliseum in 1972. Billed as the "Black Woodstock," the concert was organized by Stax Records, the legendary Memphis, Tennessee–based recording company that helped put Southern soul music on the map the previous decade. Performers at the event included Isaac Hayes, the Staple Singers, Kim Weston, Rufus Thomas, Sly and the Family Stone, and Albert King. Reverend Jesse Jackson gave a stirring invocation entitled "I Am Somebody," which was subsequently sampled in the 2005 song performed by hip-hop artists Public Enemy, Dead Prez, and Kam. "I am somebody," shouted Jackson, followed by "I may be on welfare ... I may be small ... I may have made mistakes, but I am somebody. My clothes are different, my face is different, my hair is different, but I am somebody." Jackson raised his fist in the air as he uttered these remarks and the crowd cheered. The 1973 documentary *Wattstax* features concert performances and studio footage of comedian Richard Pryor. A 30th anniversary special edition of the concert was released on DVD in 2006, and many of the performances can be found on YouTube and other online video sharing websites.

Kim Weston's performance of the "Black National Anthem" at the start of the concert is particularly notable. Partway through the performance the video cuts to images of enslaved Africans packed into slave ships, photographs of black sharecroppers and people who were lynched, as well as signs which denoted Jim Crow segregation in the early twentieth-century American South, nineteenth- and twentieth-century civil rights activists, athletes, musicians, and images of law enforcement officials brutalizing African Americans. The imagery added to Kim Weston's performance adds an additional level of depth to the concert in the way that it creates a clear association between the situation in Watts and the lengthy history of black oppression in the U.S.

At the end of Weston's performance, the video cuts to Dr. Martin Luther King, Jr.'s, last speech on April 3, 1968, wherein he explains to the crowd in Memphis, Tennessee, that he had been to the mountain top and seen the promised land, but he may not make it there. The imagery and tone in the Wattstax documentary highlighted a much different set of experiences and realities than that of the Beach Boys, the Mamas and the Papas, and other California-based music popular among white Baby Boom youth. The juxtaposition of these different musical worlds in the classroom can build a foundation for understanding social and cultural history in the second half of twentieth-century California. Whereas the hippie counterculture was based around a desire to "drop out" of white middle-class society, the latter addressed inequalities and social injustice, and illustrated a distinct desire to be more part of society.

Transnational Fusions: Chicano Rock and Popular Mexican American Music Artists

Similar to white middle class Baby Boomers and African Americans in late twentieth-century California, Mexican Americans also contributed to the popular music scene in ways that, when incorporated into a class curriculum, highlights broad social and cultural experiences rooted in "sunshine" and "noir." Los Angeles was known as a place of freeways, Hollywood, palm trees, sunshine, and the beach in the 1950s and 1960s, but the Latino/a population, made up mostly of Mexican Americans, lived in a series of barrios segregated in a similar manner as that witnessed by African Americans. The Latino/a population in the city tripled in size between 1940 and 1960, from 200,000 to 600,000, and many worked in the most difficult blue collar and low-wage service sector and manufacturing jobs. Out of this society, and built on the foundation laid by artists such as Lalo Guerrero and Don Tosti, emerged a series of popular musicians and groups. Don Tosti, a Mexican American jazz and rhythm and blues musician, mixed boogie woogie, bebop, and caló (Spanish slang popular in the mid-century American Southwest) in his 1948 song "Pachuco Boogie." The song sold one million copies, making him the first Mexican American artist to do so in U.S. history.

Ritchie Valens, the Mexican American rock and roller from the San Fernando Valley, followed in Tosti's footsteps with his chart-topping cover of the traditional Spanish language song "La Bamba" in 1958. Nicknamed the "California Kid," Valens produced a number of hits before his untimely death in a plane crash in 1959, the most notable of which, "Donna," illuminated the "noir" thread in the Mexican American experience in mid-century Southern California, while also serving as an anthem for interethnic/racial romance between Valens and his white girlfriend, Donna. Valens grew up in the barrio in Pacoima, California, and Donna's father prevented her from dating him because he was Mexican American, thus inspiring the song. This, along with the broader story of Ritchie Valens, is included in the 1987 biographical film *La Bamba*.

Yet even as Valens faced the kinds of sentiments expressed by his girlfriend's dad, as stated by Garcia (2001), "interethnic mixing on the dance floors and in parking lots broke down youths' ambivalence towards intercultural romance" (p. 208). Along with *Land of a Thousand Dances: Chicano Rock 'n' Roll from Southern California* (Reyes and Waldman, 2009) and *Mexican American Mojo: Popular Music, Dance, and Urban Culture in Los Angeles, 1935–1968* (Macías, 2008), *Barrio Rhythm: Mexican American Music in Los Angeles* (Loza,1993), *Spaces of Conflict, Sounds of Solidarity: Music, Race, and Spatial Entitlement in Los Angeles* (Johnson, 2013), and the chapter "Memories of El Monte: Dance Halls in Youth Culture in Greater Los Angeles, 1950–1974" in *A World of Its Own: Race, Labor, and Citrus in the Making of Greater Los Angeles, 1900–1970* (Garcia, 2001), are excellent resources on Mexican American popular music in California during the second half of the twentieth century. These academic studies can be supplemented with the 2008 Public Broadcasting Service (PBS) documentary *Chicano Rock! The Sounds of East Los Angeles*, and episode three of the 2009 documentary series *Latin Music U.S.A.*, "The Chicano Wave."

As the Mexican American civil rights and Chicano power movement encouraged more pride in identity and culture, Mexican American artists produced music that fused different Latin rhythms and instruments with sounds popular in the mainstream U.S., paving the way for late twentieth and twenty-first century music produced by the likes of Ozomatli, Quetzal, Los Cafeteras, La Santa Cecilia, and Prayers. From the 1970s onward, groups like Tierra, El Chicano, and Los Lobos addressed issues related to immigration, systemic problems with economics and education in urban centers, and a number of other issues in popular songs. Released in 1984, Los Lobos's third studio album, *How Will the Wolf Survive?* is a testament to Mexican immigration intergenerational relations and coming of age for second and later generation Mexican Americans in the U.S. The music video for the title-track single, and the song's lyrics, touch on issues related to border-crossing, acculturation and survival as its protagonist crosses a desert landscape into the U.S. and struggles with work as a dishwasher in a restaurant.

The section in the Mexican American history class I have taught for four years for the Departments of History and Multicultural and Gender Studies explores popular Mexican American music artists, from Tosti and

Lalo Guerrero to Los Lobos and Selena, among others, is usually the students' favorite part of the course. As in so many other classes, many are familiar with the music and claim that they listened to it growing up. They also express, however, shock that they knew nothing about the social and cultural context around the different examples we explore. Most importantly, the students, many of which are Mexican American, express in class discussions and short in-class written responses that the lyrical content in the popular music we explore relates to their own experiences and that of their families.

California Sagas in the 1970s

As music became more diverse and multicultural, the image of California in popular culture also became more complicated. Southern California, a place once romanticized with citrus crate art and promotional literature distributed by the Los Angeles Chamber of Commerce and others became the home of urban revolt, student walk-outs, multiracial protests, and environmental catastrophes. With this, the image of California in popular music became more complicated in the late twentieth century.

Popular music produced by the Beach Boys throughout the late twentieth century carried the "sunshine" torch with songs like the 1973 single "California Saga" on the album *Holland*, while artists like Carole King and groups such as the Starland Vocal Band produced songs like "Back to California" (1971) and "California Day" (1973). Simultaneously, new West Coast country folk rock songs explored the darker "noir" side of death, drug-induced burnout, struggles in dealing with an increasingly corporatized music industry in Southern California, and social alienation in the late 1960s and 1970s. As displayed in the 2007 BBC documentary *Hotel California: L.A. from the Byrds to the Eagles*, the Byrds, Buffalo Springfield, Joni Mitchell, Jackson Brown, and Neil Young led this alternative movement in popular music. "For What It's Worth" by Buffalo Springfield, for example, was written in response to the Sunset Strip curfew riots in 1966 when civic and business leaders, as well as local law enforcement officials, attempted to shut down the counterculture scene which sprouted up around popular music venues.

After his successful stint with Buffalo Springfield, and his widely successful fourth studio album *Harvest* (1972), an album which topped the *Billboard* charts for two weeks and featured the popular singles "Heart of Gold" and "Old Man," Neil Young became disenchanted with life in Los Angeles, and it showed in his music. In "L.A.," a song with appeared on Young's 1973 album *Times Fades Away*, he describes the particular uptight nature among people in greater Los Angeles, while also criticizing traffic congestion and smog in the region. His next album, *On the Beach*, released in 1974, contained songs which continued this thread of despair and alienation.

The cover for *On the Beach*, a dystopian scene on the beach with patio chair and table, a buried car, and Young in the distance with his back to the photographer in a yellow and white suit, is among the more striking album covers produced by Young throughout his long career. Under the patio table, half dug into the sand, is a newspaper with the headline "Senator Buckley Calls for Nixon to Resign." The album was released just days before the House Judiciary Committee recommended the impeachment of President Nixon. In addition to showing video footage and clips from actual songs, album covers are also a great resource for class lectures and discussion, and many can be easily found online with a quick search on Google Images. Even better is the presentation of authentic vinyl record albums in the classroom.

In 1977, the Eagles, a super-group which emerged from the West Coast country folk scene, released their signature hit "Hotel California." The song's lyrics tell the story of an arrival to California. The guest, presumably a man, is greeted by a mysterious woman at a hotel named California, and upon arrival there is confusion as to whether the destination is heaven or hell. As the song continues, the situation grows darker as the lyrics hint to the era of excess in the 1970s found especially in the world of popular music. In the end, the hotel becomes a prison, and as the protagonist attempts to escape he discovers that there is no way to exit once visitors have checked in. Similar to songs like "Surfin' U.S.A." by the Beach Boys or "California Dreamin'" by the Mamas and the Papas, students in a typical college classroom will likely have heard "Hotel California," but they may not have ever listed closely to the song's dark lyrical content and the way it speaks to the history of California's image in American popular culture.

Punk, Hip-Hop and Generation X

The Eagles took the West Coast country folk rock sound to the top of the corporate music world in the late 1970s. Released in 1976, *Their Greatest Hits (1971-1975)* is among the best-selling albums of the twentieth century. But as the music industry shifted to the West Coast, punk and hip-hop emerged out of new underground counterculture movements to take popular music by storm. While both genres started on the East Coast in 1970s New York City, by the 1980s, California, namely greater Los Angeles and the Bay Area were home to their own scenes. Like the 1960s counterculture, when it was in its infancy, punk and hip-hop on the West Coast was outside of the corporate music world in the clubs and on the streets of California's urban centers. Both scenes were driven by members of Generation X (those born between 1965 and

1980), a cohort who faced higher rates of poverty and unemployment, and unlike many Baby Boomers, two-parent working households. The social alienation and rebellion from middle class society so prominent in the alternative rock music of the 1990s was born in the punk and hip-hop of the late 1970s and 1980s.

Diverse punk artists and groups like X, the Brat, Alice Bag, and the Dead Kennedy's critiqued middle class consumer society in their music and the more conservative mainstream youth fashion styles with their dress and mannerisms, while aligning with feminist and radical political ideologies. Punk songs like "We've Got a Bigger Problem Now" (1980) by the Dead Kennedys painted Ronald Reagan as a white Christian supremacist and fascist who fought against human rights, while also acknowledging that California played an important role in the emergence of the New Right in late twentieth-century American politics.

Punk and hip-hop music in the 1980s represented the "noir" underbelly of Reaganomics. Increases in poverty and unemployment in black, Latino/a, and working class white communities showed the failures of "trickle-down economics" as urban centers deindustrialized and faced the rise of the prison industrial complex. In *Footsteps in the Dark: The Hidden Histories of Popular Music* (2007), George Lipsitz criticizes the conservative movements which targeted hip-hop music in the 1980s, while ignoring the real conditions faced by cities across the U.S. reflected in the music. Niggaz wit Attitudes (N.W.A.), a Compton-based rap group led by Dr. Dre and Ice Cube, helped found the "gangsta rap" sound with the debut album *Straight Outta Compton* in 1988. With songs like "Fuck tha Police," the group shocked the record buying public and received attention from the Federal Bureau of Investigation for, as the organization stated, encouraging violence against police—even while the song essentially criticized the long history of police brutality faced by African Americans in greater South Los Angeles. The music video was banned by MTV, and *Billboard* blacked out their name on the charts, all of which made them even more popular among youth in the era. The title track song introduced the group and helped place real and imagined notions of Compton in the pop culture lexicon for generations to come. As explained by Josh Sides (2004), N.W.A.'s hyper-popularity blinded listeners to real elements of Compton's long and sorted history with racial segregation, deindustrialization, and economic problems, and sensationalized the black experience in South Los Angeles even as their music criticized systemic racism and provided a "geography lesson" for white listeners (p. 599).

Despite the resistance by the record industry, MTV, and law enforcement organizations like the F.B.I., N.W.A. sold three million copies of their debut album. By 1992, the group, along with the help of Ice T., launched a new West Coast hip-hop sound. In 2015, N.W.A. received renewed popularity after the release of the film *Straight Outta Compton* which dramatized the lives and experiences of its members. Additionally, the 2010 ESPN *30 for 30* episode *Straight Outta L.A.* directed by Ice Cube, chronicled the rise of N.W.A., the role they played in the popularization of black Oakland Raiders football hats and jackets, and the very identity of late 1980s and early 1990s Los Angeles. After the group disbanded, co-founder Andre Young (Dr. Dre) eventually moved into a less political sound known as G-Funk, while Ice Cube continued to criticize social and political conditions in his lyrics.

Dre's stepbrother, Warren G, released his 1994 debut album *Regulate … G Funk Era* with the single "Regulate," which reached #2 on the *Billboard* chart and went triple-platinum. The album's cover painted a bleak landscape of housing projects set within the symbolic Southern California landscape of palm trees and sunshine. The imagery countered that of sunshine Los Angeles, the semi-tropical land of sunshine, health and beauty. N.W.A.'s lyrical content also mentioned numerous locations in Southern California, but in a much different way than the Beach Boys and others. I regularly encourage students to recognize the stark juxtaposition between the lyrical content in Beach Boys and N.W.A. songs, as both groups called out specific Southern California locations, albeit in different contexts.

Conclusion

The sunshine and noir of California in the popular music and festivals of the twentieth century, was carried forth with a new collection of music artists, groups, and events in the twenty-first. The century opened with a new presentation of the California dream. With the bold title of "Cali Dreamin'," Ice Cube, Snoop Dogg, and Dr. Dre appeared on the cover of the April 2000 edition of *The Source* magazine. Additionally, the Long Beach, California, ska group Sublime's description of multiracial unity in their song "April 29th, 1992," focused exclusively on rebellion in response to the Rodney King beating, signaling the rise of the new, more inclusive and diverse multicultural California of the twenty-first century. Teaching popular music about California, uncovers social and political transformations in the state's history, reflecting different generations, popular myths, regionalism, and identity formation.

REFERENCES

Garcia, M. (2001). *A world of its own: Race, labor, and citrus in the making of greater Los Angeles, 1900–1970.* Chapel Hill, NC: University of North Carolina Press.

Gregory, J.N. (1989). *American exodus: The dust bowl migration and Okie culture in California.* New York: Oxford University Press.

Johnson, G.T. (2013). *Spaces of conflict, sounds of solidarity*. Los Angeles: University of California Press.
La Chapelle, P. (2007). *Proud to be an Okie: Cultural politics, country music, and migration to southern California*. Los Angeles: University of California Press.
Lipsitz, G. (1990a). Listening to learn and learning to listen: Popular culture, cultural theory, and American studies. *American Quarterly, 42*(4), 615–636.
Lipsitz, G. (1990b). *Time passages: Collective memory and American popular culture*. Minneapolis: University of Minnesota Press.
Macías A. (2008). *Mexican American mojo: Popular music, dance, and urban culture in Los Angeles, 1935–1968*. Durham, NC: Duke University Press.
May, K.G. (2002). *Golden state, golden youth: The California image in popular culture, 1955–1966*. Chapel Hill, NC: The University of North Carolina Press.
McGirr, L. (2001). *Suburban warriors: The origins of the new American right*. Princeton, NJ: Princeton University Press.
Reyes, D., and Waldman, T. (2009). *Land of a thousand dances: Chicano rock 'n' roll from southern California*. Albuquerque: University of New Mexico.
Sides, J. (2014). Straight into Compton: American dreams, urban nightmares, and the metamorphosis of a black suburb. *American Quarterly, 56*(3), 583–605.
Szatmary, D.P. (2014). *Rockin' in time: A social history of rock-and-roll*. Upper Saddle River, NJ: Pearson.
Väkevä, L. (2017). The politics of and in teaching popular music. In C.X. Rodriguez (Ed.), *Coming of age: Teaching and learning popular music in academia* (pp. 3–29). Mountain View, CA: Maize Books.
Wyatt, D. (1997). *Five fires: Race, catastrophe, and the shaping of California*. New York: Addison-Wesley Publishing.

Remembering Tomorrow
Exploring the Deeper Transatlantic Story of the Birth of the Psychedelic Sixties

Tom Zlabinger

> [T]omorrow never knows. It remembers.
> —Author Nick Bromell
>
> If you remember the '60s, you really weren't there.
> —Comedian Charlie Fleischer

Music making never happens in a vacuum. Musicians have always borrowed from other musicians, explored older traditions, and utilized different technologies. Before the mid-twentieth century, the rate of musical change was usually slow and often localized to a specific area. This was not true, however, with the explosion of the sights and sounds of the psychedelic sixties (1967–1970). Not only did the new sights and sounds seem to arrive suddenly, psychedelic music (and all that went with it) spread across the United States, the United Kingdom, and beyond rather quickly. Guitarist and co-founder of Jefferson Airplane Paul Kantner witnessed the quick transformation in the Midwest of the U.S. while on tour:

> We went to, I think, Grinnell College in Iowa once, in 1967, and all the people came to the show in, like, prom gowns and tuxedos and then we came back to Grinnell the next year and they were having like, nude love-ins, and mud-bath parties, and acid freak-outs and all this sort of thing ... in just one year [as quoted in Robins, 2000, p. 9].

To understand what happened in and around popular music in the psychedelic sixties can be difficult. In addition to this speed of change, there are many different elements that fed into what crystalized into the Summer of

Love in 1967 in San Francisco, which transformed a generation of musicians and listeners in the Bay Area and beyond.

For two years, I taught *History of Rock Music*, which was immensely popular as students were eager to talk and write about rock music. But of all the moments within the history of rock and roll, I was surprised that the psychedelic sixties was one of the hardest eras to teach well. Many students were fans of the Beatles, the Grateful Dead, Jimi Hendrix, Pink Floyd, and other bands associated with the era. But I never felt that the students truly appreciated the seismic cultural shift of the mid–1960s. Unfortunately, much of the psychedelic sixties is swamped with stereotypes like hippies, LSD, peace signs, VW vans, and other iconic images and themes. And thus, it was hard to pierce the surface of what is a very complex and expansive development in popular music. There is also a wealth of information a half century later in books published on the subject, plus a multitude of videos available on DVD/Blu-ray and streaming on the internet. Thus, it is difficult to know where and how to best start studying the psychedelic sixties.

Jesse Jarnow's *HEADS: A Biography of Psychedelic America* (2016) helped spark the idea for this essay. The book includes Earl Crabb and Rick Shubb's famous countercultural poster *Humbead's Revised Map of the World* (1969), which depicts the cities of San Francisco, Berkeley, Los Angeles, Cambridge, and New York fused together as a supercontinent of psychedelic culture that is surrounded by the names of hundreds of people involved in the greater psychedelic scene. But the map does not include important English cities like London, Liverpool, or Canterbury. Their absence is what got me thinking about the greater, transatlantic phenomenon of the birth of psychedelic music.

In addition, Danny Goldberg points out in his book *In Search of the Lost Chord: 1967 and the Hippie Idea* (2017) that "[i]t should go without saying that no two people perceived the psychedelic sixties in the same way..." (Goldberg, p. 11). Goldberg's quote highlights the challenges of navigating through the subjective accounts and opinions (both positive and negative) surrounding the psychedelic sixties. This essay is designed to provide a resource for teachers, students, and other researchers of rock music in order to gain a quick (but intricate) understanding of some of the details of the history of early psychedelic music that led to this rapid transformation in the psychedelic sixties. The essay also intends to point the reader in the direction for further research on the era. First, the concurrent histories of Bob Dylan, the Beatles, and Ken Kesey and the Merry Pranksters from 1962 to 1967 are told as an introduction to the transatlantic dynamics of early psychedelic music. Second, using many of the historic films made during and after the psychedelic sixties, the essay then suggests three activities that can help teachers, students, and other researchers in their exploration of the psychedelic sixties: a transatlantic comparison of some relevant albums of 1967 through the lens of Dylan, a comparison of early Beatles and the Monterey International Pop Music Festival (1967), and a comparison of the hippie culture as spread by Kesey and the Merry Pranksters in light of the dark reality that was the Altamont Speedway Free Festival (1969) near San Francisco and the Isle of Wight Festival (1970) off the coast of southern England. Finally, a group project is also suggested to help examine, celebrate, and spark conversation around relevant voices surrounding the psychedelic sixties using published autobiographies.

To discuss early psychedelic music accurately, there must be some mention of lysergic acid diethylamide (better known as LSD or acid). It is no mere coincidence that the birth of psychedelic music coincides with the illegalization of LSD in both the U.S. and the U.K. in late 1966. Musicians experimented with the drug (and other recreational drugs) before LSD's illegalization, and the influence of their experiences persists in their music making afterwards. This essay's discussion will remain focused on the musicians and their music making, but LSD and other drugs will be mentioned as drug use impacts the history of psychedelic music, both as an inspiration for creativity and as a disruptive agent in the evolution of the popular music of the sixties.

The essay's title "Remembering Tomorrow" is intended to reflect the challenge of illustrating the birth of the psychedelic sixties and is intentionally paradoxical. The two epigraphs of the essay deal with memory. Nick Bromell's quote (2000, p. 165) is a variation of the title to the Beatles' song "Tomorrow Never Knows" from *Revolver* (1966). Bromell is correct that tomorrow can only remember today. Thus, we no longer really know a history after it has happened and are best aware of a time period as it is happening. After the time period, much is lost as the thrill of experience fades into the echo of memory. The epigraph from comedian Charlie Fleischer (Christon, 1982, p. M60) thus rightly questions the validity of any memory of the sixties. As an antidote to the paradox of the two quotes, and in an effort to capture the confusion (and excitement) of being in the middle of the transition of the psychedelic sixties, we can turn to John Lennon's inspiration for the lyrics of "Tomorrow Never Knows" found in Timothy Leary's book *The Psychedelic Experience* (1964):

> Trust your divinity, trust your brain, trust your companions.
> Whenever in doubt, turn off your mind, float downstream
>   [Leary, Alpert, & Metzner, 1964, p. 14].

In that spirit, please enjoy the following discussion and information in this essay as we take a journey toward a better understanding of the musicians and music at the beginning of the psychedelic sixties. And by following these transatlantic undercurrents, we can begin to grasp the deeper story of a complex time and its music that then informs the music that comes afterwards.

Early Psychedelic Music as a Transatlantic Process

In his book *Sixties Rock: Garage, Psychedelic, and Other Satisfactions* (1999), Michael Hicks asserts that garage rock and psychedelic music are "best viewed through lenses relatively free from the powerful spectres of the Beatles and [Bob] Dylan" (p. viii). Though it is true that garage rock may be better appreciated as largely independent from the Beatles and Dylan, I would argue that psychedelic music is best understood as a product of the combined output of the Beatles and Dylan, especially within the context of their transatlantic appreciation of one another. Their mutual admiration would eventually lead to a collision of their music, which then redirected both of their trajectories.

In addition to the Beatles and Dylan, there is a third "spectre" that cannot be ignored when talking about early psychedelic music: author Ken Kesey. Immortalized in Tom Wolfe's *The Electric Kool-Aid Acid Test* (1968), Kesey, the Merry Pranksters, and their 1964 cross-country trip from California to New York (and back again) aboard their multi-colored 1939 International Harvester school bus Furthur, are just as relevant (if not more so) to the birth of early psychedelic music as any moment in the careers of Dylan or the Beatles. And though both Dylan and the Beatles used drugs, it was Kesey who was first exposed to LSD (and other drugs) in 1960 as part of a government-sponsored study at Menlo Park Veterans' Hospital in San Francisco. By including Kesey, and the events that took place in respect to the Acid Tests in California after the bus trip, we are able to develop a deeper understanding of the events leading up to the birth of early psychedelic music. In a new foreword to his first and most-famous novel *One Flew Over the Cuckoo's Nest* (1962), Kesey talks about his experience of being exposed to hallucinatory drugs in a clinical environment and the world that was opened up to him as a result:

> Eight o'clock every Tuesday morning I showed up at the vets' hospital in Menlo Park, ready to roll. The doctor deposited me in a little room on his ward, dealt me a couple of pills or a shot or a little glass of bitter juice, then locked the door. He checked back every forty minutes to see if I was still alive, took some tests, asked some questions, left again. The rest of the time I spent studying the inside of my forehead, or looking out the one little window in the door. It was six inches wide and eight inches high, and heavy chicken wire inside the glass. You get your visions through whatever gate you're granted [Kesey, 2002, p. vii].

Coincidentally, just before Kesey's novel was published, the young singer-songwriter Robert Zimmerman from Minnesota moved to New York City in 1961, and soon released his first album under his newly assumed name,

Bob Dylan (1962). The same year of Dylan's debut album, the Beatles met with producer George Martin to record their first sessions at Abbey Road studios in London. Though these three histories were probably not associated with one another at the time, they would begin to converge and later impact one another over the years leading up to the Summer of Love in 1967.

Quickly, Dylan transformed from a lesser-known Greenwich Village singer-songwriter to a protest singer, releasing *The Freewheelin' Bob Dylan* (1963), which included his often-covered anthem "Blowin' in the Wind." Dylan debuted at the famous Newport Folk Festival that summer, propelling him to the status of voice of the younger generation. He also performed with Joan Baez in front of over 200,000 people at the March on Washington on August 28, 1963, alongside Dr. Martin Luther King, Jr. That same year, the Beatles' *Please Please Me* (1963) became the number one album in the U.K., which propelled the band to fame and led to their first trip to the U.S. the following year. While attending the Broadway premiere of the play adaptation of his *One Flew Over the Cuckoo's Nest* in the fall of 1963, Kesey learned about the upcoming 1964 New York World's Fair. Partially inspired by Jack Kerouac's *On the Road* (1957), Kesey concocted the idea of traveling cross-country from California to New York with a bunch of his friends to see the World's Fair, which coincided with the publication of his next novel *Sometimes a Great Notion* (1964) the following summer.

Both Dylan and the Beatles released albums at the beginning of 1964. *The Times They Are A-Changin'* (1964) further established Dylan as a protest song troubadour. And *Meet the Beatles!* (1964) contained the music that was to be broadcast across the U.S. as part of the Beatles' historic television debut in the U.S. on *The Ed Sullivan Show* on February 9, 1964. In 1971, Dylan admitted that he loved the Beatles and that the lads from Liverpool influenced his transformation from protest singer to rock and roll singer (Scaduto, 1971, pp. 203–204). The Beatles also admired Dylan after they first heard him on his album *The Freewheelin' Bob Dylan* shortly before their arrival in the U.S. The Beatles' and Dylan's mutual appreciation for each other's music would result in an exchange of musical ideas, if not an unspoken sense of competition.

On August 28, 1964, Dylan and the Beatles met for the first time at the Delmonico Hotel on Park Avenue and 59th Street in New York. Dylan is credited with getting the Beatles high on marijuana for the first time. But more importantly, the collision of their two worlds would result in a huge creative shift for both parties: Dylan would soon adopt the Beatles' electric guitar sound and the Beatles would adopt Dylan's deeper, more expansive approach to writing lyrics. Dylan had been infusing psychedelic imagery into his lyrics as early as "Chimes of Freedom" from his appropriately titled *Another Side of Bob Dylan* (1964), which began his transition away from being a protest singer after his experiences taking LSD in early 1964.

58   Part 1: Popular Music History and Genres

In late 1965, Kesey began to host what would be known as the Acid Tests in northern California after his return from his and the Merry Pranksters' historic bus trip. These events were free-form parties with live music and psychedelic lighting, with many attendees under the influence of LSD. Participants were asked: "Can you pass the Acid Test?" A new band from the Bay Area known at the time as the Warlocks performed at some of these parties. The band soon changed their name to the Grateful Dead. The music the Grateful Dead created at the Acid Tests was not only experimental, but also highly improvisational. Such long-form improvisations would be the foundation upon which the Grateful Dead would build their 30-year career.

But inarguably the first psychedelic music heard by mainstream audiences was "She Said She Said" and "Tomorrow Never Knows" on the Beatles' *Revolver* (1966). This was the beginning of the Beatles' exploration of new sounds made possible by advances in studio recording technology. After three years of a grueling schedule of live performances around the world, the Beatles gave their final live performance at Candlestick Park in San Francisco on August 29, 1966, and permanently retired from touring. They spent the remainder of their time as a band creating music solely in the studio. The Beatles started working on their first post-touring creation in the fall of 1966, using sonic possibilities they could have not easily reproduced at the time as a live quartet. Their first effort, "Strawberry Fields Forever" (1967), featured multi-track recording, backwards recording, exotic instrumentation, and additional studio trickery made possible by audio engineer George Martin. The song would set the tone for their next album *Sgt. Pepper's Lonely Hearts Club Band* (1967). The Beatles' new approach to music and image was most notably featured in Thomas Thompson's June 16, 1967, *Life* article "The New Far-Out Beatles: They're Grown Men Now and Creating Extraordinary Musical Sounds" which depicted the lives of each of the Beatles since they stopped touring. Gone were the mop top haircuts and suits, replaced by even longer hair, mustaches, and psychedelic clothing. No longer were the Beatles as interested in performing their music for the world, but rather in furthering their personal musical evolution, and exploiting the current technological advances in the studio that augmented the possibilities of music making.

As mentioned earlier, LSD became illegal in both the U.S. and the U.K. in the fall of 1966. In response, Kesey concluded his free-form parties with the Acid Test Graduation at San Francisco's famed Winterland Ballroom on Halloween of that year. But in the spring of 1967, Kesey's psychedelic world and San Francisco culture collided with the Beatles. While on vacation in California, McCartney visited Bill Graham's famed venue the Fillmore, home to many of the psychedelic bands of San Francisco. He met members of Jefferson Airplane and even jammed with them. During the experience, McCartney learned of Kesey's psychedelic bus and its adventures, and subsequently developed the basis of what would become the Beatles' next album and corresponding 1967 television special, *Magical Mystery Tour* (Gould, 2008, pp. 438-440). Instead of a bus full of Merry Pranksters travelling across the U.S., the Beatles film featured the Fab Four and other peculiar characters on a Sunday pleasure tour through the English countryside, with odd stops along the way. Despite the inclusion of new Beatles music, the mostly improvised film was not a hit at the time.

The transatlantic phenomenon discussed between Dylan, the Beatles, Ken Kesey, and other musicians is only an introductory explanation of a greater, complex musical evolution that took place at the birth of the psychedelic sixties. The following three activities are intended to provide a deeper foundation for preparing to teach or research this transitional moment of the psychedelic sixties.

Activity #1: Dylan and Relevant Albums of 1967

To gain a better understanding of the music at the time and its subsequent transformation, watch the documentary *The Other Side of the Mirror: Bob Dylan Live at Newport Folk Festival—1963-1965* (2007) that traces Dylan's historic performances across three years of the Newport Folk Festival, including his controversial electric set in 1965. Take special note of Dylan's musical transformations from year to year.

Keep Dylan's transformation in mind while examining some albums from 1967 as listed in "Table 1: Notable Albums Released in 1967 Organized by Location." The albums have been grouped into four regions: U.K./Ireland, San Francisco, Los Angeles, and New York. Los Angeles is delineated from San Francisco to help separate the groups associated with the more urban city and its movie industry, which often served as an alternative to the dominant hippie culture. Most notably, bands and musicians like the Beach Boys, the Doors, and Frank Zappa were not necessarily part of the traditional hippie counterculture. Pick two albums from each region and listen to them in a focused and isolated environment, but also listen to them passively while doing something or riding in a car. Think of these eight albums as purchases you made in 1967 for your record collection. If possible, obtain LP (or at least CD) copies of the albums so you have access to the artwork and liner notes. After watching the Dylan documentary and digesting the albums, how can you draw connections between Dylan and the birth of psychedelic music? What foundation has Dylan laid that other musicians subsequently built upon? What themes are in Dylan's music and how are they different or similar to the albums chosen? And how are the albums chosen similar or different across the four regions?

To better understand the times and how music was consumed, try to recreate some of the environment in which the music was enjoyed. Sitting in front of speakers in communion with recordings was a crucial part of the early days of psychedelia. Writing for the Seattle-based underground newspaper *Helix* in 1967, John Cunnick wrote about the ritual, depicting the listener in the iconic pose of the famous RCA Victor dog "Nipper" with ears cocked toward a gramophone's horn:

> I wake up in the morning, roll a joint, and do a [His] Master's Voice thing in front of the speakers for a couple of hours; *then* I go outside. Music defines a total environment.... Go to a house and someone hands you a joint in front of a record player, and it's assumed ... that you are going to sit for a couple of hours, not talking, hardly moving, living to music [as quoted in Bromell, 2000, p. 1].

Cunnick's account underlines the increased popularity of recorded music in the psychedelic sixties. Listening to the music created an identity for many. As to be expected, these listeners were often using drugs. (Not only were drugs used during the enjoyment of psychedelic music, drugs played a role in the creation of the music.) How can you expound on what Cunnick describes as "living to music" when listening to your chosen albums?

As mentioned previously, drugs were often involved in the enjoyment and creation of psychedelic music. In his book *Sixties Rock: Garage, Psychedelic & Other Satisfactions* (1999), Michael Hicks outlines useful parallels between psychedelic music and the experience of taking a drug like LSD:

> To understand what makes music stylistically "psychedelic," one should consider three fundamental effects of LSD: dechronicization, depersonalization, and dynamization. *Dechronicization* permits the drug user to move outside of conventional perceptions of time. *Depersonalization* allows the user to lose the self and gain an "awareness of undifferentiated unity." *Dynamization*, as [Timothy] Leary wrote, makes everything from floors to amps seem to bend, as "familiar forms dissolve into moving dancing structures"; objects become liquid, "dripping, streaming, with white-hot light or electricity," as thought the "substance and form" of the world were "still molten." Music that is truly "psychedelic" mimics these three effects [Hicks, 1999, pp. 63–64].

These three effects provide a good approach to listening to and discussing early psychedelic music. The synesthetic quality (hearing colors and seeing sounds) of psychedelic music is crucial and is often one of the first things mentioned when discussing psychedelic music, especially by non-musicians. How do your chosen albums mimic the three LSD-related effects Hicks describes? Try to imagine hearing these new sounds and someone's reaction at the time. Be very specific as to how lyrics and sound mimic the three Hicks effects.

Admittedly, this activity is very labor intensive. But one of the hallmarks of psychedelic music is long-form performance. This is one of the challenges of teaching psychedelic music beyond stereotypes. One must spend a fair amount of time listening to these long, complex songs. And the recordings also need to be contextualized within the technological transitions of the time, like the rise of the LP (long-playing) album (which allowed for such long-form performances), the introduction of stereo recordings (which widened the sonic possibilities over speakers and headphones), and the advent of multi-track recording (which provided the possibilities of layered music and synthetic soundscapes).

The visual and other non-sonic components of these albums must also be investigated. Recordings of early psychedelic music were often augmented by colorful artwork, printed lyrics, and other information found in the album's packaging, creating an enhanced audio experience. Listeners need to ponder an album's visual material and lyrics while experiencing the music to appropriately complete this activity. Engage with the artwork, lyrics, and other information. Sit back, relax, and absorb the music slowly while also enjoying the colorful artwork, the printed lyrics, and liner notes. During this activity, take notes while listening. But also be sure to take the time simply to listen and absorb the album without taking notes, alone and with others.

Activity #2: The Beatles and Monterey

During the Summer of Love in San Francisco, John Phillips of the Mamas & the Papas spearheaded the organization of the Monterey International Pop Music Festival, a three-day event held June 16–18, 1967, that included many of the most famous psychedelic musicians from the U.S. and the U.K., plus musicians from around the world. In honor of the festival, Phillips wrote the song "San Francisco (Be Sure to Wear Flowers in Your Hair)" (1967), which was recorded by Scott McKenzie and went on to be a hit single and an anthem for the Summer of Love. Monterey Pop, rock's first festival, is a microcosm of the discussed transatlantic phenomenon that happened at the birth of the psychedelic sixties. For example, Monterey was the U.S. debut of both the Who and the Jimi Hendrix Experience. Both bands were suggested by Paul McCartney, who helped program the festival with Phillips as part of the "Board of Governors" along with several other famous musicians (most notably Donovan, Mick Jagger of the Rolling Stones, Paul Simon, Motown's Smokey Robinson, and Brian Wilson of the Beach Boys). Worth noting, the Jimi Hendrix Experience was billed at Monterey as "one of the hottest bands from England," even though Hendrix was born in the U.S. The festival also featured many Bay Area bands, like Big Brother and the Holding Company with Janis Joplin, the Grateful Dead, Jefferson Airplane, and Moby Grape, as well as musicians from outside the U.S. and the U.K., like South African trumpeter Hugh Masakela and Indian sitarist Ravi Shankar. In addition, southern soul singer Otis Redding performed for a mostly white audience for the first time. And the innovative psychedelic light show at Monterey complemented the adventurous sounds heard at the festival.

In order to gain a deeper understanding of the transition that happened around the historic festival, I suggest a thought experiment that draws on two of rock's most famous films. First, watch the Beatles' first film *A Hard Day's Night* (1964) as a reference point for Beatlemania. Imagine you are a teenager in high school witnessing and falling in love with the Fab Four in all their early glory. Then imagine you are now a college-aged student in the spring of 1967 and studying in the Bay Area. You have heard that there is a large music festival that summer and you bought tickets. Watch D.A. Pennebaker's film *Monterey Pop* (1968), which includes performances at the festival by many of the musicians mentioned above. While watching each film, take notes on your observations and reactions.

After you are finished, compare and contrast the two films from the viewpoint of a music fan in the sixties. Why were the Beatles embraced and loved? What does *A Hard Day's Night* convey about youth and popular music? What additional themes and issues are presented in the Beatles film? *Monterey Pop* features the music of many different musicians, but how are the aesthetics of the festival similar to or different from the Beatles film? Granted, *A Hard Day's Night* is a fictional film and *Monterey Pop* is a documentary, but you can still examine the similarities and differences between the films as both are cultural touchstones. How are the look and the music featured in *Monterey Pop* indebted to the Beatles? And how have the look and the music of the film departed from the Beatles? Be very specific about dress, language, instrumentation, use of sound, look, and performance. How do you perceive the non–U.S. groups like the Who, the Jimi Hendrix Experience, Masakela, Shankar, and others? How are their look and sound different from the Bay Area and other U.S. bands? How do you perceive the U.S. musicians like Jefferson Airplane, Simon & Garfunkel, and others? Finally, what are you going to tell your friends and family after you return from the festival? What are the impacts of this intense musical experience?

Activity #3: Kesey and the End of the Hippie Dream

During their adventures, Kesey and the Merry Pranksters documented Furthur's cross-country trip with audio and video recordings with hopes of making a movie. But the footage was not seen by the public until the release of *Magic Trip: Ken Kesey's Search for a Kool Place* (2011). The spirit of Kesey's trip is conveyed in the footage, from Neil Cassidy's driving, to antics on and off the bus, to reactions by the people who see the bus drive by. In addition to reading Wolfe's book, we can now literally see and hear what it was like to be "on the bus."

Monterey may have been rock's first festival, but two years later the Woodstock Music & Art Fair is the event most people remember and gave birth to a group of shared dreams known as Woodstock Nation. The three-day festival held on a farm in upstate New York on August 15–18, 1969 and attended by half a million people was arguably the climax of the sixties, and featured many of the musicians from Monterey, plus others of equal stature. For a full lineup of Monterey and Woodstock, see "Table 2: The Four Major Rock Festivals of the Psychedelic Sixties." In addition to these two festivals, the table also includes information on the Altamont Speedway Free Festival (1969) and the Isle of Wight Festival (1970). Though Woodstock would be a success like Monterey, both Altamont and Isle of Wight ended in either tragedy or financial ruin. Many folks associate the end of the psychedelic sixties with the breakup of the Beatles and the deaths of Hendrix, Janis Joplin, and Jim Morrison in 1970. Lennon even declared that the dream was over in his song "God" (1970). But the end of the hippie dream is best witnessed at these festivals in late 1969 and 1970. We can see the trajectory of the rise and fall of the psychedelic sixties as a large, positive social movement via the films made about these four festivals.

For this activity, first watch *Magic Trip* to understand what Kesey and the Merry Pranksters stood for and the world they collided with. Then watch both *Monterey Pop* and *Woodstock* (1970). Compare the films of the two highly successful rock festivals. What are the differences and similarities? During your analysis, include not only information on the sound and look of the performances in the films, but also discuss the difference in size and atmosphere of the two festivals. *Woodstock* includes footage of the journey to the festival, which is not such an issue in *Monterey Pop*. We see footage of the organizers of Monterey, but nothing to the degree of the depicted journey of Woodstock's attendees. How can we speak about Woodstock in context of Monterey? How is Woodstock indebted to Monterey? And besides the size of the festival and the journey to get there, are there any other pertinent differences between the festivals?

After witnessing the positivity depicted in *Monterey Pop* and *Woodstock*, watch the two much darker films on music festivals in the psychedelic sixties: *Gimme Shelter* (1970) on Altamont and *Message to Love: The Isle of Wight Festival* (1997). In addition to their performance, the Rolling Stones' documentary highlights the tense atmosphere surrounding Altamont, due in part to the hiring of the Hells Angels as security for the free event and the subsequent refusal of the Grateful Dead to perform after Jefferson Airplane singer Marty Balin was assaulted by a member of the Hells Angels. The film also features scenes of the Stones reviewing footage of the death of concert attendee Meredith Hunter, who was stabbed by a member of the Hells Angels after Hunter had pulled out a gun at the concert. Though not as violent as Altamont, the Isle of Wight festival was a disaster financially. Despite the difficulties of being on an island off the coast of England, the event was larger than Woodstock. The film features members of a group of campers known as Desolation Row (named after the Dylan song), which repeatedly disrupted the festival, demanding that the festival be free. Festival organizer Rikki Farr is seen in the film shouting in rage at the behavior of the Desolation Row protestors, calling them "bastards" and "pigs" for tearing down the fences and other rude behavior. The film also includes footage of Joni Mitchell's plagued performance, which is forcefully interrupted by concert goer Yogi Joe, leading to Mitchell's famous speech demanding more respect from the audience and calling concert attendees "tourists."

For this activity, connect all four films into a greater story of what happened musically and socially in the psychedelic sixties. How did the look, feel, and other elements of a music festival change over the years from 1967 to 1970? Remember that these were some of the first rock festivals ever to happen. In these films, who is attending and who is performing at these festivals? What are similar and different themes and elements across the films? What (if any) conflicting themes or ideas emerge across the films? What was seen and experienced by the attendees? What became of the hippie dream? And how did it change? Be very specific and examine specific moments and dialogue in the films.

This is another labor-intensive activity. But by comparing the films we can begin to see larger tropes across the history of the psychedelic sixties, including the positive (raised social consciousness and non-violent protest) and the negative (violence and self-indulgence). This helps counter the stereotypes of psychedelic music and depicts the greater transatlantic phenomenon. Granted, three of the four festivals took place in the U.S. But we must remember that it was the British Invasion of the early 1960s that helped fuel the transformations of the psychedelic sixties later in the decade. Therefore, it is appropriate that we conclude this musical journey in England at the Isle of Wight.

Psychedelic Voices: A Group Project

In addition to the previous three activities, the following additional group project would help illuminate the complex transatlantic web of voices, perspectives, beliefs, and events surrounding the Summer of Love. Thanks to the continued interest in the psychedelic sixties, many autobiographies by musicians and others who lived through the turbulent times have been published over the last 50 years. Several of these books have been collected and organized into "Table 3: Some Autobiographies by Psychedelic Sixties Musicians."

The group project would be a discussion by three or more people using the voices of relevant musicians and others from the psychedelic sixties. Each person would select a different autobiography from Table 3 (preferably from different columns in order to gain a range of voices across the four regions). Keeping the events and attitudes leading up to the year 1967 in mind, each person would read his or her selected autobiography while paying close attention to the author's observations and comments on the era. Readers should also be aware if the author foregrounded the events of the era positively or was more critical of the time. After everyone has read his or her selected autobiography, the group would convene and discuss the information found in the voice of the person who wrote the autobiography as if he or she were attending a present-day event or conference celebrating the Summer of Love. Informed by what they read, the members of the group would engage in a discussion about what the author remembered happening in the late sixties, and how their memories relate to today's events, attitudes, and beliefs. Ideally, the people participating in the discussion would begin to unpack the many events and various viewpoints surrounding the psychedelic sixties in a meaningful way. For example, if three people selected autobiographies by Roger Daltrey, Phil Lesh, and John Phillips, how did each of these musicians remember Monterey Pop and the Summer of Love? What was important to each musician building up to the event, during the event, and after? Of the memories of each musician, what observations and issues were similar and different? Do their memories agree or disagree with one another? And how do we gain a better perspective on Monterey from the composite memories of these musicians from three different regions?

Conclusion

The psychedelic sixties will continue to be a time that many scholars, music fans, and students will further enjoy and investigate. Hopefully, the above discussion, information, suggested activities, and group project provide avenues for faculty, students, and other researchers of psychedelic music to understand better the music of the era as a transatlantic phenomenon. With all the additional resources now available since the birth of psychedelic music, we can now more easily share and more deeply investigate a music that deserves further discussion. In reflecting on Fleischer's epigraph to this essay, those of us who were not present in the sixties may actually have an advantage by not being able to remember the birth of the psychedelic sixties. Though we are dependent on how the era and its music were documented, the minds of those who were not present are not clouded by the memories of living through those turbulent times. Therefore, some of us can now begin to envision a psychedelic tomorrow that is worth remembering.

Table 1: Notable Albums Released in 1967 Organized by Location

U.K./Ireland	U.S. West Coast		New York
	San Francisco	Los Angeles	
The Animals: *Winds of Change*	The 13th Floor Elevators: *Easter Everywhere*	The Beach Boys: *Smiley Smile* *Wild Honey*	The Blues Project (feat. Al Kooper): *Projections*
The Beatles: *Sgt. Pepper's Lonely Hearts Club Band* *Magical Mystery Tour*	Country Joe and the Fish: *Electric Music for the Mind and Body* *I Feel Like I'm Fixin' to Die*		The Paul Butterfield Blues Band: *The Resurrection of Pigboy Crabshaw*
		Captain Beefheart: *Safe as Milk*	Leonard Cohen: *Songs of Leonard Cohen*
Bee Gees: *Bee Gees' 1st*	Grateful Dead: *The Grateful Dead*	Tim Buckley: *Goodbye and Hello*	Bob Dylan: *Bob Dylan's Greatest Hits*
David Bowie: *David Bowie*	Jefferson Airplane: *Surrealistic Pillow*	Buffalo Springfield: *Buffalo Springfield* (second pressing "For What It's Worth [*Stop, Hey What's That Sound?*])"	*The Basement Tapes* (released 1975)
Cream: *Disraeli Gears*	After Bathing at Baxter's	Buffalo Springfield Again	*John Wesley Harding*
Donovan: *Mellow Yellow*	Janis Joplin: Big Brother & the Holding Company	The Byrds: *Younger Than Yesterday*	The Fugs: *Virgin Fugs*
A Gift from a Flower to a Garden	Scott McKenzie: *The Voice of Scott McKenzie*	Canned Heat: *Canned Heat*	Arlo Guthrie: *Alice's Restaurant*
Jimi Hendrix: *Are You Experienced*	Moby Grape: *Moby Grape*	The Doors: *The Doors* *Strange Days*	The Holy Modal Rounders: *Indian War Whoop*
Axis: Bold as Love	Sly and the Family Stone: *A Whole New Thing*		The Lovin' Spoonful: *The Best of the Lovin' Spoonful*
The Kinks: *Something Else*		Love: *Forever Changes*	*You're a Big Boy Now* [soundtrack]

U.K./Ireland	U.S. West Coast	New York
	San Francisco	
	Los Angeles	
The Moody Blues: *Days of Future Passed*	The Mamas and the Papas: *The Mamas and the Papas Deliver*	*Everything Playing*
Van Morrison: *Blowin' Your Mind!*	The Monkees: *Headquarters*	Nico: *Chelsea Girl*
Pink Floyd: *The Piper at the Gates of Dawn*	*Pisces, Aquarius, Capricorn & Jones Ltd.*	Peter, Paul and Mary: *Album 1700*
Procol Harum: *Procol Harum*	Strawberry Alarm Clock: *Incense and Peppermints*	Simon & Garfunkel: *The Graduate* [soundtrack]
The Rolling Stones: *Between the Buttons* *Flowers* *Their Satanic Majesties Request*	Frank Zappa: *Absolutely Free* *Lumpy Gravy*	Vanilla Fudge: *Vanilla Fudge* The Velvet Underground: *The Velvet Underground & Nico*
Ten Years After: *Ten Years After*		
Traffic: *Mr. Fantasy*		
The Who: *The Who Sell Out*		
The Yardbirds: *Greatest Hits* *Little Games*		

Table 2: The Four Major Rock Festivals of the Psychedelic Sixties

FESTIVAL	Monterey International Pop Music Festival	Woodstock Music & Art Fair	Altamont Speedway Free Festival	Isle of Wight Festival 1970
DATE(S)	June 16–18, 1967	August 15–18, 1969	December 6, 1969	August 26–31, 1970
LOCATION	Monterey, CA	Bethel, NY	Tracy, CA	Isle of Wight, England
ATTENDANCE	8,500+	400,000+	300,000+	600,000+
NOTABLE PERFORMERS	The Animals The Paul Butterfield Blues Band Booker T. & the M.G.s Buffalo Springfield (with David Crosby replacing Neil Young) The Byrds Canned Heat Country Joe and the Fish The Electric Flag Grateful Dead Jimi Hendrix Jefferson Airplane Janis Joplin Al Kooper The Mamas & the Papas Hugh Masekela Scott McKenzie Steve Miller Band Lou Rawls Otis Redding Simon & Garfunkel The Who	Joan Baez The Band Blood, Sweat & Tears The Paul Butterfield Blues Band Canned Heat Joe Cocker Country Joe and the Fish Creedence Clearwater Revival Crosby, Stills, Nash & Young Arlo Guthrie Grateful Dead Richie Havens Jimi Hendrix Janis Joplin Jefferson Airplane John Sebastian Ravi Shankar Santana Sha Na Na Sly & the Family Stone Swami Satchidananda Ten Years After The Who Johnny Winter	Crosby, Stills, Nash & Young Jefferson Airplane The Rolling Stones Santana	Joan Baez Leonard Cohen Miles Davis Donovan The Doors Emerson, Lake & Palmer Richie Havens Jimi Hendrix Jethro Tull Kris Kristofferson Joni Mitchell The Moody Blues John Sebastian Sly & the Family Stone Ten Years After Tiny Tim The Who
NOTABLE CANCELLATIONS	The Beach Boys	The Doors Iron Butterfly Joni Mitchell	Grateful Dead	

Table 3: Some Autobiographies by Psychedelic Sixties Musicians

U.K./Ireland	U.S. West Coast San Francisco	U.S. West Coast Los Angeles	New York

The Animals
  Eric Burdon:
    Don't Let Me Be Misunderstood (2001)
The Beatles
  George Harrison:
    I, Me, Mine (1980)
  John Lennon:
    Lennon Remembers (1971)
  Paul McCartney:
    Many Years from Now (1997)
Cream
  Ginger Baker:
    Hellraiser—The Autobiography of the World's Greatest Drummer (2010)
  Eric Clapton:
    Clapton—The Autobiography (2007)
Donovan:
  The Autobiography of Donovan—The Hurdy Gurdy Man (2005)
The Jimi Hendrix Experience
  Jimi Hendrix:
    Starting at Zero—His Own Story (2013)
  Mitch Mitchell:
    Jimi Hendrix—Inside the Experience (1990)
	The Grateful Dead
	  John Perry Barlow:
	    Mother American Night—My Life in Crazy Times (2018)
	  Jerry Garcia:
	    Garcia—A Signpost to New Space (1972)
	  Mickey Hart:
	    Drumming at the Edge of Magic—A Journey into the Spirit of Percussion (1990)
	  Bill Kreutzmann:
	    Deal—My Three Decades of Drumming, Dreams, and Drugs with the Grateful Dead (2015)
	  Phil Lesh:
	    Searching for the Sound—My Life with the Grateful Dead (2005)
	Jefferson Airplane
	  Jorma Kaukonen:
	    Been So Long—My Life and Music (2018)
	  Grace Slick:
	    Somebody to Love? A Rock-and-Roll Memoir (1998)
	Carlos Santana:
	  The Universal Tone—Bringing My Story to Light (2014)
		The Beach Boys
		  Mike Love:
		    Good Vibrations—My Life as a Beach Boy (2016)
		  Brian Wilson:
		    I Am Brian Wilson—A Memoir (2016)
		Canned Heat
		  Fito de la Parra:
		    Living the Blues—Canned Heat's Story of Music, Drugs, Death, Sex and Survival (1999)
		Crosby, Stills, Nash & Young
		  David Crosby:
		    Long Time Gone—The Autobiography of David Crosby (1988)
		  Graham Nash:
		    Wild Tales—A Rock & Roll Life (2013)
		  Neil Young:
		    Waging Heavy Peace—A Hippie Dream (2012)
		The Doors
		  John Densmore:
		    Riders on the Storm—My Life with Jim Morrison and the Doors (1990)
		  Ray Manzarek:
		    Light My Fire—My Life with The Doors (1998)
			Joan Baez:
			  Daybreak (1968)
			  And a Voice to Sing With: A Memoir (1987)
			The Band
			  Levon Helm:
			    This Wheel's on Fire—Levon Helm and the Story of the Band (1993)
			  Robbie Robertson:
			    Testimony (2016)
			Judy Collins:
			  Sweet Judy Blue Eyes—My Life in Music (2011)
			Bob Dylan:
			  Chronicles—Volume One (2004)
			Art Garfunkel:
			  What Is It All but Luminous—Notes from an Underground Man (2017)
			Richie Havens:
			  They Can't Hide Us Anymore (1999)
			Al Kooper: *Backstage Passes & Backstabbing Bastards—Memoirs of a Rock 'n' Roll Survivor* (1998)

Part 1: Popular Music History and Genres

U.K./Ireland

Noel Redding: *Are You Experienced? The Inside Story of Jimi Hendrix* (1990)

The Kinks
  Ray Davies: *X-Ray—The Unauthorized Autobiography* (1995)
  Americana—The Kinks, the Riff, the Road: The Story (2013)

Pink Floyd
  Nick Mason: *Inside Out—A Personal History of Pink Floyd* (2005)

The Rolling Stones
  Keith Richards: *Life* (2010)
  Ronnie Wood: *Ronnie—The Autobiography* (2007)
  Bill Wyman: *Stone Alone—The Story of a Rock 'n' Roll Band* (1997)

The Who
  Roger Daltrey: *Thanks a Lot Mr. Kibblewhite: My Story* (2018)
  Pete Townsend: *Who I Am—A Memoir* (2012)

U.S. West Coast

San Francisco

Los Angeles

Joni Mitchell *In Her Own Words* (2014)

The Monkees
  Micky Dolenz: *I'm a Believer: My Life of Monkees, Music, and Madness* (2004)
  Davy Jones: *They Made a Monkee Out of Me* (1987)
  Michael Nesmith: *Infinite Tuesday—An Autobiographical Riff* (2017)

Frank Zappa: *The Real Frank Zappa Book* (1989)

New York

The Mamas and the Papas
  John Phillips: *Papa John—A Music Legend's Shattering Journey Though Sex, Drugs, and Rock 'n' Roll* (1986)
  Michelle Phillips: *California Dreamin'—The True Story of the Mamas and the Papas* (1986)

Peter, Paul and Mary
  Peter, Paul and Mary: Fifty Years in Music and Life (2014)
  Mary Travers: *A Woman's Words* (2013)

The Velvet Underground
  John Cale: *What's Welsh for Zen—The Autobiography of John Cale* (1999)

REFERENCES

Bromell, N. (2000). *Tomorrow never knows: Rock and psychedelics in the 1960s*. Chicago: University of Chicago Press.
Christon, L. (1982, June 13). The comedy column: Shandling takes the low-key road. *Los Angeles Times*, p. M60.
Goldberg, D. (2017). *In search of the lost chord: 1967 and the hippie idea*. Brooklyn, NY: Akashic Books.
Gould, J. (2008). *Can't buy me love: The Beatles, Britain, and America*. New York: Harmony Books.
Hicks, M. (1999). *Sixties rock: Garage, psychedelic & other satisfactions*. Urbana: University of Illinois Press.
Jarnow, J. (2016). *HEADS: A biography of psychedelic America*. Boston: Da Capo Press.
Kesey, K. (2002). Sketches. Included in deluxe edition of *One flew over the cuckoo's nest*. New York: Penguin Books.
Leary, T., Alpert, R., & Metzner, R. (1964). *The psychedelic experience: A manual based on the Tibetan Book of the Dead*. New York: Citadel Press.
Lennon, J. (1970). "God." *John Lennon/plastic Ono band* [LP]. London: EMI/Apple.
Robins, W. (2000). *Behind the music: 1968*. New York: Pocket Books.
Scaduto, A. (1971). *Bob Dylan: An intimate biography*. New York: Grosset & Dunlap.
Thompson, T. (1967, June 16). The new far-out Beatles: They're grown men now and creating extraordinary musical sounds. *Life*, *62*(24), 100–106.

Globalizing Jamaican Music
From Reggae to New Wave

William M. Knoblauch

In 2012, after accepting a tenure track assistant professor position at a small, private liberal arts college, I was given extraordinary freedom to update its history curriculum. For my first semester, alongside world and U.S. history surveys, I could teach any course of my choosing. Sharing this dilemma with a close friend, he simply exclaimed, "Just teach the history of rock and roll!" It was sage advice. I have been playing music since I was 16 and have been an avid fan of rock history for even longer. Delivered every two years, *History of Rock and Roll* proves to be one of my most popular courses. However, it might just as well be called *History Through Rock and Roll* because throughout the semester we examine issues of race and ethnicity, politics, gender and sexuality, and trends in popular culture. Over 15 weeks, students examine these themes through numerous units, such as "The British Invasion," "Commodifying the Counterculture," and "The Roots of Hip-Hop." For this essay I will describe the unit titled "From Reggae to New Wave."

Scheduled for one 80-minute session, "From Reggae to New Wave" combines lecture with media clips and question prompts to spark classroom interaction and guide course outcomes. The unit begins with a brief primer on the history of Jamaica, as reggae reflects numerous political, cultural, and spiritual aspects of the island. Next, it examines how Jamaican music evolved as musicians discovered American rhythm and blues. As tastes shifted, so did sounds, and thus began a triangular series of sonic exchanges between the United States, Jamaica, and the United Kingdom—exchanges that show globalization in action. The growth of a Jamaican cultural diaspora (meaning a cultural outpost which exists far away from the place of its origin) that arrived in Great Britain was driven by economics; as Jamaican immigrants came looking for employment, their music spread. In London, teens embraced a new style that intermingled reggae and punk—a raw form of rock itself imported from, and then repackaged and sent back to, the United States. By the late 1970s, these musical genres both mixed and diluted; by the 1980s, Music Television (MTV) began marketing a more Americanized (and commercialized, if less authentic) genre of this music with the label "new wave." All told, from the 1950s through the 1980s, Jamaican sounds and culture traversed the globe and transformed rock music forever. Indeed, as Chang and Chen (1998) explain:

> reggae is probably the only music not of European or American origin which can be heard in every country on Earth, and is arguably the first example in modern times of a third world country exporting its culture to such a diverse audience [p. 2].

Readers should note that, regarding reggae, there are numerous teachable angles that will not be explored in this essay. Much Jamaican music is politically-charged, with lyrics that often reflect the struggles of colonized and post-colonial peoples; some of these aspects will be examined, but this is not the central focus of my essay. There are sonic avenues left unexplored as well. For example, reggae's influence on electronic music—in genres ranging from ambient, drum and bass, and Electronic Dance Music (EDM)—is undeniable, but also lay outside the periodization of this examination. Finally, there will be numerous artist omissions; your favorite reggae artist might not appear in this essay, but the limited examples I provide, by design, trace an evolution of sounds attributable to the process of globalization. In short, I recognize this essay's limitations, but historians make choices; curious readers should reference selections in the essay's bibliography for sources that more fully examine these, and other, aspects of reggae and the history of Jamaica.

There are three goals of this unit around which this essay is organized. First, students should be able to define "globalization" and identify it as a historical process using examples from the history of Jamaican music and its exportation around the world. Second, in tracing this process, students should be able to describe how reggae provided a distinctly different rhythm than most forms of popular postwar music in both America and Great Britain, and use examples to trace how that rhythm influenced rock and roll on both sides of the Atlantic. Finally, by the end of the lesson, students should effectively provide examples—in the forms of fashion, lyrics, and music videos—to show connections between 1950s Jamaican music, 1970s British ska and punk, and finally early 1980s "new wave."

To guide course outcomes, at the outset of each class period I provide a potential future exam question, which in this instance is:

> To what extent does reggae's sonic evolution, and its influence on other genres, exemplify globalization? In your answer, consider the evolution from mento, to ska, to reggae in Jamaica, as well as the evolution of punk between America and Great

Britain. You might also want to consider the impact of emigration and technology in the postwar period.

I also provide the following terms to guide student notetaking: Globalization, Marcus Garvey, Rastafari, Haile Selassie, Zion, Babylon, mento, ska, reggae, Bob Marley, the Wailers, Lee "Scratch" Perry, punk, the Sex Pistols, the Clash, Don Letts, the Roxy, Blondie, the Police. Each of these terms appears chronologically in the pages that follow.

Globalization and Jamaican History

To begin, it is vital that students comprehend what "globalization" means. According to anthropologist Arjun Appadurai (2001), the term can be used in many different contexts. For social scientists, it can concern issues of inequality in the global marketplace; for political scientists, it refers to the blurring of cultures beyond traditional nation state borders, a phenomenon that has accelerated with the rise of social media and internet technology. For historians, globalization shows how peoples of different cultures and economies have become intermingled. Eckes and Zeiler (2003) contend that Harvard University marketing professor Theodore Levitt first used the term in a 1983 *Harvard Business Review* article. They define globalization as:

> The *process* of integrating nations and peoples—politically, economically, and culturally—into larger communities," and state that "over the centuries, [globalization] has brought people and nations closer together as technological innovations dissolved barriers of time and distance, enhanced flows of information, and promoted greater awareness and understanding [p. 1].

One of the challenges of teaching globalization's impact on Jamaica is choosing just how far back to delve into the historical record. Individual educators who choose to can go as far back as the Atlantic African Slave Trade (legally practiced between 1400 and 1833), the era of Jamaica's colonial British rule (starting in 1655), or its struggle for independence (achieved in 1962). If so, these teachers may benefit greatly from one accessible, single volume: Sherlock and Bennett's (1998) *The Story of the Jamaican People*. However, this lesson plan begins in the 1920s, the decade in which Marcus Garvey began to preach a doctrine of African resettlement. Sherlock and Bennett argue that Garvey was instrumental in breaking the psyche of colonialism by preaching a doctrine of African-ness and was:

> one of few of his time who understood how seriously the inner world of the African had been damaged, and in some cases destroyed, by the experience of enslavement combined with alienation by a transfer of authority and by total immersion in a wholly materialist society [p. 294].

Garvey's insistence on rejecting western materialism and embracing a uniquely African-based cultural identity would live on in reggae's rhetoric in the forms of rejecting "Babylon" (destructive western culture) and seeking "Zion" (peaceful African culture).

To be sure, there were important precursors to Garvey's brand of African identity formation in Jamaica, notably the Bahamian-born anti-colonialist Robert Love, who politicized the harm of the United Fruit Company's exploitative practices on the island, which lasted well into the early twentieth century (see Colby, 2011). However, it was Garvey who established ideas most clearly traceable in the Jamaican music presented below; specifically, students should be able to identify Garvey's idea that Jamaicans not regard themselves as subjects of Great Britain, but instead embrace their African roots and break their colonial bonds (Sherlock and Bennett, 1998).

Garvey's brand of Black Nationalism is apparent in a vitally important strand of Jamaican culture: *Rastafarianism*. The term is an amalgamation of "Ras" (the title of Duke) and "Tafari" (part of the given last name of the king of Ethiopia, Lij Tafari Makonnen, later known as Haile Selassie). Citing the King James Bible, Rastafari believed that Ethiopian leader Haile Selassie was not just of the lineage of King Solomon, but the second coming of Jesus Christ—a fact made apparent to Selassie during an April 1966 visit to the island (footage of which is available online). Rasta practitioners strive for a more peaceful world (Zion), one only made possible if—as Marcus Garvey preached—they reject exploitative western culture (Babylon). To do so, Rastas follow Old Testament kosher laws and adhere to a strict organic diet ("I'Tal" colloquially) as part of their worshiping of Jah (or God). They also adopted the colors of the Ethiopian flag (green, red, and yellow), which became the color pallet for early reggae artists. While they avoid alcohol, Rastas do freely imbibe marijuana (herb or "ganja"), which they consider a sacred method of improving consciousness (Szatmary, 2010). These elements should be made clear to students, as many will be traceable in this lesson.

A Different Rhythm

Students can hear an evolution of early Jamaican music by comparing the island's early folk music, mento, with its more Americanized offspring, ska. Mento is not the earliest precursor to reggae music; many other folk forms date back to the nineteenth century including Pocomania and Quadrille songs (i.e., folk forms akin to Jamaican bluegrass). As Chang and Chen (1998) point out, each of these styles reflect African influences on Jamaican music, as well as the poverty of an island that has "less than one-twentieth of one percent of the world's population and produces even less of its wealth" (p. 2). For this reason, mento musicians had to purchase inexpensive imported instruments or rely on homemade ones. Despite economic challenges, mento became "the dominant music of Jamaica from its first appearance in the late nineteenth-century up to the 1930s ... especially in rural areas" (Chang and Chen, 1998, p. 14).

At this point, I distribute some listening "prompts" to students, which helps to keep them engaged while listening to songs or watching music videos. I frequently ask that they answer the following questions:

- What type of instruments do you hear being played in Jamaican mento?
- What type of instruments do you hear being played in American jazz?
- Specifically, what are the *percussive* instruments used to keep rhythm?

Such questions focus attention on the specific, different instruments used for these styles. For example, mento was traditionally played with banjos, guitars, and piccolo—all relatively inexpensive when compared to American jazz instruments such as brass, woodwinds, pianos, and drum kits. The percussion comparison here is especially revealing, and I like to compare 1950s big band footage (especially with a drum solo—for example, any performance by Buddy Rich or Gene Krupa) with the Jamaican "rhumba box" to drive home just how homespun mento instruments were. Essentially a hollow wooden frame that percussionists would sit on to bang out beats, rhumba boxes also feature a few bent metal prongs from which to pluck a basic melody. Showing an online rhumba box performance juxtaposed with any big band performance will convey the folk nature of mento before the process of globalization influenced its evolution into ska. I recommend using Lord Messam's 1952 song "Take Her to Jamaica" as an example.

In the 1950s, globalization's influence on Jamaican music came in two forms: demographic shifts and the increased use of radio technology. Regarding demographics, economic hardships fueled Jamaican migrations. Just as early twentieth-century African American migrations from Mississippi to Chicago occurred—which morphed acoustic Delta blues into electric Chicago blues—itinerant Jamaican migrant workers frequently traveled to the American south for work, and this is where many first heard rhythm and blues. As Chang and Chen (1998) confirm, by the late 1940s "migrant sugar cane cutters, contracted for six months to a year in the American south, introduced rhythm and blues to Jamaica and it proved hugely popular with the local public" (p. 19). Travel was relatively easy, as Jamaicans were still under British colonial control, so work visas were common. As Lloyd Bradley (2000) explains, "during the 1950s, immigration to the U.K., Canada and North America was virtually unchecked," and that "over a quarter of a million people, or, astonishingly, about one-tenth of Jamaica's population, left for those three destinations during the decade" (p. 13). Emphasizing these facts can show causality for why Jamaican music sonically shifted in the 1950s.

When migrant workers returned to the island, they clamored for American music; luckily for them the 1950s was a period of slight economic improvement. Along with upticks in agricultural exports, Jamaica became a prime holiday destination for European and American vacationers. (Any cursory internet search can provide instructors with numerous, colorful travel advertisements featuring Jamaica as a holiday destination.) As disposable income increased, so did radio sales, meaning that islanders could now hear American music from stations in New Orleans and Miami, stations that played mostly up-tempo jazz and rhythm and blues. Many Jamaicans preferred American music to the offerings on the island's first commercial radio station, Radio Jamaica (going live in July 1950) which featured mostly country music and swing (Chang and Chen, 1998). For examples of American music, I recommend Roy Brown's 1947 hit "Good Rockin' Tonight" and Jackie Brenston's "Rocket 88." The point students should take away here is that in the 1950s, there was a shift: as Jamaicans embraced American rhythm and blues, interest in brass instrumentation and jauntier jazz tempos increased. These influences triggered the evolution of Jamaican mento music into ska.

Ska has a deep history, but when comparing it to mento, I specifically feature images of and songs by Prince Buster. I do so because later in the lesson, when examining ska's "Second Wave" in the 1970s, Prince Buster's influence becomes apparent. Here, the songs "Madness" and "Enjoy Yourself" work well for the prompts provided above, as do early songs by Desmond Dekker (i.e., "Israelites"). In time, ska tempos slowed down, and songs featuring a more moderate beat became international hits, such as Harry Belafonte's 1957 "Jamaica Farewell," a highly polished mento standard that reaffirmed the island's growing reputation as a vacation destination. Another "rocksteady" international hit, Johnny Nash's "Hold Me Tight," provides students yet another example of how, by the 1960s, Jamaican music was evolving because of the economic and technological forces of globalization. But it took one more step—rocksteady to reggae—to make Jamaican music truly global, especially though the music of the genre's most famous artist: Bob Marley.

Reggae Roots and Bob Marley

Before delving into reggae, I make sure that students have a basic appreciation of just how revolutionary this rhythm is. With a minimum of listening, students should be able to identify and differentiate a reggae rhythm from a standard rock beat. Here, I employ a canonical classic rock song or two to train the ears, usually songs that feature a clearly defined backbeat—meaning that the drummer hits the snare on the "two" and "four" of each measure with a common kick drum accompaniment usually on the "one" and the "and-three" of the same 4/4 measure. Some recognizable examples might include the Beatles' "I Want Hold Your Hand," and the Rolling Stones' "Jumpin' Jack Flash," but there are hundreds to choose from.

After listening to a few of these "straight" rock beats, we examine how a reggae rhythm is different. Unlike rock, reggae accentuates a kick drum beat on the "three" of a measure, while the bass frequently avoids the "one" and the guitar commonly strums on the "and's" of each measure; colloquially, Jamaican musicians refer to this as the "riddim." To explain this difference, I employ a clip of drummer Stewart Copeland of the Police. In an early 1980s interview with Jools Holland, Copeland colorfully narrates an evolution of rock drumming with accompanying performances. Then, he plays and counts a reggae beat—emphasizing that the kick drum hits on the "three" of each measure—only to conclude: "I have no idea how it ever was arrived at. It's brilliant. It's a paradigm for the cosmos!" (Jither, 2007).

With the rhythm sufficiently explained, it is time to introduce students to Bob Marley. More than any artist, Marley reigns supreme in reggae's history. Born February 6, 1945, in St. Ann (some nine miles in the interior of Jamaica), Marley himself was a product of globalization. His father was "Captain" Norval Marley, a white British government agent who provided little support to Bob's mother, Cedella Booker. Like many of his reggae contemporaries, Marley grew up in "Trenchtown," the name given to the "shanty town"—the commonly referenced colloquial term for Jamaican ghettos usually from the island's interior—of Jamaica's capital, Kingston. By the early 1960s, Marley and his friend Peter Tosh began covering American pop hits of the day by the Platters ("The Great Pretender" and "Only You"), Ben E. King ("Stand by Me"), and the Drifters ("Under the Boardwalk"). Tosh remembers those days fondly, recalling that when he came to Kingston at the age of 16, "nine out of ten singers found themselves in poverty in Trenchtown, the ghetto. It was me, Bob Marley, Bunny Livingstone, Joe Higgs, the Maytals—we'd sit around every night and just sing" (Szatmary, 2010, p. 247). They settled on the name the Wailing Wailers and began covering American R&B songs. Here, I have the class compare Dion and the Belmonts' "Teenager in Love" with the Wailer's cover (Moskowitz, 2016, p. 92).

Like many Trenchtown musicians, Marley's personal struggles led him from covers to more personal songwriting. From a young age, Marley was teased for being of a mixed-racial background, and at the age of 16 he recorded "Judge Not." Marley and the Wailers' other early singles reflect social messages about life in the Jamaican ghetto. For example, "Simmer Down" discusses gang violence, and "Rude Boy" references toughs from Trenchtown. In 1969, Marley's look, and songs, strongly reflected Rastafarianism, specifically in his dreadlocked hair, lyrical references to Zion and Babylon, and the smoking of herb. Here, audio and/or video clips from "Duppy Conqueror," "Easy Skanking" and "Stir It Up" all reinforce Marley's promotion of Rastafari beliefs.

In the early 1970s, the world was becoming enamored with Jamaican music and culture. In addition to the before mentioned reggae songs, the 1972 film *The Harder They Come* became something of a global hit with its unflinching (if low budget) look at the crime-ridden realities of life in Trenchtown. The film featured Jimmy Cliff, one of many musicians who provided songs for the film's soundtrack. Examples here include Desmond Dekker ("007—Shanty Town"), the Maytals ("Pressure Drop"), and the Melodians ("Rivers of Babylon")—each song a useful example ripe for classroom sonic and textual analysis. Around the same time, Marley released two landmark albums, and by 1973 the reggae "riddim" was influencing more mainstream artists. Examples include Led Zeppelin's song "D'yer Mak'er" (the band's most oft-mispronounced song; it is simply phonetic slang for "Jamaic-er"), and guitar legend Eric Clapton's 1974 cover of Marley's "I Shot the Sheriff." Here, a comparison with the original proves instructive, as does pointing out how Clapton diluted pure or authentic reggae rhythm for a broader rock audience. In time, however, younger British musicians would adopt a purer form of reggae rhythms, and assume a more aggressive posture in the form of punk.

Punk and Reggae in Great Britain

In the postwar period, after the devastation of World War II, Great Britain could no longer—economically, militarily, or in the face of global public opinion—maintain its colonies. Jamaica gained its independence from Great Britain in 1962, and by the 1970s, Britain was facing its own economic downturn. British teens, especially in London, began to abhor British pomp, especially in the face of rising unemployment and global decline. From the ashes of empire, U.K. punk emerged as a new, rebellious genre.

Music scholars still debate the exact origins of punk. Some cite the revival of early garage rock stylings from the early 1960s (a prime example would be the Kingsmen's "Louie Louie"), a nostalgic, fun form of rock that seemed forgotten in an age of overly complicated "Progressive Rock" (of groups like Rush, Pink Floyd, Yes, or King Crimson). Longing for a simpler sound, guitarist Lenny Kaye compiled "Garage Rock" classics for a late 1960s collection *Nuggets*, which featured tracks such as the 13th Floor Elevators' "You're Gonna Miss Me" or the Amboy Dukes' "Baby Please Don't Go." A few years later, the songwriting savant Jonathan Richman and group the Modern Lovers penned tunes with simple chord progressions ("Roadrunner") and lyrics about suburban life ("Modern World"). Others see punk arising from powerful, politically charged music of the late 1960s, especially by the MC5 ("Kick Out the Jams"). But there is no denying that wherever it started, punk gained global attention through the U.K. group the Sex Pistols (Espar et al., 1995).

By his own account, the Sex Pistols were the brainchild of Malcolm McLaren. A London shopkeeper, McLaren saw firsthand the burgeoning American punk scene that was just forming in New York clubs, such as CBGB's in the bowery district. Here, he might have seen American punk acts like the Ramones or Television. McLaren was, for a time, a pseudo-manager of the New York Dolls, a seminal punk outfit. By late 1974, he had designs on managing his own group, which led to the Sex Pistols. The group had a meteoric rise and fall, topping the charts in 1977 with "Anarchy in the U.K." and "God Save the Queen," followed by a brazen tour of the American south, after which the band promptly disbanded (Interested instructors would benefit greatly from the 2000 documentary *The Filth and the Fury*). Such exploits inspired other teens to form their own punk groups, and the early London punk scene was comprised mostly of "working class youngsters who felt at the bottom of the heap [as] unemployment in the U.K. was just becoming a fact of life" (Bradley 2000, p. 448). In these tough neighborhoods, such as Notting Hill, students can see globalization in action. Here I utilize an interview with the Clash's bassist Paul Simeon, who recalls in the 1995 WGBH documentary series *Rock and Roll* that

> when the Clash first really started I was about seventeen and really it was a strange period ... you could walk [down the street] and hear a bit of reggae out the speaker over here, and then over here they're playing Latin music and a bit further down Rockabilly. It's really quite strange because if you stand in the middle, you can hear all these influences, all at the same time [Espar et al., 1995].

You could also hear them at an early, landmark punk club, the Roxy. In 1975, the club hired Jamaican transplant Don Letts, to be DJ. According to Letts:

> It [the Roxy] held about two thousand people, and obviously they were all punks. I was the DJ, and I lived in a house with about four or five other Rasta guys. When I got the job, they all laughed at me [Espar et al., 1995].

Letts continues, recalling that it was so early in the days of punk that

> there were no punk records to play at that time, so I had to play something that I liked, primarily, and that happened to be my first love, which is reggae. And it seemed that the punk rockers could relate to it, I guess because it was the only rebellious sound around at the time [Espar et al., 1995].

In another interview, Letts remembers that "pretty soon they were telling me to forget the punk and play pure reggae. They were bringing me reggae records to play." Additionally, a nearby record shop, Honest Jon's, began "selling punk and reggae singles side by side." (Bradley 2000, p. 449). Reggae had invaded London. The connections between punk and reggae grew so strong that in 1978 Bob Marley penned the song "Punky Reggae Party," which extolled a "new wave" of musical collaboration.

By the mid–1970s, British artists increasingly identified with the themes of Jamaican reggae. For example, Junior Murvin's "Police and Thieves," with lyrics about crime in Trenchtown, was something downtrodden London teens could identify with; the Clash's famous cover of "Police and Thieves," provides a comparative example for students. The Clash was not the only U.K. group that identified with reggae's often anti-establishment message. Seeing parallels with their own economic troubles, British reggae group UB40 took their name from the government unemployment form to get on "the dole" (aka welfare)—a clear allusion to class inequality in late 1970s Britain. By the late 1970s, a so-called "second wave" of ska had emerged in Great Britain. Here, I ask students to examine both the look and the sound of the Specials. To do so, I distribute a second prompt with the following questions:

- How would you describe the look of the band? Specifically, how are they dressed?
- What is the instrument make-up of the group? Does it remind you of any previous examples from this class?
- How about the lyrics of the songs here? What are they referring to?

In an accompanying slide show, I first feature the iconic "Two Tone" label image, alongside one or two images of the band from the late 1970s. Their look is revealing, as the band traditionally dressed in some form of 1920s-style gangster regalia—a clear homage to the 1950s Jamaican artists who adopted the same style some three decades previous (e.g., Prince Buster). They also adopted the lyrical themes of early Jamaican ska, as shown in the band's live performance of "Rudy, A Message to You" (albeit slightly jumbled, as the Specials entitled their version "A Message to You, Rudy"). The song's reference to a "Rude Boy" is plucked from 1950s ska; it's a phrase repeated in another useful example: the Clash's "Rudie Can't Fail." Both songs feature bright horn sections, yet another nod to first wave ska of the 1950s. For a final example, I play the 1982 video "Our House" from British ska outfit Madness—a group that took their name from Prince Buster's 1967 ska hit "Madness." The video also nicely sets up the lesson's final section, which focuses on Music Television (MTV), the medium that would popularize "new wave" acts that embraced reggae rhythms and sounds.

MTV and New Wave

The final step in reggae's globalization—and dilution—came from Music Television (MTV). Launched on August 1, 1981, MTV was one of many theme-specific channels that benefited from then-emerging cable technology (other examples include the Cable News Network, or CNN, and the Entertainment and Sports Network, or ESPN). Although it quickly rose to cultural prominence, initially record labels were wary of MTV; they did not want to risk having their top acts appear on a channel that might fail. Instead, labels largely submitted videos by British bands that embraced reggae rhythms. What these new wave (the term came from Marley's song "Punky Reggae Party") artists had in common, besides their willingness to embrace a relatively new medium, the music video, was their slight adoption of a reggae rhythm.

For the first example, I feature New York group Blondie. Famously cutting their teeth in the NYC club CBGB's, Blondie were part of an early American punk scene alongside contemporaries Talking Heads and the Ramones. But Blondie had major breakthrough success with a string of hits, the biggest being "Heart of Glass." The song broke in 1978, but its demo version (available online) reveals that this disco song originally featured a reggae beat, and in 1980 Blondie covered the Peter Holt song "The Tide Is High." By 1981, these songs and their videos were in heavy rotation on the burgeoning music channel. Reggae had reached beyond second wave ska or punk outfits in London; it was now being heard throughout Middle America on MTV. New wave artists like the Pretenders ("Brass in Pocket") and Elvis Costello ("Watching the Detectives") were penning songs with just a hint of reggae rhythm. But there is perhaps no clearer example of reggae's reach than its adoption by Canadian Progressive Rock icons Rush. Their 1982 album *Signals* features the song "Digital Man," which both features a reggae rhythm in its chorus and lyrics referencing Babylon and Zion.

No new wave band borrowed more liberally from reggae than the Police. The group's first hit, "Roxanne" (1978) featured a reggae-inspired sparseness, while their follow-up "So Lonely" copped the rhythm and the chord progression of Bob Marley's massive hit "No Woman, No Cry." Play these examples back-to-back for students, and the influence should become clear. The group's 1979 album *Reggatta de Blanc* (a jumbled pseudo-French allusion to "White Reggae") included reggae rhythms on songs "Walking on the Moon" and "The Bed's Too Big Without You." The Police are where I end the lesson, as there is perhaps no better example of reggae traversing the globe and influencing rock music. More intrepid instructors might extend examples by including lead singer Sting's reggae-influenced solo work, such as "Love is the Seventh Wave" from *The Dream of the Blue Turtles* (1985). Regardless, the Police exemplify globalization. They were a band comprised of British and American members, who falsely claimed to be punks, but who embraced (copied, even) reggae rhythms and chord structures. By 1980, they were touring the world with new wave faux-reggae songs, and by 1983—thanks to heavy rotation on MTV—they had upended Michael Jackson's *Thriller* from atop the pop charts.

Conclusion

Reggae's remarkable influence on popular music is undeniable. As Chang and Chen (1998) write, "in many ways, reggae's most impressive achievement is to have retained its popularity among its own people amidst the unfettered cultural imperialism of the mass communication age" (p. 3). As a summary, I use a series of world maps and ask students to trace the cultural exchanges of the lesson. A successful summary will start with 1950s American rhythm and blues and its exportation to the island of Jamaica—either via laborers, or through radio technology. Here, mento evolved into ska, and later into reggae, genres that arrived in London in the form of a cultural diaspora from Jamaican transplants like Don Letts. Another line can be drawn from New York City to Great Britain, thanks to the influence of Malcolm McLaren's Sex Pistols, who themselves toured the American south. After London punks like the Clash and Second Wave ska artists such as the Specials adopted reggae looks in original songs and covers, their music went back to America. Finally, with the realization of MTV, which featured many American and British new wave acts, reggae rhythm came to dominate the airwaves and pop charts via groups like Blondie and the Police.

Students usually enjoy this class in part because most have some familiarity with the music. This is thanks to Bob Marley, a figure who became an iconic representative of Jamaican music. He remains an almost timeless conduit between the generations, and because listeners young and old have some familiarity with his music, many classroom barriers of age break down in positive ways. This examination of reggae, and in particular Marley's music, regularly fosters meaningful discussions and engagement. It also allows students to take a somewhat stale subject—globalization—and see it in action by tracing the look, sounds, and rhythm of reggae. Some students will offer examples of these trademarks in contemporary EDM or trance music. Reggae's durability as a genre makes teaching globalization via Jamaican music as relevant today as it was in the late twentieth century. Hopefully, your class enjoys its own "Punky Reggae Party."

REFERENCES

Appadurai, A. (Ed.). (2001). *Globalization*. Durham, NC: Duke University Press.
Bradley, L. (2000). *This is reggae music: The story of Jamaica's music*. New York: Grove Press.

Chang, K., & Chen, W. (1998). *Reggae routes: The story of Jamaican music*. Philadelphia: Temple University Press.

Colby, J.M. (2011). *The business of empire: United fruit, race, and U.S. expansion in Central America*. Ithaca, NY: Cornell University Press.

Eckes, A., & Zeiler, T. (2003). *Globalization and the American century*. Cambridge, MA: Cambridge University Press.

Espar, D., Bippart, V., & McCabe, D. (Directors). (1995). *Rock & roll, volume 5* [Motion Picture on VHS]. Boston: WGBH.

[Jither]. (2007, May 20). *Jools Holland interviews Steward Copeland*. [Video File]. Retrieved from https://www.youtube.com/watch?v=q45sg06K4yI

Moskowitz, D. (2016). *The 100 greatest bands of all time: A guide to the legends who rocked the world*. Santa Barbara, CA: Greenwood.

Sherlock, P., & Bennett H. (1998). *The story of the Jamaican people*. Kingston, Jamaica: Ian Randall Publishers.

Szatmary, D. (2010). *Rockin' in time: A social history of rock-and-roll* (7th Ed.). Upper Saddle River, NJ: Prentice Hall.

Teaching Black Music as a Living Tradition
Pedagogically Connecting the Past to the Present

Justin Patch

In 1971, Eileen Southern published her seminal text, *The Music of Black Americans: A History*. The textbook was a watershed moment in music pedagogy and provided a text that courses on African American music (beyond jazz) could use. The text is impressive in its depth and deserves credit for opening up spaces within the academy for African American music to be listened to and analyzed on par with European masters. However, there are two issues that later scholarship reveals. The first is the focus exclusively on the United States; the second is a narrative of historical development that does not explain or illuminate the incredible variety of modern music. While African Americans have made unique contributions to global culture, Afro-diasporic communities, people of African descent living outside of the continent, have also created unique cultures that are worth investigating. Scholarship like Paul Gilroy's *The Black Atlantic* (1993) challenged this narrative, highlighting the uniqueness of other diasporic cultures, and the aesthetic links between them. Other criticism, like Homi Bhabha's *The Location of Culture* (1994), confronted notions of linear time in the post-colonial world and among oppressed peoples, calling linear narrative histories into question and asking how history and culture should be represented. These critiques create a fundamental pedagogical question: what is Black music?

This question hangs over every decision involved in conveying the meanings, joys, struggles, intellect, and humanity contained within five centuries of music making by Afro-diasporic communities. Is Black music comprised of genres originated in Afro-diasporic communities, regardless of the racial makeup of the performers? Genres like jazz, hip-hop, bachata, and Cuban son are considered Black music, but are products of cultural exchange or mixed-race communities. Is Black music any music performed by people of the diaspora regardless of genre? This could then encompass nearly any genre, from opera and the concert tradition through heavy metal, old time, and EDM. Is Black music bounded by particular clusters of people, politics, aesthetics, spaces, and events, or does it include music made on the African continent and music of recent transnational black communities in the Americas, Europe, Asia, and Australia? The short answer is that there is no single answer and no clear lines of demarcation. Black music is, like so much African American culture, dynamic, contingent, historically rooted but existing in the moment.

The question of Black music is made even more complex with postmodern forms of Blackness and new identities that have gained acceptance (many grudgingly) within mainstream culture as individuals and communities fight for their own spaces, practices and audiences. As Touré insists in *Who's Afraid of Post-Blackness?* (2011), Blackness in the new millennium is more complicated and nuanced than ever. Because of that, narratives that encompassed Black music history and analysis, like the dialectic of Black Power and Civil Rights, repurposing remnants of hegemonic culture, and collective salvation through respect for roots and struggle; can no longer univocally explain or theorize the complex, diverse histories and experiences of Black music. But rather than see this as a point of frustration, it is an opportunity to rethink the purpose of teaching the music of the African diaspora in the new millennium, and to employ new pedagogical approaches to work through these intricacies.

For the past four years of teaching the course *Black Music*, I have wrestled with issues of global Blackness and historical narratives when teaching. Over the years I have experimented with different approaches and have chosen to use a familiar contemporary album to demonstrate the different intellectual and musical legacies of the African diaspora as it exists in the present. In the past I have used both Kendrick Lamar's *To Pimp a Butterfly* (2015) and Beyoncé's *Lemonade* (2016) as anchor texts. I can also imagine using National Public Radio's "Tiny Desk Concert" series, which features a rich diversity of Black performers in many styles from around the globe. There are many available options, artists and albums, soundtracks, or other collections of music, that can lead to productive course design. By taking this approach, I end up with a course that presents Black music as a living tradition, rather than a history of stylistic, social, and material developments of African slaves to the popular and concert music industries. This form of pedagogy begins with the present, examining styles, ideologies, and aesthetics that artists and audiences living in the contemporary moment value. This recasts modern artists as complex agents who exist within particular traditions and practices, but select their lineage and present personal histories of inspiration and experience.

For this essay, I will examine some of the theoretical and practical applications of designing a Black music course using Janelle Monae's Chase Suite trilogy: *Metropolis* (2008), *The ArchAndroid* (2010), and *The Electric Lady* (2013) as a primary text. I use Monae's music as an "anchor" text through which to examine various musical styles, critiques, and aesthetics. While there are sections of the course, like modules on spirituals, jazz, bachata, and reggae that cannot be taught through the Chase Suite, it is a helpful teaching tool for texts on the gender, sexuality, race and politics, as well as funk, R&B, hip-hop, electronica, girl groups, and other key genres of Black music. I have found that using a few contemporary works provides a necessary theme and through-line for a course that is designed to encompass long, complicated, and varied histories and communities. I will close with a note on Monae's 2018 "emotion picture" *Dirty Computer*, a 45-minute combination of original narrative film and music videos, which became part of the most recent articulation of my Black Music course.

Thinking Through the Roots of Black Music

Black music, since the mid–1500s when the first enslaved Africans were transported across the Atlantic to the New World, has been dynamic and innovative, just like diasporic linguistic, religious, culinary, fashion, dance, and social cultures. For cultural theorist Stuart Hall (1993), this dynamism and variation is representative of the many ways that diasporic culture has manifested itself for the past five centuries in rural and urban life, in North and South America, the Caribbean, and Europe, in fields, churches, barber shops, stages, dance halls, basements, and recording studios. Together, these musical cultures form a heterogeneous, multi-sectional tapestry that is not easily summarized or unraveled through linear narratives.

The complexities of the rich and varied histories of Black popular, sacred, vernacular, and concert music make courses like *Black Music* difficult to teach comprehensively in one semester. Inevitably decisions are made about which genres, artists, or works deserve special attention and which are unfortunately left for another course. While these decisions are implicit in teaching any subject, they are frustrating and leave educators with the feeling that too much is left unsaid, unexamined, or unheard. While this feeling is inevitable, there are pedagogical approaches that provide thematic coherence, do justice to the past, and introduce students to meaningful tools for analyzing the present. There are political and aesthetic decisions that are inherent with this strategy. The writing and teaching of history is a combination of narratives and silences that shape our perception of events. There is a politics in each pedagogical decision, and we are obliged to be honest with our students about our decisions and why we make them. This presents students with the possibility of assembling evidence differently to make alternative narratives, an important academic skill.

My method for teaching grows out of an anthropological consideration—in the classroom I am representing a living tradition that is part of a global history shared by tens of millions. The individuals and communities that created and nurtured the musical forms we love—from hip-hop and R&B, to funk, gospel, samba and Afro-beat—are part of diasporic communities that continue to produce innovative musical forms and sustain older ones. Many of these communities are also heirs to histories of violence, oppression, and discrimination. A purely historical approach risks neglecting relevant contemporary issues, like educational inequality, critiques of Black capitalism, police brutality and incarceration, gentrification, and valorizing the past at the expense of the present and the marginalized. By examining elements of Black musical history that are represented in contemporary works, links between the present the past are made visible without constructing a "golden age" against which contemporary music is judged.

If the purpose of teaching Black music is to valorize silenced traditions, expose students to marginalized voices, and get students to better understand and contextualize the sounds of their world, then we should begin with by examining how history is lived in the present. By centering contemporary examples Black music can be taught as art that is firmly rooted in the African diaspora, but continues to meet the needs, desires, dreams, and practices of today. Janelle Monae's Chase Suite and *Dirty Computer* exemplify how genres of Black music can be re-packaged and remixed to speak to the sexual, racial, and economic realities of the twenty-first century.

Case Study: Janelle Monae's Chase Suite

In 2007, singer, songwriter, dancer, and actress Janelle Monae released her first solo EP, *Metropolis*. The work is the beginning of a three-album set (divided into five "Suites") that tell the story of android Cindi Mayweather and her life in the turbulent, futuristic, post-apocalyptic mega-city Metropolis in the year 2719. In the narrative, Mayweather is an organic android gifted with both musical talent and a soul. In this futuristic dystopia of conflict, decadence, and excess, Mayweather becomes a pop star and the leader of the cybersoul musical movement. But her life is thrown into jeopardy when it is revealed that she is in love with a human, the robo-zillionaire Anthony Greendown. In Metropolis, androids are forbidden to know love, especially from a human, and she is sentenced to disassembly. The eight tracks on the EP chronicle the announcement of Mayweather's termination orders ("Violet Stars Happy Hunting"), through her despair ("Many Moons," "Cybertronic Purgatory") and escape into the Wunderground ("Smile").

The second release in the Chase Suite is 2010's *The ArchAndroid*, subtitled "Suites II and III." More philosophically complicated than *Metropolis*, *The ArchAndroid* combines the past, present, and future, introducing a time warp into the narrative. Over the course of the album the listener is acquainted to both Janelle Monae as a character in the narrative, and her relationship to android Cindi Mayweather ("Locked Inside," "Tightrope," "Oh, Maker"). The liner notes are written from the perspective of a present day (2010) character named Max Stellings, the Vice Chancellor of the Palace of the Dogs Arts Asylum. The fictional mental hospital has its own mythology: that it once housed both James Brown and Jimi Hendrix (perhaps the inspirations for Monae's own psychedelic soul). In the liner notes Stellings attempts to untangle the paradox that is Cindi Mayweather, as viewed from the present. His patient, Janelle Monae, claims she is from the future, that her DNA was stolen, illegally auctioned off, and implanted into android Cindi Mayweather, after which she was sent back to 2010. In 2719, Cindi Mayweather is now the ArchAndroid, whose powers of music and dance are working to liberate the citizens of Metropolis. Stellings' notes also explain the abundance of rhythm and blues and girl-group sounds on the album: that Monae, in her delusions claims to have worked with production duo "Deep Cotton," who, according to records, died in 1954.

The third release in the trilogy is *The Electric Lady* (2013), subtitled "Suites IV and V." This is meant to provide a modicum of closure to the Cindi Mayweather narrative, although the fate of Cindi Mayweather and Janelle Monae are left open ended. The narrative of the album follows Monae's magical escape from the Palace of the Dogs. Following her disappearance, the final two suites are anonymously delivered to Stellings. These are the triumphant testimonies of Cindi Mayweather, a musical weapon against oppression and a coded battle plan against the forces that divide society ("Q.U.E.E.N.," "Ghetto Woman," "Electric Lady"). Despite a clear warning from the state, Stellings released "The Electric Lady" because he has come to believe in the power of the music to bring freedom to the coming age.

What makes this series of albums an exciting tool for teaching Black music is the gamut that the music runs. The music ranges from classic film score and R&B, to soul, bossa nova, funk, hip-hop, and slow jams. In addition to the music, *The Electric Lady* features a series of interludes that feature a call-in show modeled on free-form Black radio, featuring a jive-talking DJ, a group of Cindi's android sisters, and callers of all persuasions from Metropolis. These musical styles cover many facets of Black vernacular and popular music (although by no means exhaustive), connect the Black American experience to Afro-diasporic music from the Caribbean and South America, and include sounds from other media, like film and radio, that are crucial to the formation of musical and social aesthetics and identities. There are also a number of thoughtful and creative music videos that accompany the albums. Videos like "Many Moons," "Tightrope," "Q.U.E.E.N.," and "Electric Lady" provide an opportunity to view Monae's narrative and politics expansively, and to utilize the visual medium, which many students are more comfortable working with than purely with sound. Finally, Monae's brief "Inspired by…" liner notes for each song on *The ArchAndroid* and *The Electric Lady*, provide singular statements that connect the music to a host of popular culture referents that demonstrate the social embeddedness of music.

A Critique of History

Perhaps the most effective way to teach these albums as a single, complete work is to begin with the future, to view Black music as an expression of aspirations, hopes, and dreams, as well as a repository for the individual and social histories of Africana people. Dreams of the future are always rooted in narratives of the past (empirical, mythical, or folkloric) and the experiences of the present. They are also shaped by the expressive cultures that current creatives find meaningful and useful. Contemporary artists ventriloquize artists from the past (think of Prince or Living Colour guitarist Vernon Reid channeling Jimi Hendrix, The Weeknd and Michael Jackson, Jennifer Hudson and Whitney Houston, Beyoncé and Tina Turner, or Brit Howard and Memphis Minnie) as a way of claiming lineage, and communicating with audiences through shared culture. In futuristic music like Monae's the past and the present are filtered into the imaginary space of the future, where expectations are manifested. Everything from dreams of fame, fortune, and notoriety, to utopias of freedom, universal love, communication with other worlds, and transcendence of time and space are woven into the fabric of music.

Monae follows in the steps of notable Afro-futurist bandleader and jazz keyboardist Sun Ra, and the iconic 1960s Marvel comic book *Black Panther*, whose expressions of futurism, unlike European futurists, combined imagined noble primitivism of the past with technological utopias of the future. However, Monae's past is rooted in 1954, rather than the pre-industrial past of *Black Panther*, or the Egyptian kingdoms of Sun Ra. The year 1954 is significant in popular music history. It is the birth of rock and roll as a genre apart from rhythm and blues, a manifestation of the color line in popular music, particularly broadcast media. The transition from rhythm and blues to rock and roll emphasized white male musicians and appeal to white audiences and patriarchal notions. Bill Haley records "Rock Around the Clock," Elvis Presley records "That's Alright (Mama)" and "Blue Moon of Kentucky" at Sun Studios, and Carl Perkins moves to Memphis with the hopes of recording at Sun. "Shake, Rattle and Roll," a Big Joe Turner classic penned by rhythm and blues songster Jesse Stone, was made popular by Bill Haley. Pat Boone's career also began, which included numerous hits originally written by Little Richard and other rhythm and blues artists.

In the segregated world of rhythm and blues, a seminal recording by guitar virtuoso Johnny "Guitar" Watson, called "Space Guitar," is released. This up-tempo rhythm and blues track features guitar lines with heavy doses of reverb, a new analog effect that adds the auditory illusion of distance (and no doubt influenced the sound and imagination of both young Jimi Hendrix and Ernie Isley whose signature psychedelic guitar sounds pervade the latter two Monae albums). Additionally, one of the great soulful voices of futuristic psychedelic funk-rock, Glen Goins, of Parliament-Funkadelic, was born, and a youthful firebrand named James Brown was captivating audiences in Georgia and South Carolina with the Famous Flames, on the verge of a breakthrough that would come a year later.

By tracing her own futuristic history to this pivotal year, Monae runs counter to long-established narratives of Black music that emphasize spirituals and the blues traditions. These outgrowths of African American slave songs and early religious practices are the basis for gospel, soul, rhythm and blues, funk, rock, jazz, and various forms of fusion. Many scholars locate the African-ness in these practices through their emphases on rhythm, improvisation, pitch bending, double entendre and word play, intensely emotional spirituality, or expressions of freedom (Cone, 1972; Dargan, 2006; Davis, 1998; Ramsey, 2003). In the scholarly literature, attempts are made to connect practices of the Civil Rights Era—soul, funk, hard bop—to a timeless tradition that connects Africana peoples to a pre-colonial past, and to a history of struggle and triumph (Baraka, 1963; Floyd, 1996). Monae downplays these histories, instead establishing her own genesis in 1954, and nodding to male performers James Brown and Jimi Hendrix as inspirations rather than imitating female icons from the same era like Tina Turner, Aretha Franklin, Abbey Lincoln, or Nina Simone. Monae also includes little musical material from jazz and gospel, instead leaning heavily on the girl-group sound, psychedelic funk, ballads, hip-hop, R&B, and film scores.

This short-circuiting of long (pre-colonial African or slavery) historical referent is reminiscent of philosopher Kodwo Eshun's "Operating System for the Redesign of Sonic Reality." In the 2012 essay, Eshun rejects "roots" music in favor of a pure, electronic, post-human futurism, one that is freed from the constraints and limitations of history and human identity. He rejects the naturalistic redemption of Afro-utopian movements like Rastafari and the essentialist cultural nationalism of Black Power in favor of electronic liberation, which starts with futuristic sounds and massive, otherworldly electronic beats and bass frequencies. While Monae's history is not as radical as Eshun's, it resists and tempers narratives of "the changing same," while selectively participating in a subjectively curated Black musical history. This process presents its own liberatory form: critiquing both present injustice and forms of oppression that are carried within liberation movements.

Monae's Chase Suite narrative presents critiques of modernity, particularly the loss of personal autonomy experienced by people of the African diaspora in the form of slavery and then in various exploitative practices like Jim Crow and contemporary forms of systemic discrimination. This is metaphorically embodied in the relationship between the decadent society of Metropolis and the Alpha Platinum 9000 androids. The music video/short film "Many Moons" from *Metropolis*, features a scene that is reminiscent of a slave auction, where wealthy buyers bid on different versions of the Alpha Platinum droids, each with different appearances and skills. The auction takes place in a set that appears like a fashion runway, with the different androids strutting and posing on the catwalk while buyers bid on them, while Cindi Mayweather and her cybersoul band provide 1960s rhythm and blues style music. The theme of voyeuristic sexuality and fetishization is obvious, as many of the android models are strikingly dressed and pose with obvious sexual allure while onlookers and bidders gawk.

The video for "Electric Lady" also portrays a vision of Afro-futurism that is rooted in a technologically augmented past. The video is set in a fraternity/sorority party that is literally timeless. The subjects push candy cars reminiscent of the refurbished 1970s muscle cars and big-bodied luxury cars favored in 1990s G-funk culture. Monae's crew are attired in outfits that index fashions from four decades, from 1950s letterman jackets to halter tops, crop tops, cut-off shorts, and skinny jeans. When Monae emerges to meet her crew, she takes a group picture of them with an apparatus that looks like a smart watch with a camera on it, and then examines it on her Samsung smartphone. When the crew piles into the car, they insert an 8-track tape of *The Electric Lady*, and the songs kick into gear. They arrive at a house party with features of Black Greek culture—elaborately choreographed step dancing (including a group of cyborg-attired women dancing with light sabers), fly solo and pair dancing, and a cipher featuring Janelle Monae. In another nod to Black collegiate culture, the video ends with a marching band featuring Monae as their drum major with "South Atlanta" on her cape. The characters in the video represent the many modes of Blackness that Touré writes about— from Afro-centric and hip-hop, to geek chic, throwback, bougie sophisticated, and athletic. The music is squarely in a 1970s vibe, with horn hits, additional percussion, Ernie Isley–like fuzz-wah guitar, responsorial backup singers, and a bass-forward mix, but also features a verse of Monae rapping. The lyrics extoll a space-age woman with the ability to captivate her audience and take them to interstellar regions.

These two songs/videos connect Monae to other forms of Black music, from seventies funk to marching bands, pop, Motown, R & B, hip-hop, and disco. They show an intellectual amalgamation of what the living history of Black music means to one performer. "Electric Lady" can be taught alongside tracks like Stevie Wonder's "Golden Lady," Jimi Hendrix's "Angel," Ma Rainey's "Prove It on Me Blues," the Isley Brothers' "Who's That Lady?," Duke Ellington's "Sophisticated Lady," Willow Smith's "Female Energy," Baaba Maal's "African Woman," Celia Cruz's "La Negra Tiene Tumbao," or Beyoncé's "Run the World (Girls)" for comparative celebrations of women in Black popular music. Likewise, "Many Moons" can be taught alongside tracks like Taj Mahal's "Follow the Drinking Gourd," Bob Marley's "Slave Driver," Damian Marley's "Slave Mill," Chico Science's "Monologo Ao Pe Do Ouvido," or Charles Mingus' "Meditations" as musical confrontations with slavery and its legacies. Monae's music connects to these histories but adds a fresh voice that incorporates political and social movements from the present and recent past to create a distinct feminist artistic statement on music history and female empowerment.

The Chase Suite also centers a narrative that dates back to early African American culture: that of forbidden love and the denial of Afro-diasporic peoples' right to freely express their love. Cindi Mayweather's love (rather than simply pleasure) with and for human Anthony Greendown is cause for termination orders in Metropolis. Androids, even those with souls, are not allowed to love humans, under penalty of dismantlement. The monologue that opens *Metropolis,* "March of the Wolfmasters" and "Violet Stars Happy Hunting!!!" feature an orchestral march over which a peppy voice joyfully announces the charges against Mayweather and the penalty lodged against her. It ends with specific instructions about who is allowed to hunt the famous android and which weapons are to be used to perform the disassembly (the barbaric-sounding "chainsaws and electro-daggers"). The joy with which the voice announces the hunt is a dark parody of lynching and the brutal, ineffable realities of slavery, Jim Crow, and into the present, as reflected in incidents like the murders of Emmitt Till, Treyvon Martin, and those by law enforcement that led to the rise of the Black Lives Matter movement, and the unlawful incarcerations of the Scottsboro Boys, Kalief Browder, Sandra Bland, and the Central Park Five.

The topic of love that transcends the arbitrary structures that society holds dear, is not only historical, but also casts light on contemporary issues of sexuality, queerness, and non-heteronormative expressions, along with continued repression of communities of color. While Loving vs. Virginia, which banned anti-miscegenation laws, passed its 50th anniversary two years after marriage quality became national policy, many still struggle with the social stigmas associated with interracial relationships, not to mention sexual variation, same sex and non-binary relationships. Canonical Black artists and thinkers like James Baldwin and Angela Davis have chronicled this struggle for autonomy within the confines of both the Black and mainstream American culture, and Monae's narrative is in continued dialogue with contemporary movements for autonomy, recognition, and respect. The tracks "Cold War," "Sir Greendown," "Q.U.E.E.N.," and "Oh, Maker" all tackle the emotions and politics of forbidden love and the sense of being that love provides. While Monae's more recent *Dirty Computer* tackles the issue of sexual liberation more fully, the Chase Suite does contain tracks like "Mushrooms and Roses" that hint at broadened the sexual politics (which will be discussed in the postscript).

The topic of forbidden love, or love denied, is one that has captivated many other artists. From the longing portrayed in the music of Ma Rainey, Bessie Smith, and Billie Holliday (covered extensively in Angela Davis' 1988 *Blues Legacies and Black Feminism*), to Body Count's "KKK Bitch," James Carr's "At the Dark End of the Street," Clarence Carter's "Slip Away," and Miles Davis' "He Loved Him Madly," there is a long history of songs that reflect the pain of loss and denial of emotional expression, or the vengeance embodied in prohibition (in the case of Body Count). The topic is relevant to modern life, even in the wake of marriage equality. Monae's takes on the notion of social rejection on the basis of queerness and non-traditional sexuality and often appears in both male and female coded outfits (more on this below).

In *The ArchAndroid*, Monae pursues another topic that pervades the history of Black music: that of appropriation. The fact that the liner notes describe the stealing of her DNA, leading to the creation of the wildly successful and soulful Cindi Mayweather, as "genoraped" is significant. The theft of Black intellectual property, particularly in the musical realm, is well-documented, from Pat Boone in the 1950s enjoying success with songs written and originally performed by Little Richard, Fats Domino, Ivory Joe Hunter, and Charles Singleton, to the 1960s British Invasion taking the United States by storm using long-ignored classics by blues artists (Carosso, 2013), and Vanilla Ice's *To the Extreme,* which sold over 15 million copies worldwide in the early 1990s, making a white rapper from suburban Dallas the biggest selling hip-hop artist of his era. (In a 2017 interview with Dan Patrick, Rob Van Winkle, aka Vanilla Ice, claimed to have sold 160 million records internationally.) Referring to this act of stealing artistic ability as both an assault and a theft adds a complex dimension to scholar Eric Lott's dialectic in *Love and Theft* (1993). Lott, among other scholars, looks at the widespread imitation of African American culture, from music to language, fashion, body language, and affect, as a complex interplay of appropriation (and at times a violent one) and acts of genuine inspiration. Monae's critique questions the "love" aspect of this by reframing the theft of musical intellectual property as rape, asking if the inspirational acts of love are not something far darker, which perform a violent violation and are not harmless imitations.

While this position is difficult in its accusations, it is worth considering. For example, hip-hop, a genre hatched out of transnational relationships between African Americans from the U.S. and the Caribbean and urban Latino communities, has become a pillar of international youth culture. However, with these stylistic innovations and extraordinary production of art, music, dance, fashion, and other types of intellectual property, only a select few from the hip-hop generation and after reap the full benefit. Many artists are signed to recording and distribution contracts that favor the industry over the artist, and the shelf-life of hip-hop and pop artists is short. Artists like Ice Cube, Dr. Dre, Sean Combs, Jay-Z, and Beyoncé who have succeeded in the industry since the 1990s owe their accomplishments in part to their business savvy outside of the music industry, something that many artists do not have. This reflects Timothy Taylor's 2012 critique of the sounds of advertising: that the pop music industry and the advertising industry share the same sounds and motives—to sell commodities—and that these have become almost indistinguishable. Under modern monopoly capital, artists are forced into the marketplace of commodities and transnational business rather than an exchange between those who make music and those who consume it through listening, dancing, sampling, and imitating.

This critique of modernity is carried through tracks like "Dance or Die," "Faster," "Tightrope," and "Come Alive" from *The ArchAndroid*, and "Electric Lady" and "Dance Apocalyptic" from *The Electric Lady*, where the act of dancing is portrayed as both liberating and dangerous. As Angela Davis writes in *Blues Legacies and Black Feminism* (1998), the pleasures of the body are a refuge from the grueling and demeaning nature of wage labor and alienation. Dance is a way to reconstitute community, share knowledge, and salvage remnants of humanity through sensual contact and meaningful interaction that exist outside systems of exchange and valuation.

Monae's critique connects to one of the seminal moments in Black public culture: the establishment of Don Cornelius' hit television program *Soul Train* (1971–2006). In *What the Music Said* (1999), Mark Anthony Neal points to the seminal music, dance, and fashion program as the first time that hip Black secular culture was represented in mass media in a way that was empowering, positive, and responsive to community. In the combination of new music, fly dance moves, fresh outfits (many homemade), and beautiful faces, Black audiences saw a celebration of life and a valorization of style and community. Monae takes Neal's celebration of Black representation in dance and combines it with trenchant critiques of racial and sexual repression and exploitation to create a unique integration and message: dance like your life depended on it.

Finally, *The Electric Lady* brings Monae's critique of sexuality and sexual politics mixed with racial and gender politics, to the fore (something that she pursues in 2018's *Dirty Computer*). The song/video "Q.U.E.E.N." (an acronym for queer, untouchables, emigrants, excommunicated, negroid) is an expression of liberation from below. The song text runs through myriad issues of inclusion and exclusion, by those who would police morality and sexuality, to the realities of discourses that exploit Black or feminized bodies only to recast these same bodies at needy when compensation is demanded. Monae asks who has the power to perform acceptance and why these rules are in place. The video is a masterpiece of the genre. It takes place in the future, where tourists come to see a display of time-travelling rebels from past times in a tableau, à la The Museum of Natural History. The virtual tour guide explains that these members of Wondaland and their Project Q.U.E.E.N. created music and emotion-pictures as part of a covert weapons program and freedom movement. Two young women sneak in and place a record on a skull-with-gold-tooth record player, which re-animates Monae, Erykah Badu, the Cotton Brothers, and a guitar and drum set rhythm section. Monae and Badu then proceed to take over the exhibit and testify. Monae's followers subdue the guards and her music animates herself, the Cotton Brothers and Erykah Badu. They proceed to hold a dance party in the museum, advocating for freedom and justice.

Perhaps the most mature and challenging work in the trilogy, "Q.U.E.E.N." combines elements that encapsulate struggles within the Black community—historically and into the present moment. The video's referencing of "freedom movements" captures the broad umbrella of Monae's argument, from economic independence to personal and sexual freedom, gender and racial equality, economic and social justice. She also emphasizes the role that expressive culture plays in these struggles for autonomy and representation but literally showing music bringing rebels to life, by lyrically confronting repression and injustice, and asking if her audience will take action. This video is rich in semiotic detail, as is the song, and connects with everything from civil rights songs like Abby Lincoln's "Freedom Suite" and Sam Cooke's "Change is a Coming" to Rasta theology of "chanting down Babylon," the "free your mind" discourses of Parliament-Funkadelic and En Vogue, and the unapologetically queer performances of Bounce artist Big Freedia.

As a statement on the complex present of liberation movements,

"Q.U.E.E.N." presents a critique of the present from the periphery, a bombastic but beautiful advocacy for those at the margins of modernity who are systematically and structurally silenced. This is the legacy and the purpose of Black music, to let these voices resonate in the present, and to put them in conversation with past and ongoing struggles and joys of Afro-diasporic communities through music and music culture.

Course Discussions

There are many ways that discussions about Janelle Monae's Chase Suite can go. In the past, I have emphasized both style/genre and lyrical content, drawing lines between the mythologies of her characters and figures from Afro-diasporic history. From parallels to slavery to sharing futuristic visions, The Chase Suite makes connections between the rich history of Afro-diasporic culture and the present moment. I have had success connecting her oppression to freedom narrative to the Old Testament (often purveyed musically in spirituals, hymns, and gospel), Rastafari musical practices from Count Ossie, Bob Marley, and Kabaka Pyramid, music of the Civil Rights movement (hymns, Aretha Franklin, Sam Cook, Nina Simone), and to the Afro-futurism of Sun Ra, George Clinton, and contemporary EDM and house. The class has also had vibrant discussions on representations of gender and sexuality, looking at Janelle Monae in relation to Ma Rainey, Bessie Smith, Grace Jones, Big Freedia, Little Richard, Celia Cruz, and Prince.

Conclusion

One album alone cannot comprehensively teach Black music, nor sum up its complexities. But neither can a single textbook, or a single course. When approaching the impossible, we must first ask, why is teaching Black music important and how can we take these points of emphasis and convey them to students? I believe that examining Black music as a living tradition with a canon that is dynamic and contemporary brings music, politics, aesthetics, and artistry to life. This prioritizes the nervous urgency of the present and engages students in the process of progressive understanding—one that does not judge by hallowed historical models and notions, but assesses the present as an object in and for itself and asks: how does this artist enunciate themselves and to what purposes? Janelle Monae's Chase Suite is an excellent example of contemporary racial, sexual, and liberatory politics, many which are rooted in the past and connect to older forms of music. There are many other examples of artists, collectives, albums, and tracks that can be employed for the purposes of understanding and analyzing Black music, rather than attempting to define it. In this process, Black music pedagogy can be inclusive in the present and conscious of the past.

Post-Script: Dirty Computer

In April 2018, Monae released *Dirty Computer*, an "emotion picture" that combines narrative film with music video. The work takes place in a dystopic totalitarian future where a repressive technology-enabled regime controls the population through erasing memories and "cleaning" bad habits. The narrative begins in a cleaning facility with cleaners scanning and erasing Monae's memories. The film consists of regime agents watching Monae's memories, which consist of her enjoying life with a band of flamboyantly attired youths who enjoy dancing, partying, and loving in desert locations away from the prying eyes and robots of the regime. The themes of sexual and personal freedom run through *Dirty Computer*. In the plot, Monae has a relationship with a woman and man who rebel and love together. Lyrically, Monae also relates her own treatment at the hands of those who criticized her for looking too manly and dismissed her talent. She also continues to confront systemic racism that keeps African Americans in low-wage low-respect positions in contemporary society and lifts up the achievements of Black women. Late in the spring 2018 semester we turned to this work as we wrapped up the class. It was a pedagogically effective way to see a contemporary take on culture, politics, sexuality and representation, particularly as we are collectively contemplating contemporary politics and the role of civil rights in the past, present and future. This also helped to put spirituals, the blues, jazz, soul, and funk into context: talking about Janelle Monae's criticisms and position in society was an excellent way to revisit artists like Marian Anderson, Paul Robeson, Count Osssie, Master Juba, John Coltrane, or KRS-One when they performed music as political and artistic statements.

REFERENCES

Alexander, M. (2012). *The new Jim Crow: Mass incarceration in the age of colorblindness*. New York: The New Press.
Baker, H.A. (1987). *Modernism and the Harlem renaissance*. Chicago: University of Chicago Press.
Banfield, W. (2004). Black artistic invisibility: A black composer talking 'bout taking care of the souls of black folk while losing much ground fast. *Journal of Black Studies, 35*(2), 195–209.
Baraka, A. (LeRoi Jones). (1963). *Blues people: The negro experience in white America and the music that developed from it*. New York: William Morrow and Company.
Campbell, H. (1987). *Rasta and resistance: From Marcus Garvey to Walter Rodney*. Trenton, NJ: Africa World Press.
Carosso, A. (2013). Recolonizing the blues. The paradox of the British invasion of American

popular music. In B. M'Baye & A.C.O. Hall (Eds.), *Crossing traditions: American popular music in local and global contexts* (pp. 121-138). New York: Scarecrow Press.

Chang, J. (2005). *Can't stop won't stop: A history of the hip-hop generation*. New York: St. Martin's Press.

Charry, E. (Ed.). (2012). *Hip-hop Africa: New African music in a globalizing world*. Bloomington: University of Indiana Press.

Coates, T., & Stelfreeze, B. (2016). *Black Panther: A nation under our feet, book one*. New York: Marvel.

Cone, J.H. (1972). *The spirituals and the blues: An interpretation*. Maryknoll, NY: Orbis Books.

Dargan, W.T. (2006). *Lining out the word: Dr. Watts hymn singing in the music of black Americans*. Berkeley: University of California Press.

Davis, A.Y. (1998). *Blues legacies and black feminism: Gertrude "Ma" Rainey, Bessie Smith, and Billie Holiday*. New York: Vintage Books.

Eshun, K. (2012). Operating system for the redesign of sonic reality. In J. Sterne (Ed.). *The sound studies reader* (pp. 449-453). New York: Routledge.

Floyd, Jr., S.A. (1996). *The power of black music: Interpreting its history from Africa to the United States*. Oxford, UK: Oxford University Press.

Gilroy, P. (1991). Sounds authentic: Black music, ethnicity, and the challenge of a "changing same." *Black Music Research Journal*, *11*(2), 111-136.

Gilroy, P. (1993). *The black Atlantic: Modernity and double consciousness*. Cambridge, MA: Harvard University Press.

Goodman, J. (1993). *Stories of Scottsboro*. New York: Vintage Books.

Hall, S. (1981). Notes on deconstructing "The Popular." In R. Samuel (Ed.). *People's history and socialist theory* (pp. 227-240). London: Routledge.

Hall, S. (1993). What is this "Black" in black popular culture? *Social Justice*, *20*(2), 104-114.

Krims, A. (2000). *Rap music and the poetics of identity*. Cambridge, UK: Cambridge University Press.

Lipsitz, G. (2007). *Footsteps in the dark: The hidden histories of popular music*. Minneapolis: University of Minnesota Press.

Lott, E. (1993). *Love and theft: Blackface minstrelsy and the American working class*. Oxford, UK: Oxford University Press.

Marcus, G. (1989). *Lipstick traces: A secret history of the twentieth century*. Cambridge, MA: Harvard University Press.

Mintz, S.W., & Price, R. (1976). *The birth of African-American culture: An anthropological perspective*. Boston: Beacon Press.

Monae, J. (2008). *Metropolis* [Compact Disc]. New York: Bad Boy Records.

Monae, J. (2010). *The ArchAndroid* [Compact Disc]. New York: Bad Boy Records.

Monae, J. (2013). *The Electric Lady* [Compact Disc]. New York: Bad Boy Records.

Monae, J. (2018). *Dirty Computer* [Video]. New York, NY. Wondaland Arts Society. Bad Boy Records: Atlantic Records.

Moore, R. (1997). *Nationalizing blackness: Afrocubanisimo and artistic revolution in Havana, 1920-1940*. Pittsburgh, PA: University of Pittsburgh Press.

Neal, M.A. (1999). *What the music said: Black popular music and black public culture*. New York: Routledge.

Peterson, J.B. (2016). *Hip-hop headphones: A scholar's critical playlist*. New York: Bloomsbury.

Ramsey, G.P. (2003). *Race music: Black culture from bebop to hip-hop*. Berkeley: University of California Press.

Rivera, R.Z., Marshall, W., & Pacini-Hernandez, D. (Eds.). (2009). *Reggaeton*. Durham, NC: Duke University Press.

Rose, T. (1994). *Black noise: Rap music and black culture in contemporary America*. Middletown, CT: Wesleyan University Press.

Szwed, J.F. (1998). *Space is the place: The lives and times of Sun Ra*. New York: Da Capo Press.

Taylor, K.Y. (2016). *From #BlackLivesMatter to black liberation*. Chicago: Haymarket Books.

Taylor, T.D. (2012). *The sounds of capitalism: Advertising, music, and the conquest of culture*. Chicago: University of Chicago Press.

Touré. (2011). *Who's afraid of post-blackness?: What it means to be black now.* New York: Free Press.

Trouillot, M.R. (1995). *Silencing the past: Power and the production of history.* Boston: Beacon Press.

Van Winkel, R. (2017) Interview. *The Dan Patrick Show.* https://www.vladtv.com/article/230507/vanilla-ice-on-selling-160-million-copies-still-selling-4-million-this?page=2

Whitfield, S.J. (1998). *A death in the Delta: The story of Emmett Till.* Baltimore: Johns Hopkins University Press.

PART 2

Artists and Icons

Good Rockin' in the Classroom

Teaching Elvis Presley and Popular Music

Jay Scott Chipman

Elvis Presley remains an iconic figure in cultural imagination. His music is distinctive and stylistically diverse. People continue to listen to his songs. His image and music is at the center of a commerce industry that generates multimillions annually. To some, he is an object of fantasy. To others, he is the object of ongoing controversies. Still others view him an object for artistic inspiration. He is worshipped. He is reviled. He is collected. He still provokes response. As Peter Guralnick, author of *Careless Love: The Unmaking of Elvis Presley* (1999), has stated:

> You don't have to like Elvis Presley—but it's impossible, if you listen to his music, not to recognize both his achievement and his originality ... [His] music exists, like all art, without explanation ... [and that inspires a sense of] mystery that will continue to reward repeated explorations, long after the frenzy of the fame is finally gone [p. xv].

In many ways, Elvis Presley is a perfect subject for academic study.

And he has been for many decades. An International Conference on Elvis Presley was organized in 1995 and held annually the next three years. Though short-lived, these conferences generated an eclectic mix of scholarly articles and personal narratives such as those collected in the edited anthology *In Search of Elvis: Music, Race, Art, Religion* (Chadwick, 1997). More recently, in August 2017, an international event titled *New Perspectives on Elvis* was held at the University of Memphis in celebration of the fortieth anniversary of Presley's death. One goal of this event was to recontextualize Presley's music, career, and cultural legacy in terms of recent scholarly developments.

It is not unusual to find courses that offer scholarly examinations of Elvis Presley's life and career among the curricular offerings at colleges and universities. A course on Elvis Presley can draw upon an ever-expanding Presley and popular culture scholarship, including not only meticulously-researched biographical studies, but also books and articles that consider Presley in the context of history, musicology, socio-economics, popular culture, and politics as well as those that investigate the culture industries that have emerged to capitalize upon his enduring status.

That's All Right: Elvis, Archway Seminar, Pedagogical Contexts

Elvis Presley: The Man, the Music, the Movies was developed as a course for the Archway Seminar program at Nebraska Wesleyan University (see also essays by Mohr and Whitt in this volume). The Archway Seminar is a requirement for all first-year students and is designed to orient students to the expectations of collegiate academics. Teaching an Archway Seminar is enticing for faculty because it opens the possibility to teach content they are passionate about but which may lie outside their academic discipline. This results in a wide range of appealing, often interdisciplinary, topics available from which incoming students may choose. Topics related to popular culture have proven attractive to both professors and students. All Archway Seminars, however, share a common set of course objectives that guide the development of curriculum. These goals include developing the capacity for critical thinking, conducting research and communicating the results of that research orally and in writing, and learning and practicing collaboration skills. There is the additional expectation that the Archway Seminar will also acquaint students with campus resources and future academic and co-curricular opportunities, as well as be the main source of academic advising during their first semester. One challenge for professors, therefore, involves an interesting balancing act of utilizing the course content as the foundation for achieving the required course outcomes, while preserving time for the other key informational sessions.

As the title *Elvis Presley: The Man, the Music, the Movies* suggests, the course was ambitious in scope. Presley's music was always envisioned as the central hub of the class, with plenty of listening opportunities incorporated into class time and assignments. The music, however, needed context, which necessitated students acquiring fundamental biographical knowledge of Presley's life and career as well as a sense of the cultural histories that shaped the music. Compared to his music, relatively little attention has been focused on Presley's movies. Frequently mentioned only in passing, or dismissed as inferior products designed primarily to sell the soundtrack albums and other Elvis music, the films provided a vital visual element as well as means for students to expand their thinking about Presley's identity and celebrity. The movies also, in practical terms, became another way for students to encounter and engage with popular music.

Teaching a class on Elvis Presley, his music, and his films to twenty-first century undergraduates is not without its challenges. Even though they are surrounded by ample evidence of Elvis culture, the fact that he died in August 1977 after a sustained career in the '50s, '60s, and '70s raises very real questions in the minds of contemporary students about Presley's continued relevance. Students should be encouraged to voice these doubts, which can become sources of debate about the persistence of Presley's popularity and the merits of learning about a significant historical figure from a contemporary perspective. It may also be worth urging students to consider contemporary parallels among singer songwriters of their generation and what societal factors have contributed to their success and popularity. The biographical details of Presley's life and career also sometimes leads students to a rush to moralistic judgments that open interesting opportunities for conversation about the personal impact of fame, fortune, and celebrity status. The goal of teaching a course like *Elvis Presley: The Man, the Music, the Movies* was not to persuade students to like Presley or become fans of his songs or his films, although in some cases that may, indeed, have happened. A more realistic aim was for students to develop an appreciation for what Presley accomplished during his career as well an understanding of the cultural factors leading to Presley's personal successes and shortcomings as an artist and why his music has continued to be so popular.

One factor potentially working in favor of a class on the life and career of Elvis Presley is the age of first-year college students. Presley achieved success with his first singles for Sun Records in 1954 when he was 19 years old, the average age of many beginning their collegiate studies. At the same age, he was booked to play those hits at venues throughout the South and traveled extensively, developing a strong regional fan following. At age 20, he was quickly starting to achieve national attention, signed a major label contract with RCA, and made television appearances on *The Milton Berle Show*, *The Steve Allen Show*, and *The Ed Sullivan Show*, which led to international stardom. Although circumstances for young adults in the 1950s were very different from those of today's college students, it may be worth exploring age similarity connections. Young adults, as well, comprised the majority of Presley's avid fan base in those early years. Good opportunities for conversation may be cultivated by drawing parallels to fan-followings of contemporary young celebrities, including those favored by members of the class.

Many young adults of college age currently listen to popular music and began forming strong connections to popular music from a young age. Fewer have engaged in systematic critical thinking about the elements or features that characterize and categorize certain compositions and recordings as popular music. Working with popular music in the classroom would seem to require intentional consideration of popular music's characteristics and categories, as well as thinking about who is making such decisions and how that changes over time. Depending on specific circumstances, it might be advisable to begin such a conversation early in the semester and return to it periodically as the class progresses. Fortunately, sources such as Donald Clarke's *The Rise and Fall of Popular Music* (1995) and Simon Frith's *Performing Rites: On the Value of Popular Music* (1996), among others, offer coherent discussions of popular music that can serve as starting point for helping students begin to formulate hypotheses about the characteristics of popular music without resorting to rigid definitions. Professors may choose to share portions of such texts to stimulate conversations. An additional option might be to take a less direct approach by asking students to read and draw conclusions about popular music from Greil Marcus's extended essay "Elvis: Presliad" from his volume *Mystery Train: Images of America in Rock 'n' Roll Music* (2008). Utilization of this text also has the additional advantage for a class focusing on the music of Elvis Presley as it could also be used to stimulate thinking about the construction of myth and celebrity in the popular imagination.

Pieces of My Life: Elvis, Biography, First Assignments

Selecting textbooks for the class was a major challenge, not only because of the sheer volume of books published about Elvis Presley, but because the chosen texts would help students acquire foundational knowledge about the subject as well as shape class discourse and help provide the means to accomplish course objectives. A book with a biographical focus was essential. Ideally, students would read Peter Guralnick's *Last Train to Memphis: The Rise of Elvis Presley* (1996) and its companion volume *Careless Love: The Unmaking of Elvis Presley* (1999). These two books offer the most comprehensive overview and critical analysis of Presley's life and career. They are also carefully researched and documented, providing excellent examples of academic writing geared toward a broad reading public. Guralnick (1999) also, admirably, tries to give readers "a new basis for understanding by delineating the context in which frequently well-known events occurred" (p. xiv). This focus pushes the biography of Presley in the direction of cultural history.

Although ultimately not selected as course textbooks for practical reasons involving page length and course design, Guralnick's two books, because of the wealth of detail and cultural context, proved to be a valuable resource for research in the Archway Seminar for students and for me as the professor. Instead, the students read *Fortunate Son: The Life of Elvis Presley* (2006) by Charles L. Ponce de Leon. While not as nuanced, Ponce de Leon's biography of Presley is a well-written and researched, compact text that allowed class members to quickly and efficiently gain a fundamental sense of Elvis's life and career trajectory. Ponce de Leon (2006), like Guralnick, also investigates how Presley was a "product of history" whose decisions were shaped, not only by "his temperament, background, and life experiences" (p. 7), but also "by the times in which he lived" (p. 8). This was the first textbook read by students in the Archway Seminar. Ponce de Leon's attention to the cultural contexts of Presley's life and career helped acquaint students with historical circumstances from times far removed from their lives in the early twenty-first century.

Fortunate Son: The Life of Elvis Presley is also an example of effective academic writing and, as such, provided the opportunity to point out how Ponce de Leon constructed arguments and supported them with evidence from research. Doing so became part of the writing instruction that was fundamental to the class. In addition, this textbook, as might be expected, makes frequent references to the titles of Presley's hit recordings and the recordings of other artists such as Little Richard, Carl Perkins, the Beatles, and the Rolling Stones in each essay. As students completed reading assignments, it was expected that they take time to listen to the recordings as they are mentioned and described in the book. This activity, coupled with in-class listening as each essay was discussed, kept engagement with popular music as a central focus for the class. There was also in-class viewing and analysis of Presley's early television performances.

Having read and discussed *Fortunate Son: The Life of Elvis Presley* and the attendant listening exercises in the first weeks of class, students were ready to undertake their first research and writing assignment for the Archway Seminar. Based on their reading of the biography, students were asked to choose one aspect or moment of Presley's life and career to investigate further. This gave each student considerable flexibility for selecting topics based upon what interested them from the reading and/or connected in some aspect to their anticipated area of academic study. In keeping with the goals of the class, students were asked to incorporate discussion of music into their essays whenever possible. The target length of this research project was 10–15 pages so, in practical terms, it meant it would be necessary for the essay to have a narrow focus. Given this was the first written assignment, writing instruction was incorporated into several class periods to review thesis writing, documentation of research, supporting claims with evidence, proper citation, and the fundamentals of essay style and structure. Proposed topics and theses were collected and revised and then students began to work outside of class on their own time with the goal of submitting a first draft two weeks later. These drafts were shared in peer review, graded, and returned for revision. This assignment served the express purpose of engaging students in the process of thinking critically about history and culture in relation to Brode's (2006) contention that Presley is "the most influential [musical] performer of the twentieth-century's second half" (p. 1). The students also began to grapple with how to effectively write about Presley's music. It is worth noting as well, although it was not done for this Archway class, that students potentially could make oral presentations based on this written assignment.

Raised on Rock: Elvis, Cultural History, Second Assignments

Textbook selection for the *Elvis Presley: The Man, the Music, the Movies* was also fueled by a desire to go beyond biography to focus more specifically on Presley's music. This led to the adoption of Michael T. Bertrand's *Race, Rock, and Elvis* (2005), an examination of how rock and roll emerged amidst the societal transitions following World War II. Bertrand is especially interested in how rock and roll impacted regional and national perceptions of race, class, and gender. Although actively integrating aspects of the history of rock and roll and Presley biography into his study, one of his stated goals is to investigate "how popular culture affected the racial attitudes of white southerners who lived during a period of unprecedented possibilities ... to initiate a dialogue and to suggest that we look at the South's past from a fresh perspective" (Bertrand, 2005, p. 13). Such a focus potentially takes dialogue about the popular music of Elvis Presley in productive directions that are in line with current attention to the intersectionality of cultural identities.

From a pedagogical standpoint, *Race, Rock, and Elvis* was strategically placed as the second textbook so that students encountered it with some fundamental knowledge of Presley's life and career in hand. They could now revisit and expand that knowledge by considering the implications of Bertrand's extensive research into popular culture's impact on the dynamics of social change. He offers, for example, valuable insight into why there has been a general tendency to marginalize popular culture in historical studies, and how that tendency has complicated scholars' efforts to place an artist like Elvis Presley into a historical context that takes into account changing attitudes about race, class, and perceptions about Southerners and southern culture. In addition, he notes that historians "have been slow to acknowledge that rock 'n' roll may have signaled a time of change regarding racial attitudes" (Bertrand, 2005, p. 231). Bertrand argues otherwise, and considers a range of phenomena including the rise of youth culture and consumerism in the 1950s, mechanisms of racial inequality that were embedded in traditions of Southern etiquette, aesthetic standards of taste that were used to discredit rock and roll music along class and regional affiliations, and the economics of the mass entertainment industry that shaped the actions of artists and audiences.

Race, Rock, and Elvis, as a text, stands in distinct contrast to *Fortunate Son: The Life of Elvis Presley*. Geared toward more of an academic readership, the writing style is more complex with considerably more embedded sources and documentation to support Bertrand's arguments. As such, the book models a different kind of effective scholarly writing and offers different opportunities for writing instruction. It was also many students' first encounter with a more challenging academic text, requiring different reading strategies they likely would be expected to employ in future classes. Because of the stylistic differences, it was not feasible to assign full chapters for each class period. Openly acknowledging the density of the text and that it would require more time to read, each chapter was subdivided and taught over several class periods in order that more class time could be spent unpacking Bertrand's analysis and discussing the implications of the evidence, as well as continuing to listen to and discuss the music mentioned in the text. Given the emphasis on race, class, gender, and regional identity, it was also necessary to navigate and accommodate a range of student comfort zones and opinions about these topics in order to ensure that students were thinking and writing critically about viewpoints that differed from their own beliefs. These chapters opened up many interesting opportunities, as well, to discuss contemporary parallels concerning popular culture, music, and social justice.

Bertrand regards Presley as possessing "the unusual combination of talent, charisma, and luck that made it possible to become an extremely popular and influential individual" (2005, p. 231). Presley's relationship to race and class was enigmatic during the time he was performing and recording. With the passage of time, as reading and discussing *Race, Rock, and Elvis* evidences, much of the enigma remains intact even with an expanded range of analytical tools at one's disposal. Even so, Presley's "greatest talent" with regard to the societal tensions and changes of the times, as noted by Bertrand, "may have been an ability to epitomize the emotions, aspirations, thoughts, feelings, tastes, and particularly contradictions of a large segment of his audience" (p. 231). For students in the Archway Seminar, *Race, Rock, and Elvis* effectively brought expanded focus on Presley as a singer, performer, and celebrity, while simultaneously foregrounding his music within the context of the dynamics of popular culture and social change.

Reading and discussing *Race, Rock, and Elvis* led into the next research and writing assignment. Students were asked to select topics drawn from or inspired by the text and develop them within the parameters of a 12–15 page essay. This opened up a range of topics connected not only to Elvis Presley, but also the civil rights movement, historic events of the '50s and '60s (rise of nuclear power, formation of NASA, Cuban Missile Crisis, protest movements on college campuses), and other aspects of popular culture (the Beat Generation, fashion, dance crazes, other celebrities, the beginning of color television). Students also had the option this time to investigate more contemporary societal concerns such as voter's rights, progress on gender equity in wages, political climate and social justice for underrepresented groups, and viewpoints on same-sex marriage. Once again, if possible, students incorporated discussion of music into the essay, forging connections based on principles and avenues of discussion drawn from the class. Class time, as before, was devoted to writing instruction, with attention paid to addressing some of the difficulties students encountered with their previous assignments. Because of the social justice dimensions of Bertrand's text, this essay required both incorporation of a different array of source material, as well as thinking about history and popular culture in more challenging ways.

Some of the stronger essays arising from this assignment utilized the contexts provided by Bertrand to investigate the careers of specific African American recording artists such as Willie Mae "Big Mama" Thornton, B.B. King, and Little Richard, incorporating discussion of the systemic challenges they encountered because of racial inequities and discrimination. Some of the same contextual information was incorporated, by a business administration major, into an examination of economic and political obstacles faced by record label (Stax, Chess, Atlantic) executives that promoted African American artists. One student interested in political science brought together evidence about Cold War politics and McCarthyism to explore the cultural anxieties and dynamics of flawed decision-making that surrounded the 1961 Bay of Pigs incident. More contemporary investigations tended to center on music celebrities. A essay that considered comparisons of Presley to Tejano music singer and songwriter Selena Quintanilla-Perez was one of the most successful, as it fostered analysis based on how celebrity culture intersected with Selena's gender, class, and Mexican American ethnicity.

Fame and Fortune: Elvis, Cinema, Presentations and Final Projects

While students began work on their second writing assignment, the focus in class shifted to consideration of films starring Elvis Presley. In mid-career following his return from military service in Germany in 1960 until he began appearing in concert again in 1969, the films and the accompanying soundtracks became the primary source of access to Presley's music and image. During that 10-year span, he made 27 films, frequently averaging three a year. Presley's film career was only occasionally mentioned in the texts students had previously read for class, so the films represented a different avenue of popular culture in which Presley's life, career, and music could be analyzed. The unit also begins to integrate consideration of visual culture. Once again this unit sought to address the goals of broadening student perspectives, knowledge acquisition, and building critical thinking skills.

Selecting a text for this unit was more difficult. Only a handful of books have taken the films of Elvis Presley as their focus. As Douglas Brode suggests in *Elvis Cinema and Popular Culture* (2006), "In-depth analysis of Elvis films did not take place at the time [they were produced], nor has it after the fact" (p. 3). Brode's own text certainly was an option and represents a notable step toward pulling "Presley's films out of their oblivious position in our pop culture world" (p. 278). His discussion of the individual films, however, proved idiosyncratic and grounded too heavily in the context of Presley's biography, an approach that would potentially steer students in unproductive directions. Likewise, *The Elvis Movies* (2014) by James Neibaur, while incorporating considerable research and making strong arguments for the films' relevance in assessing Presley's career, lacked analysis of broader cultural contexts in targeting its general readership.

The decision was made to move in a slightly different direction by selecting Erika Doss's *Elvis Culture: Fans, Faith, & Image* (1999) as the text to accompany the cinema unit. While Doss makes minimal reference to Presley's films, her book is centered on an examination of visual culture. As Doss notes:

> Clues to Elvis's abiding cultural symbolism are not to be found, in other words, only in his music or his biography, but among his many diverse and conflicted images and what they mean to the people who look at them, make them, and collect them: his fans [p. 4].

Drawing upon extensive research and personal interviews, Doss assembles and considers a wide array of visual culture: Elvis fan clubs and fan magazines, collection of Elvis memorabilia, Elvis tribute artists, Elvis-inspired artworks, Elvis rooms and shrines, pilgrimages to Graceland, and Elvis Presley Enterprises and its marketing of the Elvis culture industry. Through her investigations Doss draws conclusions about construction and production of visual images as well as how people respond to, develop relationships with, and produce meaning from them. Films, too, are an aspect of visual culture and Doss's analyses can be applied to students' viewing experiences of Elvis Presley cinema.

The chapters of *Elvis Culture: Fans, Faith, & Image* were interspersed between discussions of assigned film viewings in the unit. This pedagogical strategy helped to ensure that students continually situated and analyzed Elvis Presley film artifacts, and the music contained in them, within the parameters of visual culture. Shared viewings required of all class members included *Love Me Tender* (1956), *Loving You* (1957), *Jailhouse Rock* (1957), and *King Creole* (1958). These were the four films Presley completed before leaving for military service in 1958, and display Presley's initial potential as an actor and screen musical performer. Discussion of these films in class afforded ample opportunity to model effective film analysis, addressing the multiple facets of the collaborative filmmaking process and the function of the songs, as well as tying in observations about Presley from previous readings and points about visual culture in *Elvis Culture: Fans, Faith, & Image*. The remainder of Presley's films became options for oral presentations.

To address the Archway Seminar course objectives involving speaking and collaboration, students chose partners for two-person teams to compose, rehearse, and present 8–10 minute persuasive speeches about an Elvis Presley film of their choice. Having first viewed the film, they would select evidence from articles and film reviews, as well as film clips, to present a structured oral presentation with the goal to convince the class to watch the film. Students were required to utilize the original trailer for the film as well as at least one additional video clip in their presentation. Class time was dedicated to speaking instruction, including viewing an instructor-led sample speech. The grading rubric was distributed and discussed so that students knew they would be assessed on speech structure, use of evidence for persuasion, appropriate source citation, strategies for incorporating media, interpretation of evidence, and effective delivery techniques.

This speaking-instructive and collaborative activity allowed all students to work with one of Presley's visual culture artifacts. While drawing inspiration and principles from *Elvis Culture: Fans, Faith, & Image*, the project required original research about the selected film and shrewd decision-making about what evidence to present so that they made the strongest persuasive argument for viewing for the film. Although not possible for this Archway Seminar, it would be beneficial to structure the class so that students would do a second oral presentation to refine and practice their speech writing and delivery skills. Given that *Elvis Presley: The Man, the Music, the Movies* was taken in the students first semester, the activity gave them an introduction to effective speaking and collaboration, and alerted them to which aspects of oral presentation that were going well, and which would require more attention in future speaking-instructive classes.

The speaking presentations occupied a significant portion of the second half of the semester. The end-of-semester project, however, was designed to bring popular music back to the forefront of the class. For this project, students were asked to plan a 30-minute radio broadcast featuring the songs of Elvis Presley. Students had the option of working by themselves on this final project or working with a partner. Having read about, discussed, and listened to Presley's music for the entire semester, they were in the position to make informed choices about selections for their broadcast. The broadcast was to have a coherent focus, thus encouraging careful planning rather than assembling a random collection of songs. Once I approved their set list, students would write the lead-in material with clear, concise transitions between each song. This step required basic research about recording details and cultural context for each song. Once the text was written, the next step would be for the students to record the entire broadcast utilizing GarageBand or an alternate music production app. The project was then submitted online or on a CD, accompanied by a personal guided reflection about the process and its outcomes. This assignment could be modified to be a podcast project or, if the campus has a radio station, it could be designed for a live broadcast with students as guest disc jockeys. Another venue for a project such as this might be non-commercial, listener-supported community radio stations which might, as part of their mission, be willing to carve out air time for a limited series featuring the music of Elvis Presley and moderated by guest college student program hosts, either live or pre-recorded.

As a culminating project, this assignment involved research, writing, oral communication, and the option of collaboration, thus touching once again on each of the skills required of the Archway Seminar core curriculum. It also required students to make creative use of technology, drawing upon existing cultural artifacts (some of Presley's songs) and assembling them in such a way that a new artwork emerged. It tapped into their creative energies, let them exercise some artistic freedom and gave them another perspective on Presley's music, career, and place in popular culture. Several class periods were set aside for students to work in-class on this final project. Other class periods were effectively utilized to screen Presley's concert films, *Singer Presents ... Elvis* (also known as the *'68 Comeback Special*) and *Elvis: Aloha from Hawaii* (originally aired in 1973), which gave students the opportunity to view and discuss examples of Presley's concert persona and performance style.

What Now, What Next, Where To: Elvis, Teaching Popular Music, Conclusions

The aim of this discussion about the *Elvis Presley: The Man, the Music, the Movies* class was to provide an example of how popular music might be incorporated into an academic classroom. By providing concrete examples of assignments, perhaps readers may imagine how they might utilize popular music in the classroom either as a stand-alone assignment or as the basis for an entire class. Very specific to my particular university, the class was designed to address specific learning outcomes as well as allow me to teach a subject in which I had a strong interest that lay well outside of my own academic discipline of theatre arts. That the students were all first-year students taking the course in their first semester on campus guided content, the structure of curriculum, and the ways they could be challenged academically. It goes without saying that the material could be shaped differently for a different student population.

Reading three entire books, writing two research papers, viewing several films outside of class, preparing an oral presentation, and envisioning and recording a radio broadcast project meant that the class moved at a fast pace. Some students, in the course evaluations, acknowledged that they found the pace of the class too challenging. Others, however, commented that it provided a stronger insight into the demands of collegiate academics. Many believed they had gained skills in writing, speaking, and time management, and there was enthusiastic reaction to the creative broadcast assignment. As might be expected, in terms of studying Presley's music and films there was a mixed response. It was evident that some students gained a greater appreciation for Elvis as an artist and as a celebrity, especially when considering the historical and cultural contexts in which he was working. Others found it difficult to get past Presley's eccentricities and addictions, but still demonstrated an ability to engage critically with the readings.

What are the benefits from teaching popular music in the classroom? In this case, since the course was centered around the life and career of an individual musical artist, one benefit involved the opportunity to look in-depth at that individual and think critically about the factors that contributed to their successes and failures. Taking time to do so potentially enables students to extend those observations to more contemporary musicians and analysis of their musical compositions and recordings. Interesting conversations can be fostered from such questions as: What factors account for a musician's increase or decrease in popularity? Why are some artists able to sustain a career over time and why do some artists fade quickly from the public view? How does acquisition of fame and wealth impact how an individual perceives themselves as well as how they are perceived by others? What does it mean to be a fan and participate in fan culture?

Additional benefits accrue from thinking critically about popular music as a category of music, and even being able to begin to articulate what popular music is. What are its defining characteristics? How does it sound? In what ways do people respond to it differently than other kinds of music? Who sets the standards? How does what is perceived as popular music change over time? What factors contribute to its valuation? How does the artist who is making the music influence its characterization? Pondering and reflecting in writing and class discussion upon these and additional questions have the potential to expand knowledge not only about the music of iconic artists such as Elvis Presley but also the music of more contemporary musicians students encounter on a regular basis, deepening not only appreciation for popular music, but listening pleasure as well. What a wonder it would be if that could be an outcome of college class.

REFERENCES

Bertrand, M.T. (2000). *Race, rock, and Elvis.* Urbana: University of Illinois Press.
Brode, D. (2006). *Elvis cinema and popular culture.* Jefferson, NC: McFarland.
Chadwick, V. (1997). *In search of Elvis: Music, race, art, religion.* Boulder, CO: Westview Press.
Clarke, D. (1995). *The rise and fall of popular music.* New York: St. Martin's Press.
Doss, E. (1999). *Elvis culture: Fans, faith & image.* Lawrence: University Press of Kansas.
Frith, S. (1996). *Performing rites: On the value of popular music.* Cambridge, MA: Harvard University Press.
Guralnick, P. (1994). *Last train to Memphis: The rise of Elvis Presley.* Boston: Back Bay Books.
Guralnick, P. (1999). *Careless love: The unmaking of Elvis Presley.* Boston: Back Bay Books.
Marcus, G. (1991). *Dead Elvis: A chronicle of a cultural obsession.* Cambridge, MA: Harvard University Press.
Marcus, G. (2008). *Mystery train: Images of America in rock'n'roll music.* (5th Ed.). New York: Plume.
Neibaur, J.L. (2014). *The Elvis movies.* Lanham, MD: Rowman and Littlefield.
Ponce de Leon, C.L. (2006). *Fortunate son: The life of Elvis Presley.* New York: Hill and Wang.
Reed, J.S. (1997). Elvis as Southerner. In V. Chadwich (Ed.), *In search of Elvis: Music, race, art, religion* (pp. 75–91). Boulder, CO: Westview Press.

Teaching the Beatles!

Jeff Mohr

It has been argued that no band has had more impact on popular music and culture than the Beatles. Despite disbanding nearly five decades ago John Lennon, Paul McCartney, George Harrison, and Ringo Starr remain a ubiquitous presence as evidenced by the numerous publications and films that continue to be released expounding upon their music and influences on popular culture. The two most recent examples include Ron Howard's film, *The Beatles: Eight Days a Week—The Touring Years* (2016) and Mark Lewisohn's first of three planned tomes entitled, *The Beatles—All These Years, Volume 1, Tune In* (2013). Just when it seems there is nothing more to analyze or discover another book, film, or Internet revelation appears. As Lewisohn (2018) states: "It all boils down to this. They were four war babies from Liverpool who really 'did change the world, and whose music and impact still lives on in so many ways, after all these years'" (Q & A with Mark Lewisohn, www.tuneinbook.com).

Academic courses on the Beatles have been taught at several colleges and universities. In 2010 Liverpool Hope University in the United Kingdom began offering the first master's degree on the topic with "The Beatles, Popular Music, and Society." The idea of looking at a rock band as an academic pursuit worthy of serious study is apparently not so far-fetched.

As a college professor, the number of incoming, first-year students expressing interest in the Beatles and wearing Beatle gear has amazed me. This observation only encouraged me to embark on exploring the possibility of teaching a first-year seminar on the topic of my favorite band. Fortunately, Nebraska Wesleyan University gives professors an opportunity to teach a first-year seminar for incoming students in topic areas outside of their normal academic discipline in which they may have expertise or personal interest.

This essay examines my experience in teaching a first-year student seminar course at Nebraska Wesleyan University (see also essays by Chipman and Whitt in this volume) on the Beatles, which I have taught on two occasions. I will outline the pedagogy of how students and I explore the history of the band, their musical catalog, their tremendous sociocultural influence, as well as the challenges, failures, and successes involved in such an undertaking. I will include specifics such as considerations in constructing the course syllabus, selections of primary and supplemental texts, incorporation of media and film, use of guest speakers, and the challenges of taking a topic of obvious interest to many students and ensuring that the broader objectives of a first-year undergraduate seminar are met.

General Course Construction/Considerations

The syllabus for my Beatles course contains the following course description:

> This seminar will take a scholarly look at the music of *The Beatles* within its historical, social, and cultural context. We will explore how these "four lads from Liverpool" gained such worldwide fame and popularity and why they remain relevant today. Not only will we look at how *The Beatles* shaped their time in history, but how history shaped them. The class will be multi-media in nature including film, video, Internet, and, of course, the most important component—the music itself. A splendid time is guaranteed for all!

I have several course objectives which include: describing the childhood influences and backgrounds of each band member, understanding the causes and sources of the Beatles' unprecedented fame and success, identifying each album and its musical importance, understanding how the band evolved as songwriters and singers, understanding how the Beatles changed popular music and culture, and why they continue to be a major influence on popular music.

In the syllabus I state that this is a seminar class, which will rely heavily on class discussion of the assigned readings and listening material (including listening to each song on each album). Other methods of instruction include lectures, small group work, guest speakers, and viewing of audio-visual material. Students are graded on attendance and participation, administered four exams which include a listening section where parts of selected songs are played and students are expected to identify the song title, write reviews of the Beatles' first two movies, complete a major research paper, and complete a group project/presentation where students are divided into four groups, one for each member of the Beatles (i.e., John, Paul, George and Ringo groups). Students are provided with guidelines for giving a presentation, which addresses each band member's unique contribution to the band and also provides a profile of that individual's solo career. For the research paper students are asked to develop a thesis statement on a topic of interest to them. I ask them to think about what intrigues or interests them about this band. I hesitate to provide a list of potential topics as I want the idea to come from the student, but to assist them I include ideas such as writing about: a particular album or phase of the Beatles' development, someone in their inner circle who was instrumental in their success, going more in-depth regarding a musical innovation or early influences on the band, or the influence their experimentation with drugs and meditation had on their music and band dynamics.

Course Texts and Media

There have been more than 1,000 books written to date about the Beatles from a variety of perspectives. This makes choosing "texts" for a course like this a somewhat daunting task and one that I will, no doubt, continue to revisit. Most recently I have used four "texts" although legitimate arguments can be made for a variety of other options. These include *The Beatles: Illustrated and Updated Edition* (2006) by Hunter Davies, *Meet the Beatles* (2005) by Steven Stark, *A Hard Day's Write* (2005) by Steve Turner, and *The Beatles Anthology* (2003) eight DVD collection.

Legitimate arguments can be made for and against each of these selections. Davies wrote the first "definitive" Beatles biography. He was given unprecedented access to the band, family members, friends, and associates from 1967 to 1968. This gave him insights unavailable to many, but also a somewhat sanitized view of events, especially from John Lennon's Aunt Mimi who essentially raised him in his formative childhood years. The book also ends in 1968 before the band broke up in late 1969/early 1970. The "updated edition" published in 2006 does include an "end bit" that covers 1969–70, but it is not as detailed or informative as the rest of the book. Stark's book is relatively unknown, but presents the best socio-historical-cultural analysis of the impact of the group in a single volume. It is available in paperback, more academically focused, but highly readable. I rely on this text to cover much of the material related to the social and cultural impact the Beatles had including influences on youth and gender. Turner not only addresses every song the band wrote and its origins (some of which are debatable), but also contains excellent photographs of the band demonstrating how they evolved in appearance over their time together. Finally, the eight DVD anthology series, put together in the 1990s by the surviving band members in cooperation with Lennon's widow, Yoko Ono, represents *their* version of the definitive story (The Beatles, 2003). I use clips from this series in nearly every class. Again, when a band tells its own story there is bound to be bias and some "sugar coating." However, the series includes not only testimony from band members, but also archival interviews from many other important players in the story and their musical performances stretching over their entire career. I find these four texts create a balance that covers the main objectives for the course.

Lewisohn (2013) can lay claim as the most authoritative expert on the Beatles and, as was stated earlier, has completed the first of three planned volumes on the band. If I were only teaching a course about the bands origins and early years I would certainly use his book, which is the most exhaustive and comprehensive chronicling of this period. However, it is over 800 pages and would be too detailed and nuanced for a first-year college class. Plus, as stated, it only covers their formative years. With *The Beatles: The Biography*, (2006) Mark Spitz has written a generally well-received biography, but it has been criticized for several factual errors. Phillip Norman wrote *Shout: The Beatles in Their Generation* (1981) which was once considered the definitive biography, but it was later roundly critiqued as being biased towards Lennon and anti–McCartney. While many other books would make appropriate choices for a Beatles class, no single volume addresses all the objectives for this course. (The Appendix lists many other primary or supplemental options for the reader to consider including both books and web sites.) Students are provided all of this information on the course syllabus as potential references for their major research paper. For the paper students are required to come up with a basic thesis statement and then support their facts with research. I provide a list of possible topics including writing about: a particular album or phase of their career, someone in their inner circle who was instrumental in their success, a more technical aspect of their music, early musical influences that shaped the band, the influences the group has on other musicians, the influence of drugs on the band, or any of the numerous cultural and historical trends that impacted the group and its music. Students are not limited to this list, but it gives a place to begin their thinking and find something that is of interest to them. I use information from some of the sources listed in the Appendix to supplement the main texts, especially books from "insiders" who have compelling stories to tell that fill in the gaps from "authorized" biographies (Bramwell, 2005; Brown & Gaines, 2002; Emerick, 2006; Garry 1997; Harry, 1977, 2000; Shotton & Schaffner, 1984).

Other examples of instructive "media" for this course are the required movie reviews for *A Hard Day's Night* (1964) and *Help!* (1965). At the time these movies where made, the critics where ready to pounce on the notion that pop stars could be actors. By viewing these historical films, students are provided the opportunity to not only see and hear music performances, but how director Richard Lester put the band members in positions to essentially "be themselves" and receive near unanimous critical acclaim. This assignment is designed to get a fairly early sample of both the students' writing ability and critical thinking. In these two-three page papers students are asked to summarize the plot in one paragraph, address whether the film has a message, what emotional or sensual effect the film had on them, and make a recommendation on whether people should see this film.

The final "text" is my own experience as a Beatles fan since my first conscious hearing of their music in the sixth grade (I had a teacher who let us bring in records to listen to while studying). I did not own a Beatles record at that time, but I had friends who did. I have also made two separate trips to Liverpool where I spent several days doing my own research. Both trips included extensive, private tours led by native Liverpudlian and certified tour guide Jackie Spencer (www.jackiespencerbeatleguide.com). Jackie has been, and continues to be, a fountain of information for me, especially when it comes to the Beatle's upbringings in Liverpool. On my last visit in 2013, she arranged for me to have a one-hour sit down interview with Len Garry, an original member of the pre–Beatles band, The Quarrymen. Garry knew John Lennon well as they were classmates. He was invited into the band by Lennon when they were initially formed and before Paul McCartney and George Harrison were asked to join (Garry, 1997, 2013). This time spent with someone who knew Lennon when he was 15, and McCartney when he was 14, lends me a bit of "street cred" when we talk about the early pre–Beatles days in the classroom.

The tours with Jackie Spencer have also allowed me to collect an extensive digital photo archive of the relevant sites around Liverpool, which I use in the classroom including the Beatles' childhood homes, pubs where they hung out, and interiors and exteriors of the original Casbah Club and remade Cavern Club where they had the majority of their earliest musical performances before becoming famous outside of Liverpool.

History/Sociocultural Influences

The Beatles' biography, in addition to their musical catalog, is the core of the course. I approach the course from a chronological standpoint. We begin with the lives and early childhood experiences of each band member. They all grew up in post–World War II Britain in the city of Liverpool, both heavily bombed by the Nazis. Harrison, McCartney, and particularly Richard Starkey (Ringo Starr) grew up in impoverished, lower working-class conditions. While Lennon had a more comfortable existence living with his Aunt Mimi, he was lower–middle class at best. In *The Beatles Anthology* (2003), Harrison reflects on his childhood by stating, "You couldn't get a cup of sugar let alone a rock n' roll record." McCartney remarks on the social class differences by stating how impressed he was that Lennon lived in a house with an indoor toilet.

Students tend to think that the Beatles came to success relatively quickly and had the same four band members from day one. In class we spend the first month reading about and discussing the band's formative years, early musical influences, the culture of Liverpool in post–World War II Britain, their struggles in forming and keeping a band together, early audience indifference, and the key people in their early lives who shaped and influenced them. *The Beatles Anthology* DVDs are particularly helpful during this part of the class in hearing directly from all the band members, early managers, family members, and listening to the music of early American rock and roll that had a huge influence on their development. Especially poignant in their early development was family trauma (Lewisohn, 2013; Norman, 1981, 2008, 2016; Starr, 2015). Lennon experienced the deaths of his mother (hit by a car as a pedestrian by an impaired off-duty policeman) and his Uncle George (heart attack) who had served as a surrogate father figure. His biological father rarely saw him during his childhood, and only attempted to establish a serious relationship when he learned his son became famous. McCartney's mother died of breast cancer, a diagnosis which was kept a secret from the children until her death. Starr's father abandoned the family when he was only three years old. Only Harrison is spared tragedy and raised in an intact family, albeit in near poverty conditions.

The role of strong women in the Beatles' lives is also explored and is a fascinating topic given the fact that these four young men were raised in what was a very patriarchal culture (Stark, 2005). The women who served as surrogate mothers and romantic partners shaped these young men and their attitudes towards women and patriarchy, which slowly and gradually changes them, and is reflected in their musical development. Other women of importance in their lives include Astrid Kirchner, who took what would become some of the most famous photographs of the early Beatles and befriended them during their several tours of Hamburg, Germany in the early 1960s. Mona Best, the mother of their first, real full-time drummer, Pete Best, acted as one of their first informal managers, and made them the feature act in her Casbah Coffee Club in Liverpool (Lewisohn, 2013).

There is also the long-standing argument of who qualifies as the "fifth Beatle" in terms of influence and impact on the band. Candidates for this title abound depending on how it is defined, but would include: Brian Epstein (manager from December 1961 until his untimely death in August 1967), George Martin (record producer), Neil Aspinall (road manager and principal architect of *The Beatles Anthology*), and Mal Evans (trusted roadie). All of these men shaped their path in different ways.

Questions can be posed to students about whether the Beatles would have become so famous and influential had not certain historical events occurred when they did. One primary example is their television appearance on *The Ed Sullivan Show* in February 1964 shortly after the assassination of President Kennedy in November 1963. The argument can be made that America, and especially its youth, were in a deep funk after this tragedy, and the Beatles entered upon a perfect atmosphere for the emergence of a young pop band with outrageously long hair (for the time), youthful exuberance, and catchy, high energy songs (Stark, 2005).

Musical Catalog

I am not a musician, although I play a bit of guitar and ukulele for my own enjoyment. Although this is not a course in music theory we do discuss the Beatles' early musical influences, the evolution of their song writing, including many of their musical innovations. As mentioned above, students are required to listen to each Beatles album in chronological order and gain familiarity with each song. This includes their early work before they became internationally known, which is now available through releases such as *The Beatles Live at the BBC* (1994), *The Beatles Anthology 1* (1995), and *The Beatles Live at the Star Club in Hamburg, Germany* (1977). By carefully listening to each album we are able to explore how they changed as musicians, quickly becoming both performers and composers (rare at the time), evolved from simple to more complex lyricists, and incorporated more sophisticated sound and recording techniques with the help of producer George Martin, and engineer Geoff Emerick (Emerick, 2006; Martin & Hornsby, 1994). We discuss the importance of their evolution from an incredibly hard working, touring band, to musicians who honed their craft in the recording studio. With this part of the course having guest speakers who can speak to the nuances of the music is a great help. I have a few local musicians bring their guitars and demonstrate to students some of the musical and recording techniques that are evident especially around the time of the *Revolver, Sgt. Pepper's Lonely Hearts Club Band* and *Magical Mystery Tour* albums.

What will also be helpful for this course in the future are Scott Freiman's new series of lectures now available through streaming and on DVD titled *Deconstructing the Beatles* (2016). These are multi-media presentations that delve deeper into the production and song writing of the Beatles. There are separate DVDs for songs on *The Beatles (White Album), Sgt. Pepper's Lonely Hearts Club Band, Revolver, Rubber Soul,* and *Magical Mystery Tour* albums. These resources are highly entertaining and informative, teaching students how to listen with a critical ear to recording techniques such as the "fade in" (as opposed to a "fade out") on "Eight Days a Week," the use of a fuzz bass on "Think for Yourself," the incorporation of horns on "Got to Get You into My Life," random tape loops on "Tomorrow Never Knows," and the creation of the over 40-second piano chord at the end of "A Day in the Life," just to name a few of their many innovations in the recording studio.

Challenges

When one is a fan of a musical artist or group you are teaching it is not possible (at least for me) to hide your own enthusiasm, nor should you. Your excitement for the topic should be a positive contribution to creating a stimulating learning environment. However, this creates a challenge when you are also charged with teaching students how to be critical thinkers, and in this case, critical listeners. My approach to this dilemma is to balance my views with those of others including authors, critics, the band members themselves, guest speakers, and other important players in the story. Getting students to listen to the music and form their own views and opinions about what they like or dislike allows them to engage in critical thinking and express their views both orally and in writing. My job is to critique the expression of their views and arguments, not their opinions. One method I use is to give them a list of my 20 favorite Beatle songs. I make this list up every year and show students that it changes. Some songs are always there, but many are dropped and added over the years. This demonstrates to students that critical thinking, in addition to personal tastes, can change over time. The important skill is the ability to explain these changes and I openly share mine. Hopefully, it also shows students that I am not some old dinosaur, unchanging and set in my ways.

One challenge is students accepting the idea that it is important to spend time being immersed in the time period "before they were Beatles." The biographies of Lennon, McCartney, Harrison and Starr, their childhoods, the culture of Liverpool in the 1950s, their musical influences, gender roles of the times, changes taking place within media, the important people who influenced their career paths, and even luck and chance occurrences are all critical in understanding how these four young men morphed into superstardom that had never been seen before. Many students just want to listen to the Beatles music that they have already come to love before they set foot in my classroom. However, being instructed to listen with a critical ear is often a new and unfamiliar experience for first-year college students. Therefore, I find myself often in a balancing act between biography and music. My approach is to emphasize that the two cannot be separated, but in fact are integrally intertwined. Again, this cycles back to mixed instructional methods of lecture, listening to the music, watching performance, and hearing the views of the other significant players in the story including the Beatles themselves.

Another challenge is my own academic and professional discipline as a social worker. The social work profession's core values of integrity, service, social justice, the dignity and worth of the individual, the importance of human relationships, and competence are central to my being (Reamer, 2006). These are biases that carry into my perspectives on teaching this course. For example, as the Beatles matured and the turbulent 1960s unfolds, their music not only shaped, but is also influenced by the cultural tides shifting around them. For example, what does Lennon's reference to Chairman Mao in the song "Revolution" really mean? Is McCartney really singing about the plight of African American women in the southern United States in the song "Blackbird"? And, even earlier in their career, what is the significance of a clause in their American touring contract that specifically states they will not play to segregated audiences? Social justice themes emerge in these and other songs. As a social worker I cannot help but point them out as examples of the sociocultural and historical influence of the band on history, and history on the band.

Even though students are often quite interested in the Beatles or may even consider themselves "fans" they also come with their own contemporary musical tastes. Often these are musicians with whom I am not familiar. To this point I have not reached out to examine the students' musical preferences and address how they might connect with an interest in the Beatles. I am aware that there are numerous testimonials of current musicians who discuss the influence of the Beatles on their work. These are sources I need to explore and utilize more to connect especially with the students who may be less enthused about the course than others.

Appropriate topics for the research paper, outlined above, can be a struggle for some students and I have regretted some topics that I have approved in the past. For example, one student wanted to write about the conspiracy theory that John Lennon was assassinated by the United States government for his radical political views dating back to the early 1970s. I want students to be able to choose a subject they are interested in, but that also has the potential for academic rigor and sound research. Some of the best research papers have examined everything from a more extensive look at the Beatles' films, to the production influences of George Martin. I have also created a handout with guidelines to avoid problematic paper topics, and how to develop a clear and concise thesis statement.

Student Reactions/Evaluation

Unfortunately, due to my teaching schedule and other academic demands I have only been able to teach *The Beatles!* twice. However, I have had students and faculty approach me about when the course will be taught again. Thus, "word of mouth," to some extent, has been an indicator that the course has been well received. Student course evaluations have included comments about how some had little appreciation prior to the course how difficult the path to fame was for the Beatles, and how much struggle, hard work, and fate are necessary for success in any endeavor. Students have also expressed the downsides and high costs that come with stardom. As we explore how the Beatles were formed, rose to massive popularity and then eventually split, the students express an understanding of the sacrifices and heartache that come with the rewards. It has also become evident to me that many students come to a more sophisticated appreciation for Beatles music, and especially how the band developed their musical expression over time. Since this is a first-year seminar, I will typically not ever see these students again in the classroom. However, the chance encounters in a hallway have included, "I loved that class," "Check out my new Beatles shirt!," or just a smile, which communicates volumes. These alone have convinced me that I have brought some joy and also knowledge to students about the band I love. A small number of students have expressed criticisms about having to listen to the music with a critical ear ("music is supposed to be fun"), having to retain a fair amount of chronological history, and learning all about the other major players in the story including their names and the important roles they played. One student evaluation said, "I just wanted to learn about The Beatles!" If I could have had a conversation with that student I think my reply would have been, "I am sorry it was such a hard day's night. I wish you would have asked for some help earlier, and I hope it wasn't too much of a long and winding road."

Conclusion

This essay has reviewed my approach to teaching a first-year seminar course on the Beatles. I have offered my thoughts and considerations in teaching such a course including course content, texts and media, historical and sociocultural themes, the music catalog and musical innovations, and the general challenges and rewards that I have experienced. I have found that the rewards far outweigh the challenges in undertaking such an endeavor, and continue to learn from my own previous teachings of this course. Encouragement from student feedback and faculty peers motivates me to offer this course again when my schedule allows. As stated in the introduction, the Beatles have influenced generations of musicians and fans. If you attend a Ringo Starr or Paul McCartney concert today you see gray hairs, middle-aged folk, teens, and even younger children. The music and influence continues to be timeless 50 years and beyond its creation. As author Kurt Vonnegut stated, "I say in speeches that a plausible mission of artists is to make people appreciate being alive at least a little bit. I am then asked if I know of any artists who pulled that off. I reply, 'The Beatles did'" (www.beatles.net).

Appendix: Additional Recommended References

Books

Baird, J. (1988). *John Lennon: My brother*. London: Grafton.
The Beatles. (2000). *The Beatles anthology*. San Francisco: Chronicle Books.
Best, R., P. Best, and R. Best. (2003). *The Beatles: The true beginnings*. New York: St. Martin's Press.
Carlson, B. (2007). *The Beatles: A one-night stand in the heartland*. Nashville, TN: Cumberland House.
Carr, R., and T. Tyler. (1978). *The Beatles: An illustrated record*. New York: Harmony Books.
Coleman, R. (1984). *Lennon*. New York: McGraw-Hill.
Coleman, R. (1996). *McCartney: Yesterday and today*. Los Angeles: Dove Books.
DiLello, R. (2004). *The longest cocktail party: An insider account of the Beatles and the wild rise and fall of their multi-million dollar empire*. Los Angeles: Alfred Music.
Doggett, P. (2009). *You never give me your money: The Beatles after the breakup*. New York: Harper/Collins.
Doyle, T. (2013). *Man on the run: Paul McCartney in the 1970s*. New York: Random House.
Epstein, B. (1964). *A cellarful of noise*. London: Doubleday.
Everett, W. (1999). *The Beatles as musicians: Revolver through the Anthology*. New York: Oxford University Press.
Everett, W. (2001). *The Beatles as musicians: The Quarrymen through Rubber Soul*. New York: Oxford University Press.
Freeman, R. (2003). *The Beatles: A private view*. New York: Big Tent.
Giuliano, G. (1991). *Dark horse: The private life of George Harrison*. New York: Plume Books.
Giuliano, G. (1992). *The Beatles: A celebration*. London: Wellfleet Press.
Giuliano, G. (1994). *The lost Beatles interviews*. New York: Penguin Group.
Giuliano, G. (1999). *Two of us: John Lennon & Paul McCartney behind the myth*. New York: Penguin.
Goldsmith, M. (2004). *The Beatles come to America*. Hoboken, NJ: Wiley & Sons.
Gottfridsson, J. (1997). *The Beatles from Cavern to Star Club*. Stockholm, Sweden: Premium Publishing.
Gould, J. (2008). *Can't buy me love: The Beatles, Britain and America*. New York: Three Rivers Press.
Hanton, C., and C. Hall. (2018). *Pre:Fab*. Kibworth, UK: The Book Guild Ltd.
Harrison, G. (1980). *I, Me, Mine*. New York: Simon & Schuster.
Harry, B. (2000). *The Beatles encyclopedia*. London: Virgin.
Harry, B. (1977). *Mersey beat: The beginnings of the Beatles*. London: Columbus Books.
Hertsgaard, M. (1995). *A day in the life: The music and artistry of the Beatles*. New York: Delacorte Press.
Kane, L. (2005). *Lennon revealed*. Philadelphia: Running Book Press.
Kane, L. (2003). *Ticket to ride: Inside the Beatles' 1964 tour that changed the world*. Philadelphia: Running Press Book.
Lennon, C. (2005). *John*. New York: Crown.
Lennon, J. (1964). *In his own write*. London: Johnathan Cape.

Lennon, J. (1965). *A Spaniard in the works.* New York: Simon & Schuster.
Lewisohn, M. (1988). *The Beatles recording sessions: The official Abbey Road studio session notes: 1962-1970.* New York: Harmony Books.
Lewisohn, M. (1990). *The Beatles day by day.* New York: Harmony Books.
Lewisohn, M. (1996). *The complete Beatles chronicle.* London: Chancellor Press.
MacDonald, I. (1995). *Revolution in the head: The Beatles' records and the sixties.* New York: Owl Books.
McCabe, P., and R. D. Schonfeld. (1972). *Apple to the core.* New York: Pocket Books.
Miles, B. (1997). *Paul McCartney: Many years from now.* New York: Henry Holt.
Porter, A. (2003). *Before they were Beatles: The early years 1956-1960.* Bloomington, IN: Xlibris.
Riley, T. (2002). *Tell me why: The Beatles: Album by album, song by song, the sixties and after.* Boston: De Capo Press.
Rolling Stone. (2002). *Harrison.* New York: Simon & Schuster.
Schaffner, N. (1997). *The Beatles forever.* New York: MJF Books.
Sheff, D. (1981). *The Playboy interviews with John Lennon and Yoko Ono.* New York: Playboy Press.
Solt, A., and S. Egan. (1988). *Imagine: John Lennon.* New York: MacMillan.
Sounes, H. (2010). *Fab: An intimate life of Paul McCartney.* Cambridge, MA: Da Capo Press.
Starr, M.S. (2015). *Ringo: With a little help.* Milwaukee, WI: Backbeat Books.
Starr, R. (2004). *Postcards from the boys.* San Francisco: Chronicle Books.
Starr, R. (2015). *Photograph.* Guilford, UK: Genesis.
Taylor, D. (1973). *As time goes by.* London: Davis-Poynter Ltd.
Trynka, P. (2004) (Ed.) *The Beatles: Ten years that shook the world.* New York: DK Publishing.
Turner, S. (2006). *The gospel according to The Beatles.* London: Westminster John Knox Press.
Vollmer, J. (2004). *The Beatles in Hamburg.* Munich, Germany: Schirmer/Mosel Verlag.
Wenner, J. (1971). *Lennon remembers.* San Francisco: Straight Arrow Books.

Websites

Abbey Road Studios Official web site, www.abbeyroad.co.uk/
Astrid Kirchner Interview, www.retrosellers.com/features10.htm
The Beatles Official website, www.thebeatles.com
Beatles Story Museum in Liverpool, www.beatlesstory.com
British Beatles Fan Club, www.britishbeatlesfanclub.co.uk
Casbah Coffee Club website, www.casbahcoffeeclub.com/
George Harrison's Official website, www.georgeharrison.com
George Martin website, http://members.pcug.org.au/~jhenry/
Jackie Spencer, Liverpool Beatle Tour Guide website, www.jackiespencerbeatleguide.com
John Lennon's Official website, www.johnlennon.com
Lyrics of all Beatles songs, www.beatleslyricsarchive.com/
Paul McCartney's Official website, www.paulmccartney.com
Pete Best's Official website, www.petebest.com
Ringo Starr's Official website, www.ringostarr.com

REFERENCES

The Beatles. (2003). *The Beatles anthology* [8 DVD]. Hollywood, CA: Apple Corps Ltd.
Bramwell, T. (2005). *Magical mystery tours: My life with the Beatles.* New York: Thomas Dunn Books.
Brown, P., & Gaines, S. (2002). *The love you make: An insiders story of the Beatles.* New York: NALTrade.
Davies, H. (2006). *The Beatles: Illustrated and updated edition.* New York: W.W. Norton.

Emerick, G. (2006). *Here, there and everywhere: My life recording the music of the Beatles.* New York: Penguin.

Freiman, S. (2016). *Deconstructing The Beatles.* [8 DVD series]. www.deconstructingthebeatles.com.

Garry, L. (1997). *John, Paul and me: Before the Beatles.* London: CG Publishing.

Garry, L. (2013). *Personal communication.*

Howard, R. (2016). *The Beatles: Eight days a week—The touring years.* [DVD]. White Horse Pictures & Imagine Entertainment.

Lewisohn, M. (2013). *The Beatles: All these years, Volume I: Tune-In.* New York: Crown. Martin, G., & Hornsby, J. (1994). *All you need is ears.* New York: St. Martin's.

Norman, P. (1981). *Shout! The Beatles in their generation.* New York: Simon & Schuster.

Norman, P. (2008). *John Lennon: The life.* New York: Ecco.

Norman, P. (2016). *Paul McCartney: The life.* New York: Little, Brown and Company.

Q & A with Mark Lewisohn. Retrieved from www.tuneinbook.com.

Reamer, F.G. (2006). *Ethical standards in social work: A review of the NASW code of ethics.* (2nd ed.). Washington, D.C.: NASW Press.

Shotton, P., & Schaffner, N. (1984). *The Beatles, Lennon, and Me: The intimate insider's book.* New York: Stein & Day.

Spencer, J. *Jackie Spencer Beatle* guide. www.jackiespencerbeatguide.com

Spitz, M. (2006). *The Beatles: The biography.* Boston: Back Bay Books.

Stark, S.D. (2005). *Meet the Beatles: A cultural history of the band that shock youth, gender, and the world.* New York: Harper/Collins.

Turner, S. (2005). (3rd Ed.). *A hard day's write: The stories behind every Beatles song.* New York: HarperCollins.

People, Hell and Angels
The Sociocultural Contributions to the Rise and Demise of Jimi Hendrix

IGNATIUS CALABRIA

It must have been the summer of 1993 when I was digging through my older brother's CDs and found an album called *Radio One*. The cover brandished a photo of a peculiar-looking black fellow wearing what I thought was a pirate coat, twisting his face in concentration while squeezing notes out on his red guitar. I am sure I had heard his name before and thinking back probably heard "Foxy Lady" in the 1992 film *Wayne's World* and "Purple Haze" on an episode of the ABC television series *The Wonder Years* (1988–1993), but the music passed right by me. This time my 14-year-old brain had matured enough to find value in this record, leading to a lifelong dedication to studying guitar, music education and the life and career of Jimi Hendrix. *People, Hell and Angels* is a college course I developed from these interests, and have taught to different levels for over 15 years with hopes to educate those who have "never been experienced."

Despite his enormous contributions to popular music Jimi Hendrix is sparsely mentioned in academic studies, and occasionally overlooked in music history. He is not as widely studied by historians or sociologists as Elvis or the Beatles because his work was specific to the electric guitar. His discoveries, nevertheless, affected all succeeding guitarists and therefore much of rock music as we know it, making his contributions and influence worth considering as part of varied curriculum and essential to teaching popular music in the classroom.

One immediate challenge for educators is the lack of Hendrix scholarship available to conduct research and find pedagogical inspiration. It can be difficult to find articles discussing him and his work, instead often using his allure and image as a departure for sprawling discourses on lofty topics related to race or black identity that reach far and wide for interpretation, pushing the most essential element, the music itself, out of focus. While his face is familiar in guitar and pop culture publications and magazines like *Rolling Stone, Guitar Player* and *Guitar World*, his name is sometimes uncommon in the relevant fields of education. This requires educators to gain an understanding of his life and career in relation to major sociocultural events and surroundings to help construct a supportive foundation for devising curriculum. He was active from 1965 to 1970 and the many political and social challenges of this time have produced vast resources for reference to balance the lack of Hendrix material. Regarding Hendrix himself, *Room Full of Mirrors: A Biography of Jimi Hendrix* (2005) by Charles Cross is by far the most detailed and thorough examination of his life, while *Jimi Hendrix: Starting at Zero* (2013) and Steven Roby's *Hendrix on Hendrix* (2012) provide firsthand insight from letters, interviews and diary entries from Hendrix himself, presenting a personal perspective of his daily life, thoughts and feelings. *Hendrix: Setting the Record Straight* (1992) by Edward Kramer and John McDermott dives deep into his career from a historical perspective and provides valuable insight into the many unspoken details of his business.

Because of these obstacles, I break the class into units that educators could incorporate into their respective disciplines. The focus of the educator can also sway to accommodate expertise, which I will point out as this essay develops. Units from *People, Hell and Angels* will therefore be very different if taught by a musician as opposed to an historian or sociologist. I would also encourage educators to consider incorporating a unit into an existing curriculum if unable to teach the class as I have from top to bottom. For example, Hendrix was confronted with racial challenges during his career as detailed in the unit *Bold as Love,* which could be an interesting addition to a class on African American studies, race in pop culture or African Americans in music. If teaching a class or unit on jazz history, early American music or composing, *The Blues* may provide some insight. *Voodoo Child*, which examines his innovations on the electric guitar could be incorporated into lessons on rock history, acoustics, music technology or recording. Another approach is to isolate a specific social event such as the American Civil Rights movement, zoom out and question how Hendrix may or may not have reacted if teaching a class like *The Summer of Love* or *Music of the '60s*. The late 1960s was a tumultuous time for the United States, but created some of the most powerful musical and cultural movements in our history, and Hendrix was a figure of leadership. How did Jimi feel about the war in Vietnam? Check out *Machine Gun* for this or similar topics such as blacks in the military. How did Hendrix influence the hippie counterculture? Read *Monterey and Woodstock*.

First and foremost, I hope this essay will reveal and support the educational potential of Jimi Hendrix the Visionary, who vaulted the barriers of race and discrimination with the sole intention of sharing the music he believed would improve the lives and souls of his fans. Or Jimi Hendrix the Sonic Innovator, who discovered unknown potential in the electric guitar and constructed a platform on which to support all guitarists in his wake. Or, perhaps, educators will be intrigued by Jimi Hendrix Pop Icon, Peace Activist, or Acid Rocking Sex Symbol. He encompassed all of these personae which is why he is still popular today, decades after his death, and remains a valuable figure to reference when teaching popular music.

First Rays

Born November 27, 1942, young James Marshall Hendrix faced immediate challenges. He was raised primarily by his father and bounced between relatives in Seattle, Washington's, predominantly black Central District. Like so many African Americans, Seattle's residents suffered racism and poor housing, but nevertheless looked out for each other as a community. This proved crucial for Jimi's development and helped him throughout his early years as a musician. It was Hendrix's first experience in social order, and one common to many: difficult circumstances bringing like-minded people together with common goals. His first encounter with a guitar was with a neighbor at age 15. One lucky friend was given an electric guitar that Jimi adored, so his father eventually bought Jimi strings for an old family acoustic. Jimi was left-handed, but learned to play both ways because his father condemned his dominant preference, finding left-handedness "evil." With time, Jimi would commit as a leftie, but more desirable, more affordable and better-quality right-handed guitars were easily available, so he would just play them upside-down and string them accordingly. The upside-down Fender Stratocaster would eventually become one of his signature trademarks (Cross, 2005).

Hendrix's humble roots are common to many pop icons. Few came from wealth and comfort, which I keep in mind when teaching this unit. Remember to observe his development from various perspectives, inviting students to contribute their own thoughts and experiences. How does an unstable home affect a child's interests and creativity? What role does tragedy play at this stage of development? Jimi's mother, Lucille Jeter, died when he was 15. Might this affect his perception of women both personally and professionally? Hendrix had many female companions, and his songs "Little Wing" and "Angel" showcase similar female saviors/ guardians, perhaps inspired by his departed mother. John Lennon suffered a similar loss that contributed to his compositions, and I would encourage similar comparisons when examining the mother/son aspect to Hendrix's personality.

Community is another significant contributor to Hendrix's youth worth discussing. How does a student's community contribute to their development and ambitions? Without a stable household, young Jimi found food, friends, and security along a wandering path that primed him for life on the road. Conversely, the experience also left him poorly prepared for fame and wealth. I assigned students a short paper at this point on any celebrity's early years and its weight on their professional careers. Key topics included family life, financial support, encouragement, community and education and some excellent discussion came from essays on Adele, Michael Jackson, Amy Winehouse and Jay-Z.

The Blues

After a brief stint in the Army, Hendrix was discharged in 1962 and stranded in Tennessee where he learned the intricacies and culture of the blues, which would become the foundation of his music. I have always found great success in teaching blues history, theory, composing, and performance. The blues provide a simple platform for great virtuosity, emotional songwriting, and a foundation for jazz. Hendrix loved the blues and the early bluesmen and claimed, "(Nashville) is where I learned to play, really" (Hendrix, 2013, p. 31). T-Bone Walker and Muddy Waters records whetted his interest as a teen in Seattle, but southern living and culture immersed Hendrix in the blues and exposed unknown roots; it was a time of self-discovery and extreme musical growth. Since the blues are such an important part of Hendrix's music, I always start by teaching the basic form of a 12-bar blues and listen to a Hendrix recording such as "Red House," and compare it to a vocalist and instrumental recording differing in style and meter. When the 12-bar blues format is understood, I then like to discuss what the blues really is. Why blue? Why not a different color? Why and when did blue become a color representing sadness? This conversation sets the stage for the significance of song content and the story a blues composition can tell. Basically, not all blues songs are about sad or melancholy topics. The blues is first and foremost a structured formula, and if you call a 12-bar blues at a club in New York, London, or Tokyo, everyone will be on the same page. Regarding verses and interpretation, a blues could be about a breakup, an unfortunate or difficult situation, or winning the lottery. Here's an example I composed for a class:

> I woke up this morning and couldn't find my shoe
> I woke up this morning and couldn't find my shoe
> My feet are bare and lonely
> I'm not sure what I should do

Or perhaps:

> I won a million dollars, and I don't know what to do
> I won a million dollars, and I don't know what to do
> I bought a red Ferrari, and I think I wanted blue

Both examples fit the necessary format of a 12-bar blues. The chords for the first lines are the I-IV-I-I, the second line is IV-IV-I-I, and the last is V-IV-I-V while the verses in my example follow an AAB format. In 4/4 time each chord gets four beats. When teaching the blues, do not be afraid to dive right into the theory. It is very basic, easy, and essential to an accurate performance. For those unfamiliar with music theory, the Roman numerals represent a chord, which is played on piano, guitar or bass and establishes the harmony on which to sing verses. All chords are in relation to the one (1) or I chord making it the most important to remember because it establishes the key and all other chords. In the key of C, C is the I chord. With this established, if C is I, then just count to find the name of another chord, remembering to count C as 1 (very important). If C is the I chord, D is the ii (2) chord, E is the iii (3) chord and onward, no further detail is needed for the sake of the unit. As outlined earlier, the 12-bar blues is constructed of three chords repeated in a specific order, the I, IV and V chords. In the key of C, these respective chords are C, F and G (I, IV and V). Next, you plug these chords into the form giving each 4-beat bar one chord as detailed above, and you have a blues in C to work with. If you are unable to play an accompanying instrument, free software and music websites can provide background playback for group performances if you provide the correct form with the correct chords. Some nice, clear-cut examples of a 12-bar blues are Tracy Chapman's "Give Me One Reason" (1995) or Stevie Ray Vaughan's "Texas Flood" (1983).

It is the most basic formula that has been used for decades. Jazz musicians such as Dizzy Gillespie and Charlie Parker have altered some of the chords for more harmonic movement, but the form stays intact. If the measures add up and certain chords are where they should be it is a 12-bar blues. Often in jazz and bebop, verses are discarded and the blues is instrumental and functions as a means to improvise extended solos. I usually dedicate at least two full classes to the blues. We discuss blues history, examine the structure, listen to samples, and finally compose and perform a blues in groups. Students write their own blues that will be performed for the class, while I provide accompaniment on the guitar or piano if necessary. I am always so impressed by the content of their blues compositions. They quickly learn the format and are consistently successful in composing individually or in small groups and explore personal topics relevant to their lives. It is a fun way to learn the fundamentals of this genre, while also being candidly expressive with verses. While Hendrix only recorded one 12-bar blues to an album ("Red

House"), the blues would be the sound, feel, and foundation of his music, opening the door to many educational opportunities including black American history, West African music, composing, song-writing, music theory, and class performance.

The Circuit

As an aspiring musician, Hendrix worked on the Chitlin' Circuit, a trail of clubs and venues stretching from the South to Central/Northeast U.S. organized by and for black musicians. The Chitlin' Circuit provided steady work, safety, and comfort, freeing musicians to boldly be their music and perform freely. It is a fascinating page of music history that laid the foundations for American rock and roll, and plowed a path for the British Invasion in the 1960s. For further research, Preston Lauterbach's *The Chitlin' Circuit and the Road to Rock and Roll* (2011) is excellent.

One easy and successful project for this unit is to have students choose a graduate from the Circuit and write an essay following their path to their success. Consider Aretha Franklin's time on the Circuit. Whom did she sing with? What did she learn as a musician? How did the experience influence her career? Students love hearing recordings and watching footage of famous musicians before they made it big, and the Chitlin' Circuit was a stomping ground for many performers from Duke Ellington to Tyler Perry. Additionally, many genres of pop music can be traced back to the Circuit, making it a fertile subject for further research.

Since the Circuit repertoire was often simple and repetitive, Hendrix occupied himself with more complicated lead-like rhythms, developing his own style in the process. Examples of what I call "melodic rhythm guitar" could be found in "Wait Until Tomorrow," "Little Wing," "Castles Made of Sand," or "Bold as Love" on his second record, *Axis: Bold as Love* (1967). These songs showcase skills Hendrix mastered along the Chitlin' Circuit and are discussed in detail in the unit *Voodoo Child*.

Harlem and the Village

After the Circuit, Hendrix settled in Harlem. I begin this unit with a brief history of the neighborhood since its culture motivated Hendrix to stay in New York City. By 1965, Harlem was predominantly black, and Hendrix found comfort in his immediate integration. His immersion in the Circuit helped him socially, and he quickly made connections in the Harlem scene.

While a black male, Hendrix was compelled to create music that was not "black," which is important. Teachers should compare Hendrix's music to the hits of other time-appropriate black superstars, such as Hendrix's breakthrough "Hey Joe" alongside the works of James Brown, Wilson Pickett, and the Temptations. List the characteristics of the selections and compare them. Deconstruct each song, identifying instrumentation, structure, vocals, tempo details, song length, and dynamics. To balance the study, compare "Hey Joe" to popular "white" music from 1965, like "(I Can't Get No) Satisfaction" by the Rolling Stones, "Help!" by the Beatles, and Bob Dylan's "Mr. Tambourine Man." Hendrix was nowhere near to the popular Motown Sound or soul bands dominating black radio at the time, and Harlem was not the testing grounds for his music. While Harlem provided a safe, temporary residence, Hendrix saw more potential for musical success in Greenwich Village.

At this point, discuss Harlem and Greenwich Village as two culturally, historically and socially rich and diverse environments. People ventured from afar to immerse themselves in both areas, but Harlem was largely populated by a vibrant black community with a strong foundation laid by the Harlem Renaissance of the early 1920s. The Village attracted bohemians, artists, musicians and leftover beatniks of every style and color. To understand the music and identity of Jimi Hendrix, examine the social and cultural atmosphere of both neighborhoods during the mid–'60s. Focus on Harlem first, specifically the Harlem Renaissance. Ask how and why the Harlem Renaissance happened and the significance of the Great Migration, the relocation of millions of African Americans from the rural Southern United States to the urban Northeast, Midwest and West that occurred from 1915 to 1970. To balance this, do the same with Greenwich Village. John Strausbaugh's *The Village: 400 Years of Beats and Bohemians, Radicals and Rogues, a History of Greenwich Village* (2013) is detailed, comprehensive, and chronologically broken down by the populations that created the social and cultural movements.

It is fascinating to compare the two neighborhoods and their respective music and culture. Another successful project could be to find another Hendrix-type such as Rahsaan Roland Kirk that started in Harlem and found success in the Village, or vice versa. How have these neighborhoods changed today? Have other NYC boroughs become settlements for musicians? These are questions that can guide lectures on this unit and support class discussion.

An American in London

Hendrix was discovered by producer Chas Chandler in Greenwich Village in 1966 and brought to London, England, to assemble, produce, and record The Jimi Hendrix Experience. For this unit, ensure students explore the history and impact of the British Invasion on American pop culture and music industry, and how the global image and sociocultural influence of the U.K. affected the music world. Discuss how and why the British Invasion happened. What social atmosphere allowed the British Invasion, specifically Beatlemania, to unfold? Make more recent connections that students will appreciate. Discuss how Bronx housed hip-hop, Prince pioneered the Minneapolis sound and Seattle spawned grunge. A short paper could compare the British Invasion to one of these smaller pop movements, focusing on their sociological triggers and contributions. Another fun assignment could compare '60s British groups like the Troggs, the Zombies, or Herman's Hermits to later British bands like Depeche Mode, Radiohead, or Oasis. Ask for listening samples honing on specific influences while examining how pop music evolves in a specific area over decades. There are many possibilities, especially when discussing topics like the influence of the Beatles, the Who and the Rolling Stones on musicians in the U.K.

When discussing how and why Hendrix quickly conquered London there are many contributing factors to unpack and different points of departure, but one detail I expand on is that aside from the excitement of his music, Hendrix was successful in London because he was a black American. While race can be an uncomfortable subject in the classroom, I use this opportunity to teach students that confrontation and communication is a great way to address difficult but important topics such as this because Hendrix's African American heritage helped facilitate his acceptance in the London social network.

There are a few crucial details to expand on when discussing how and why Hendrix thrived in London. I like addressing how, aside from his music, Hendrix's African American heritage helped facilitate his acceptance in London's social network. Consider using this to make students reflect on race and American nationality abroad. Many British musicians who nurtured Hendrix idolized American black musicians like Chuck Berry, Howlin' Wolf, and Muddy Waters, whose brash style contrasted stiff British norms and provided a much-needed release. As an exercise, challenge students to find southern blues influences in early songs from British groups like the Rolling Stones ("Stoned") or the Yardbirds ("Louise"), and then present a short analysis, including listening samples. It is important to read and research these influences, but hearing it makes an immediate connection that drives through the main objective of this unit: that Hendrix personified early British rock's interest in black American blues.

With the support of the U.K.'s music elite like Mick Jagger, Paul McCartney, and Eric Clapton, the only thing standing between Hendrix's success and impeding fame was the Atlantic. Once he crossed it for the Monterey Pop Festival, Jimi Hendrix, an American, became the next conquering member of the British Invasion.

Monterey and Woodstock

The Monterey International Pop Music Festival, held June 16–18, 1967, was the brainchild of record producer Lou Adler, Paul McCartney, and John Phillips of the Mamas and the Papas, who believed rock music should be given the same attention and exposure as jazz, folk, and classical music (McDermott, 2007). Bands quickly assembled, and the stage was set for the three-day festival at the fairgrounds in Monterey, California. Many political and social factors intersected at this event, making Monterey paramount when teaching pop music and culture of the '60s. Educators should question how and why Monterey happened, why it was successful, and discuss the aftermath. Points of interest should include the influence of the Silent Generation, the Baby Boomers, the effects of the Vietnam War, hippies, and their contributions to popular music culture.

This part of the '60s was bursting with colorful life, so take advantage of film footage. D.A. Pennebaker filmed the festival for his documentary *Monterey Pop* (1968), an excellent resource on hippie culture. Explore the origins of the movement by discussing how Monterey was populated by Baby Boomers raised by members of the Silent Generation with strict morals and expectations regarding gender and occupation. This fueled frustration and awakened anti-establishment sentiments that songwriters like Joan Baez and Bob Dylan brought to the forefront. Highlight this generational divide by asking students about their demographic and upbringing. Is there a voice like Bob Dylan for their generation? What are their views, and why? From here, you can move by decade to the 1970s and discuss message musicians like Marvin Gaye, Bob Marley, or Crosby, Stills and Nash. In the 1980s, Bruce Springsteen celebrated American patriotism with "Born in the USA.," while across the pond, the Irish band U2 made clear statements about their interests in social and political activism, and Reagan's War on Drugs was a catalyst for groups like N.W.A. In the 1990s, Rage Against the Machine brought serious political issues to suburban houses through their inimitable combination of rap and hard rock. Educators can explore these routes, stay with Monterey in the 1960s, or unpack later musical movements/subcultures that made other big outdoor concerts like Lollapalooza, which first began in 1991, possible.

The sheer gravity of The Monterey Pop Festival may be difficult for students to comprehend. It was *the first* pop music festival. Such events have become so commonplace that educators need to underscore how Monterey was a risky, yet successful experiment. The town feared war protests and riots, and many residents opposed it altogether. Monterey's peaceful execution provided a moment of calm amidst a tumultuous political climate and inspired future festivals in Miami and Atlanta. The youth defined these events, so ask students how they shape their musical culture. How has the Internet and digital music influenced both themselves and the music industry?

Many students do not remember the pre–Internet world and may have difficulty processing it. Emphasize that Monterey was successful without instant messaging: no email, Facebook, or texting. To illustrate this, I once broke students into groups and asked how they would organize a festival today without the Internet. They were stumped at first, but as expected, they fell back onto the most basic means of communication. They looked each other in the eye and collaborated, designed posters without computers, rehearsed a radio broadcast, and directed a short television commercial. It was an active exercise in music history.

Monterey was a huge success that served as a template for the larger Woodstock Music & Art Fair on August 15–18, 1969 in Bethel, New York. If Monterey was the beginning of the Summer of Love and the hippie movement, Woodstock was its climax, and was headlined by Hendrix himself. He went from a late arrival to counterculture's fearless figurehead in just two years, famously flashing the peace sign during his iconic rendering of "The Star-Spangled Banner"—itself a relic of U.S. military history. It is thrilling to watch Hendrix pull human screams, ambulance sirens, and explosions from a simple Fender Stratocaster, several effect pedals, and some Marshall stacks. Just as noteworthy were the 500,000 attendees who packed Max Yasgur's dairy farm compared with the 200,000 who attended Monterey. It was a clear message to the country that its counterculture had grown in numbers, and their message was simple: peace and love. The 1970 documentary *Woodstock* is another great visual resource for students.

If focusing on Hendrix, discuss how he and his music matured between the two festivals. Come Woodstock, he was tired of leading The Experience and was experimenting with additional musicians, attempting to broaden his sound and release some weight from his own shoulders. The same man who fronted the power trio in Monterey now filled the stage with his original drummer Mitch Mitchell, Billy Cox on bass, two hand percussionists and of all things, a rhythm guitarist named Larry Lee. In those two years between Monterey and Woodstock, Hendrix's rock star lifestyle stretched him to the limits of his emotional and physical endurance, and he was painstakingly searching for his new sound. After Woodstock, Billy Cox was now his bass player, an old friend Buddy Miles was briefly on drums and Hendrix removed himself from the bill, renaming the now all-black trio The Band of Gypsys. Fans paid to see Hendrix the guitar-burning wild man and wanted to hear the hits, but never considered Hendrix the over-worked, exhausted, frustrated artist who was juggling court dates for possession charges and contract disputes, while desperately trying to record between tours. This conversation is important to understand Hendrix the person, and translates to any celebrity and is relevant in *The Tragedy,* a later unit addressing his death. Fans selfishly forget the needs of our idols and may not really care about their artistic needs and desires. We often want more of what has been done and this is usually contrary to the needs of any artist. Use this opportunity to examine artists with long careers and discuss their perseverance. Easy examples include the Rolling Stones, Bob Dylan, Aerosmith, U2 and Madonna. Common characteristics often unrelated to artistic creativity include good management and promotion. This will help students understand factors conducive to prolonged success in the music industry.

Bold as Love

Hendrix's British beginnings presented him with a dilemma he never completely untangled: his predominantly white audience. This is a major topic that still challenges me after years teaching this unit. We know his music appealed to black and white fans. *Rolling Stone* archives show *Are You Experienced?* reached #10 on the Billboard R&B chart, proving that he was selling records in black neighborhoods. Why were his live audiences predominately white? Educators should press the question both in class and as researchers.

It is important to understand racial and social undertones in the mid–1960s when approaching this subject. Clear lines of segregation were ever-present in the Jim Crow south and southwest U.S., and racial tensions could have dwindled mixed-race audiences. If Hendrix was cornered as white music, it would have discouraged black fans from attending his concerts. Cost is another factor. It is possible many inner-city fans could not afford tickets to Hendrix shows, further dwindling their presence. Knowing this, Hendrix performed several free concerts in Harlem and Seattle, but his management would not allow much else.

Educators should note that his original rhythm section, John "Mitch" Mitchell on drums and Noel Redding on bass, were white. This made The Jimi Hendrix Experience the only multiracial supergroup of the British Invasion, something worth developing in conversations on Hendrix as a black role model. I always presented the possibility of black youths finding inspiration in Hendrix as the leader of the trio guiding two white musicians. While not on his agenda, Hendrix became a figure representing racial equality and diversity, something also worth discussing. Appropriate statistical and historical resources, particularly questioning Hendrix's influence on '60s black youths, would be helpful for further research.

Voodoo Child

This unit deconstructs Hendrix's style and underscores his significance as a rock guitarist. Since his style was rooted in the blues, explore this through early vocal examples like Bessie Smith, and then blues guitarists. Some early Robert Johnson and Howlin' Wolf recordings help at identifying Hendrix's techniques, such as call-and-response type fills (the guitar echoes a vocal phrase) and voice-doubled guitar soloing (when a guitarist plays what he is singing on the guitar simultaneously). Choose examples like Johnson's "Dust My Broom" or "Cross Road Blues" for discussion, or compare Howlin' Wolf's "Killing Floor" to Hendrix's livelier version.

Blues form, harmony, and culture should be understood as integral to Hendrix's style. His melodic tools were just as basic. Like many guitarists, Hendrix relied heavily on the minor pentatonic scale—including some modes and variations—when composing and soloing. The minor pentatonic consists of a root or tonic note, a minor third, a 4th, a 5th, and a dominant 7th. In A minor, these notes are A, C, D, E, and G respectively. It is simple harmonically, easy on the untrained ear, and a great scale to present to unfamiliar students. It also lays nicely on the fretboard with two octaves in an easy-to-grip shape—the pentatonic box—making it a favorite for guitarists. That Hendrix rarely deviated from this scale is a testament to his creativity when improvising and composing. After listening to a minor pentatonic scale on a keyboard, piano, or computer, listen for it in Hendrix's music. The intro and main riff of "I Don't Live Today" perfectly outlines the minor pentatonic scale descending from the dominant seventh. "Gypsy Eyes" is minor pentatonic in harmonic structure and provides a good example of voice-doubled guitar soloing. As educators become familiar with his music, many more examples will emerge. I once had students spend a week searching for Hendrix trademarks—feedback, tremolo bar dives—in his and other music, and they returned with many recordings, several of which I will identify.

When teaching this to musicians, "Hear My Train a Comin'" is a great example of Hendrix's technique and style. The form is further simplified from the 12-bar blues of "Red House" to a vamp or repeating phrase in E with verses and a hook to get back to E, usually G to A. This song also provided Hendrix time and space to lay back and jam. He loved the blues vamp and indulged in lengthy interpretations of "Hear My Train a Comin'" during live performances. Its subject, a heartbroken man awaiting a train—some say his fate—follows a recurring theme to other hard luck wanderers in Hendrix's "Highway Child," "Wait Until Tomorrow," and "Bleeding Heart." The verses set the stage for explosive solos that meandered through various dynamics and sounds—depending on his mood. "Hear My Train a Comin'" showcases all of Hendrix's styles and capabilities, including feedback, pick slides (when a guitarist scrapes the edge of a guitar pick up or down a wound string to create a buzzing sound), glissandos (a steady, continuous slide up or downwards between two or more notes), guitar-doubled singing (when a guitarist sings what he or she is playing on guitar with verses or wordless vocalizing), call-and-response guitar/vocal interplay, and both delicate and screaming strings bends. It is an excellent listening example when featuring Hendrix in Rock or Blues History classes.

"Hear My Train a Comin'" was a blank canvas for Hendrix to adorn and experiment with: a perfect showcase of his ability. A more up-tempo version recorded as "Voodoo Child (Slight Return)" appeared in his 1968 double *Electric Ladyland.* Hendrix begins "Voodoo Child" with a simple but effective technique: he mutes the strings with his right hand—remember, he is a leftie—and strums while rocking the wah pedal (an electric guitar effect pedal that imitates the sound a trumpet or trombone player makes by moving a plunger mute in and out of the instrument's bell while playing notes or melodies) from heel to toe, creating a scratchy rhythmic pattern of treble and bass. If anyone had used this technique before, Hendrix was the first to record it. Another up-tempo showcase of his style is "Drivin' South." Several versions appear on his posthumous *Radio One*, a collection of live, on-air performances on the BBC by the early Experience. One particular take beautifully captures Hendrix's virtuosity in a solo where he masterfully leads Mitchell and Redding, building intensity with countless repeated patterns and phrasing.

Beyond the blues, Hendrix's time on the Chitlin' Circuit showed that his rhythm playing was just as powerful as his soloing. He did not need a rhythm guitarist: he handled both while singing. He was the first singer-songwriter/guitar hero in '60s London, a Clapton/Dylan/Townsend with added confidence and machismo. He performed behind his head and with his teeth with more speed and emotion than anyone had seen. Better put by Clapton, "I've got a lick that's better than Jeff Beck's, and Jeff has a lick that's better than mine, but Jimi Hendrix is better than either of us" (Stein, 1988, p. 3).

Machine Gun

To avoid jail time for a vehicular incident in 1961, a 19-year-old Jimi Hendrix joined the Army. It was his first major life decision and influenced one of his later compositions, "Machine Gun," a stand-out composition for a musician primarily interested in promoting peace and social harmony. I chose to name this unit after the song because the musical impact he delivers with "Machine Gun" is just as powerful and significant as the political.

I have taught this unit in several ways. Originally, I introduce *Machine Gun* as a one-day feature in an introductory course: *Music of the '60s*. The class was divided into segments exploring message and protest music. I often isolate the song "Machine Gun" when teaching '60s music because it brings Hendrix and his innovations into discussion. It is also interesting to examine the Vietnam War through the ballads of a former soldier. Although Hendrix never saw combat, his immersion in Army life gives many of his songs extra depth.

"Machine Gun" is a valuable example of Vietnam-era music and Hendrix's growing brilliance. It features some of his greatest innovations, including the use of feedback and the tremolo bar, making it essential to classes detailing the electric guitar's evolving usage. As in the intro to "Voodoo Child (Slight Return)," he imitates the clatter of an assault rifle by muffling the strings and strumming nine staccato 32nd note rhythms doubled by the snare drum. This not only mimicked the atmosphere of battle, it generated feedback he eerily bent up and down between gun bursts with the tremolo bar. It was another instance of Hendrix indulging as a soloist, making it another great sample of his style and technique. His January 1, 1970, recording at the Fillmore East is an especially good exhibition of his acoustic mastery. I like to think of this unit as an accessory to previous units as it is relevant in discussing stylistic recognition as well as political and racial awareness.

The Influence

Few musicians revolutionized their instruments the way Hendrix did his, and this discussion stretches beyond rock and pop. I group Hendrix with musical innovators like Niccolo Paganini, Franz Liszt, Miles Davis, Charlie Parker, Les Paul, and Jaco Pastorius, who mastered their instruments while unlocking unexplored potential. Hendrix's contributions, meanwhile, are sometimes overlooked by musicologists due to his image, chaotic life, and shortcomings. His influence on other musicians is also difficult to pinpoint due to widespread—and often unwanted—comparisons of later guitarists. Stevie Ray Vaughn, for example was enormously influenced by Hendrix and recorded several of his songs, while guitarist Joe Satriani sounds nothing like Hendrix, but uses many techniques he pioneered, including the whammy bar dives and doppler-like use of the wah pedal. If one plotted all of rock guitar's influences, many lines would likely begin with Hendrix.

This unit should be taught close to or alongside *Voodoo Child*, or at least while keeping its main ideas in mind. A great way to understand Hendrix's influence on rock guitar is to study the styles and techniques of notable guitarists before and after his career. Specifically, try to find a song like Albert

King's "Born Under a Bad Sign" or Muddy Waters' "Mannish Boy" performed by an earlier guitarist, Hendrix, and then a later one. A 12-bar blues is also a great starting point because the traditional form and harmony sets a perfect stage for analysis. I once compared an early Clapton blues to a Hendrix, and then a Stevie Ray Vaughn blues. My students found that Clapton was clean and composed, and Hendrix more impetuous. SRV was a mix of both: aggressive and confident, but also with shorter, calculated solos. For a project, choose a guitarist to compare with Hendrix, be it Stevie Ray Vaughn, Pearl Jam's Mike McCready, John Frusciante of the Red Hot Chili Peppers, or Steve Vai. Set clear guidelines and expectations, a two-page bio of both musicians, and maybe a list of shared or conflicting styles and techniques, with appropriate listening examples. I kept presentations to ten minutes and found students gaining a solid understanding of Hendrix's musical significance after this unit.

The Tragedy

When discussing Hendrix's death, I unpack his later life and music to better understand the *musician* rather than the rock star who overdosed. The world lost Hendrix at a creative time in his career unfortunately saddled with stress and frustration. Combined with his drug use, mounting legal bills, corporate greed, and the overwhelming depression that often haunts celebrities, the accident that took his life could have easily been avoided. Nevertheless, Hendrix died a successful musician filled with hope, promise, and ambition—not a devastated junkie. I emphasize this in the classroom by discussing his demise as an isolated event, and then backtrack to understand how and why it happened.

Before his death, Hendrix turned a major creative corner. His compositions were more developed and complex, with brass parts, multiple harmonic sections, percussion, rich vocal harmony, and multi-layered tracks. He pushed his engineers to explore new recording techniques and was introduced to new effect pedals, like the rotating speaker-inspired Uni-Vibe to bring the sounds in his head to the mixing board (Heatly, 2009). He also addressed more serious topics, like the importance of life ("Power of Soul"), community ("Message to Love"), the world's health ("Earth Blues"), and his own mortality ("Angel"). Sadly, people still wanted to hear "Hey Joe" and "Foxy Lady," and fans grumbled if he did not smash his guitars or amps. He often turned to drugs as an escape, and his intake of questionable narcotics led to his death at age 27 in London on September 18, 1970.

Hendrix thus became a founding father of the "Forever 27 Club," a list of rock stars who died at 27 that includes Brian Jones, Janis Joplin, Jim Morrison,

Kurt Cobain and Amy Winehouse. Rather than romanticize this sad community—which, in truth, only exists on paper—I focus on the circumstances behind the deaths of so many young musicians so that students can learn from past mistakes. Depending on the maturity of the class, this unit may not always be appropriate, but death is a topic that often intrigues students. I find it is best approached head-on.

I also like to remind students how lucky we are to have so many recordings to preserve and enjoy his work. Many gems from Hendrix's Electric Lady Studios were released posthumously—and controversially—by producer Alan Douglas, including *Hendrix: Blues* (1994), *Jimi Hendrix: Woodstock* (1994), and *Voodoo Soup* (1995), revitalizing Hendrix's music in the 1990s. If teachers only discuss the overdose, this is all students will remember about his final days. I have taught this unit as part of *People, Hell and Angels* to help students understand the fragility of life, its value, and to look beyond the image of iconic rock stars. Every one of them started off as people very much like us.

The Legacy

The encounters and obstacles Jimi Hendrix both faced and overcame throughout his career gives rise to valuable in-class discussion. I find students enjoy exploring his life and career while discussing his lasting influence, and many find his concert footage captivating. Visually, he typifies equality as the leader of a mixed-race rock trio bedecked in colorful '60s fashion. His poetry probes the mysteries of life and space, explores relationships, sexual interests, and addresses the realities of war. There is no shortage of captivating material when examining the life and career of Jimi Hendrix in class, and I maintain a list of readings for further research. Once the ball in class gets rolling, his work and era pave the way for educators to guide their students. His music is an encyclopedia of the times he lived through.

People, Hell and Angels is a class that examines and interprets how specific social settings, events, and culture in the '60s influenced Jimi Hendrix's music and career decisions. While this approach to music education can be applied with almost any musician, Hendrix stands out because his innovations paved the way for countless rock guitarists. Many of Hendrix's techniques can be easily duplicated and performed by a skilled guitarist, but he saw the musical potential first and pioneered it.

I also discuss the style and technique of living innovators. Among them, Tom Morello, guitarist for Rage Against the Machine, is masterful and uses the DigiTech Whammy pedal to harmonize melodies and rhythmically rubs the strings during solos like a DJ "scratches" vinyl records. His solo in "Bulls on Parade" is a good example of this unique approach to the guitar. Other greats who similarly pushed the electric guitar to new boundaries would include Jeff Beck, Eddie Van Halen, and U2's the Edge. The objective is the benefit of the student and what you hope he or she will take from the class. My goal is to share what I have discovered these many years examining the life and work of a sometimes-overlooked innovative genius.

I have always wondered how and why Jimi Hendrix's life and career unfolded as it did, and studying his sociocultural surroundings creates a more accurate, complete, and meaningful portrait of a timeless rock icon. As I gained a better understanding and appreciation of Hendrix's music and message, that mysterious face I discovered on the cover of *Radio One* as a teenager would reveal a sensitive, driven, brilliant musician whose impact on popular music was enormous and essential to understanding its evolution and development.

References

Adler, L., & Phillips, J. (Producers), & Pennebaker, D.A. (Director). (1968) *Monterey pop* [Motion picture]. USA: Leacock-Pennebaker.

Balk, B. (2014). As Seattle gets richer, the city's black households get poorer. *The Seattle Times*, November 12, 2014. Retrieved from http://blogs.seattletimes.com/fyi-guy/2014/11/12/as-seattle-gets-richer-the-citys-black-households-get-poorer/

Cross, C.R. (2005). *Room full of mirrors: A biography of Jimi Hendrix*. New York: Hyperion.

Heatley, M. (2009). *Jimi Hendrix gear: The guitars, amps & effects that revolutionized rock 'n' roll*. H. Shapiro (Ed.). Minneapolis: Voyageur Press.

Hendrix, J. (2013). *Jimi Hendrix starting at zero: His own story*. P. Neal. (Ed.). New York: Bloomsbury.

Lauterbach, P. (2011). *The chitlin' circuit and the road to rock 'n' roll*. New York: Norton.

McDermott, J. (2007). *The Jimi Hendrix experience: Live at Monterey*. Santa Monica, CA: Experience Hendrix, L.L.C.

McDermott, J., & Kramer, E. (1992). *Hendrix: Setting the record straight*. New York: Warner Books.

Redding, N., & Appleby, C. (1990). *Are you experienced?: The inside story of the Jimi Hendrix experience*. London: Fourth Estate, Ltd.

Roby, S. (Ed.). (2012). *Hendrix on Hendrix: Interviews and encounters with Jimi Hendrix*. Chicago: Chicago Review Press, Ltd.

Stein, L. (1988). *Jimi Hendrix experience: Radio one*. Salem, MA: RYKODISC.

Strausbaugh, J. (2013). *The Village: 400 years of beats and bohemians, radicals and rogues*. New York: HarperCollins.

Songs of Ascent

Teaching the History, Music and Activism of U2

DAVID WHITT

I am not ashamed to admit I miss the '80s, particularly the music from my high school years (1981–1985). While I was a fan of artists like the Police, Journey, and INXS, the Irish rock band U2 made an especially powerful impression on me beginning in 1983. In only their early 20s at the time, the four members of U2—Bono (Paul Hewson), Edge (David Evans), Adam Clayton, and Larry Mullen, Jr.—had a sound, message and attitude that, for some reason, spoke to me. I remember watching U2's video for "Sunday Bloody Sunday" on MTV, proud that I was the only student in my high school with an *"Under a Blood Red Sky"* t-shirt, and driving around my hometown of Marquette, Michigan, on a Saturday afternoon in October 1984 listening to a cassette of their latest release *The Unforgettable Fire*. U2's energetic songs of protest and unity were a source of inspiration during those awkward and formative years. In the early '80s my teenage self could never have guessed that over the next 35 years U2 would become "the biggest band in the world," with millions of albums sold, record-breaking tours, dozens of music industry awards, and an impressive track record of global activism. I also could never have guessed that 35 years later I would be a college professor teaching a class about U2, and writing about this experience for a book.

History and Rationale: The Archway Seminar

Each fall semester from 2015 to 2018, I taught a class at Nebraska Wesleyan University titled *Songs of Ascent: The Music and Meaning of U2*. The course was part of the Archway Seminar (AWS), a requirement for all first-year students (see also essays by Chipman and Mohr in this volume). The purpose of the AWS is to "introduce students to intellectual practices that will help them make the most of their liberal arts education." As an introduction to the college experience, students develop skills in reading, speaking, writing, conducting research, group collaboration, critical thinking and using technology. The AWS topics vary depending on the interests of the instructor. For example, some course titles have included: *Mindfulness Theory to Practice, The Olympics, The Necessity of Wilderness, Hamlet, The Obama Presidency, Atheism, Hamilton and the Story of America*, and *1968*. Before *Songs of Ascent*, I developed an AWS on *Star Trek* and, a few years later, comic books. In terms of their historical, political and sociocultural significance, classes like *1968* or *The Obama Presidency* would never be questioned for their academic value. However, with U2 many students, and even some parents, wondered what makes a rock and roll band worthy of being a course for college credit?

My justification for *Songs of Ascent* was multifaceted. In addition to U2's commercial and critical success, the past several years have seen an increase in U2 scholarship. For example, editor Scott Calhoun's *Exploring U2: Is This Rock 'n' Roll?: Essays on the Music, Work, and Influence of U2* (2012) and *U2 Above, Across, and Beyond: Interdisciplinary Assessments* (2015), and Timothy Neufeld's *U2: Rock 'n' Roll to Change the World* (2017), provide critical and insightful analyses of U2's history, songs, tours, and activism. Academic journals such as *Biblical Interpretation, Journal of Documentation, Popular Music History, Journal of Contemporary Religion, Popular Music & Society, Social Semiotics*, and the *Journal of Applied Social Psychology* have also published articles about U2. There have even been U2 conferences held in Durham, North Carolina (2009), Cleveland, Ohio (2013), and Belfast, Northern Ireland (2018), where educators, theologians, rock journalists and fans discuss a diverse range of U2-related subjects (I was fortunate to attend the 2018 U2CON in Belfast to discuss my U2 class). Given U2's impact upon music and culture, it is actually surprising there have only been a handful of college classes about the band. I know of only a few: Timothy Neufeld of Fresno Pacific University developed *Theology, Culture, and U2*, Sam Lovato's *U2: Mediated Discourse and Invention* at Colorado State-Pueblo, and Marshall Welch of Saint Mary's College of California taught *Spirituality and Politics of U2*.

I had been thinking about teaching a class on U2 for several years, but a notable musical event finally motivated me to do so. In September 2014, U2 released their 13th studio album, *Songs of Innocence*, and the following year were on their *Innocence + Experience* tour. Therefore, my academic exploration of U2 seemed timely. Additionally, I had a wealth of resources to supplement the course including several scholarly books, journal articles, concert DVDs, radio and television interviews, music videos, and documentaries. If anything, I had too much material, which only bolstered my belief that a course on U2 was credible and relevant. The course description in the syllabus provided additional rationale for the value of U2 as a subject of study:

> In the history of rock and roll few acts have had the longevity, popularity, and impact of U2. This course will trace the musical journey of U2 from their humble beginnings in Dublin, Ireland in the 1970s, to selling out arenas and stadiums around the world today. Along the way, we will examine U2's diverse musical catalog, their critical and commercial highs and lows, as well as the social consciousness exhibited in their songs and activism.

While there were a variety of ways to organize the course, I decided to follow a straightforward chronological pattern. I began with the early years of the individual band members and their formation as a group in Dublin, Ireland in the 1970s, then moved through the decades to discuss each U2 album in the order of its release, subsequent tour, and ended with a focus on their activism. Doing so allowed students to understand how important events (e.g., the death of Bono's and Larry's mothers, the Troubles in Northern Ireland, attending Mt. Temple Comprehensive School in Dublin), and musical artists (e.g., David Bowie, the Ramones, Rory Gallagher) influenced U2's personal and musical development, while also placing their activism within a larger social and political context. In other words, *Songs of Ascent* was really a history course, with papers, discussions, videos and music, lots and lots of music. While extensive reading, research and writing are an inevitable part of college education, my hope was that the music component made *Songs of Ascent* more enjoyable and memorable for students.

Tryin' to Throw My Arms Around U2

As stated earlier, *Songs of Ascent* was more than a class about U2; as an AWS it was also an introduction to the first-year experience and the opportunities available for students during their time at Nebraska Wesleyan. There were class periods devoted to writing and conducting research, public speaking, study abroad, internships, applying for prestige scholarships (e.g., Fulbright, Truman, etc.), registering for classes, and selecting a major or minor. As a result, instead of having a full 16 weeks to cover their particular subject matter, the AWS instructor has roughly only 13–14, which means efficiency and simplicity are the keys to success. After each semester teaching *Songs of Ascent*, I tweaked my syllabus, cutting or adding readings, assignments and activities. The following is a description of what worked, and what did not, over four years teaching the course.

Readings

What perhaps surprised students the most when it came to reading about U2 was that there were readings at all. In a class about U2 students expect to listen to music and watch live concert performances, but when they buy their books and discover there has been serious commentary and criticism published about the band, their initial attitude toward the course changes. The majority of scholarly articles came from two edited volumes, both by Scott Calhoun: *Exploring U2: Is This Rock 'N' Roll: Essays on the Music, Work, and Influence of U2* (2012) and *U2 Above, Across, and Beyond: Interdisciplinary Assessments* (2015). Of the two books, students read more from *Exploring U2* as the various chapter topics fit better into course material and class discussions. Early chapters discuss the history of the band growing up in Dublin, Ireland (Boy to Man: A Dublin-Shaped Band by Neil McCormick), and how lyrics for the band's second album *October* (1981) were lost, and later found (My Voyage of Discovery: Returning *October*'s Lost Lyrics by Danielle Rheaume). The other chapters read from *Exploring U2* focus on the analysis of songs (Playing the Tart: Contexts and Intertexts for "Until the End of the World" by Daniel Kline, and "Bullet the Blue Sky" as an Evolving Performance by Steve Taylor) and how U2's consistent and innovative vision helped develop their global brand over the decades (U2: An Elevated Brand by Michele O'Brien).

In addition to Calhoun's compilations, I used other books in *Songs of Ascent*. In the first year of the course we read *We Get to Carry Each Other: The Gospel According to U2* (2009) by Greg Garrett. While I appreciated Garrett's analysis of how U2 weaves Biblical references and spirituality into their song lyrics, the majority of students were less interested in this subject. Fortunately, a replacement was soon found in Alan McPherson's *The World and U2: One Band's Remaking of Global Activism* (2015). This book was published shortly before the Fall 2015 semester, so I was unable to use it for the class that year. However, it provided the perfect supplement to the end of the semester unit on U2's social and political activism, and was used in all future classes.

Arguably, the most valuable book we read was *U2 by U2* (2006). Author Neil McCormick interviewed Bono, Edge, Adam and Larry, along with their manager Paul McGuinness, to create an "in their own words" narrative. U2 share memories of growing up in Dublin, their first band meeting in 1976, the process of making albums with various producers like Steve Lillywhite and Brian Eno, their tours across the United States, and, eventually, the journey to becoming global superstars. Band members also candidly discuss family tragedies, interpersonal tensions, and coping with criticism from the public and press. Students liked *U2 by U2* as it unfolds in short, personal stories and reflections, making it a relatively quick and easy read. The only problem with the book is that it ends in early 2006, over a year after the release of the album *How to Dismantle an Atomic Bomb* (2004). This meant the discussion of U2's next three albums—*No Line on the Horizon* (2009), *Songs of Innocence* (2014) and *Songs of Experience* (2017)—as well any news or information about the band, had to be found in current periodicals or online sources. That said, I would argue *U2 by U2* was *the* foundational book for *Songs of Ascent*, and an invaluable resource. Hopefully, McCormick and U2 will someday publish an updated edition to make the U2 story complete.

Music, Concerts and Documentaries

Over U2's 40-plus year career they have released 14 studio albums, one live album, EPs, remixes, and the 1995 experimental side project *Original Soundtracks 1* with Brian Eno under the pseudonym Passengers. The individual members of U2 have also created music outside of the band. For example, Bono has sung duets with Frank Sinatra ("I've Got You Under My Skin") and Italian tenor Luciano Pavarotti ("Ave Maria"), Larry Mullen, Jr., and Adam Clayton contributed to the *Mission: Impossible* (1996) movie soundtrack, while Edge was part of the documentary *It Might Get Loud* (2008). With such an extensive and diverse music catalog the problem with *Songs of Ascent* was never what to listen to, but what *not* to listen to. As stated earlier, as an AWS instructor I only had 13–14 weeks to cover course content, which meant listening to an album, and sometimes two, per week. Students typically listened to U2's music on streaming services like Spotify or Amazon, moving in chronological order from their first album *Boy* (1980), to their latest release, *Songs of Experience* (2017).

To complement various U2 albums, we also viewed portions of U2 tours on DVD. We began with *U2 Live at Red Rocks*: "Under a Blood Red Sky" (1983). In the early 1980s U2 made a minor splash on MTV with their music video for "Gloria" from *October* (1981). However, during 1983's *War* tour, supporting the album of the same name released that year, the video for "Sunday Bloody Sunday" from their concert at Red Rocks Amphitheatre in Colorado, arguably broke U2 in the U.S. The music video was put into heavy rotation on MTV, and *Rolling Stone* listed the performance as #35 on the "50 Moments That Changed Rock and Roll" (Cave, 2004). Filmed June 5, 1983, *Live at Red Rocks* captures U2's youthful energy and remarkable ability to connect with a live audience, despite the fact the concert was filmed on a cold and rainy day in Colorado.

U2 would eventually release several more concerts on VHS and then DVD (see Appendix; many can also be found on YouTube), each coinciding with a new U2 album. The DVDs contain a great deal of supplementary features such as documentaries, music videos, and bonus live tracks. I found these extras to be quite valuable in not only in discussing a specific tour, but also as resources for students when writing their U2 concert critiques (discussed later). The concerts that generated the most interest from students were: *ZooTV: Live from Sydney* (1993), *PopMart: Live from Mexico City* (1997), *360° at the Rose Bowl* (2009), and *Innocence + Experience: Live in Paris* (2015). Compared with the more minimalistic *War, Unforgettable Fire,* and *Joshua Tree* tours of the 1980s that showcased U2 on stage, their tours in the 1990s began to incorporate cutting edge technology with video screens, prerecorded imagery, props, and other special effects. U2 concerts became stunning multimedia spectacles, gaining critical acclaim and setting attendance records.

The most difficult challenge showing concert clips was deciding which songs to highlight. I typically played the first two to three songs so the class could feel the crowd's energy at the beginning of a show. After that I selected another song or two to highlight a performance from the secondary, or B-stage, or if U2 was making some sort of socio-political statement (e.g., "MLK/Walk On" from *360°*). I tried to stay away from showing their more popular songs like "With or Without You" or "Beautiful Day" as there are so many more remarkable performances to analyze (e.g., "October/Bullet the Blue Sky/Zooropa" from *Innocence + Experience: Live in Paris* 2015 is one of my favorites).

On a personal note, I enjoyed showing these live DVDs as I could share my experiences as an avid U2 concert goer. From *ZooTV* in 1992, to *Experience + Innocence* in 2018, I have been fortunate to see every U2 tour, sometimes at multiple venues, for a total of 18 shows. I tell stories of buying concert tickets at a local record store for *ZooTV* in 1992 when a lottery system determined my place in line, standing in the ellipse 15 feet from the stage for the 2005 *Vertigo* tour in Omaha, and getting dumped on by torrential rain in Minneapolis in 2011 during *360°*. When developing *Songs of Ascent* in 2015 I hoped students might have the opportunity to see U2 live to better appreciate the U2 concert experience. Fortunately, they played Kansas City for *The Joshua Tree 2017*, and Omaha during *Experience + Innocence* in 2018. Students who attended these shows told me after they were "breathtaking," "electrifying," and "emotional…. I felt like I could change the world after the concert"—exactly what I was hoping to hear.

In addition to viewing concert clips, we also watched a variety of documentaries. The first, which can be found on YouTube, was *Live Aid: Against All Odds* (2010), and tells the story of Live Aid, the July 13, 1985, benefit concerts at Wembley Stadium in London and JFK Stadium in Philadelphia, raising money for Ethiopian famine relief. After showing Part 1 of the documentary, I played U2's performance of "Sunday Bloody Sunday" and "Bad" (both can be found on YouTube). When watching U2 students are initially more impressed by the crowd size at Wembley than they are the band's performance. Then, approximately seven minutes into "Bad," Bono suddenly jumps off the stage to assist a young girl who was being crushed by the crowd, and slow dances with her. At this touching moment, I turn around, look at my students, and notice many have a slight smile on their face. U2's set was one of the most talked about after Live Aid, introducing them to a worldwide audience. Just like "Sunday Bloody Sunday" from *Live at Red Rocks*, U2 at Live Aid is also must-see viewing. Additionally, understanding the significance of the Live Aid, within the context of 1980s global activism, and the popularity of songs like Band Aid's "Do They Know It's Christmas?" (1984) and USA for Africa's "We Are the World" (1985), provides a starting point from which to discuss U2's future involvement in organizations such as Jubilee 2000, ONE, Music Rising, Mencap, and the Angiogenesis Foundation.

The next two films, both available on DVD, are more U2-centric. *Rattle and Hum* (1988) is a rockumentary about U2's 1987 *Joshua Tree* tour of America, which includes interviews with band members, and performances in Denver, Colorado and Tempe, Arizona. While the film did not earn much at the box office, and was not well received by many critics, the *Rattle and Hum* album would eventually sell 14 million copies. *Rattle and Hum* captures a time when U2 would make the April 27, 1987, cover of *Time* magazine (headline "U2 Rock's Hottest Ticket"), move from playing arenas into stadiums, and achieve global superstardom. Students generally enjoy *Rattle and Hum* as they like seeing the band interviews (to get to know them a little better), and are particularly impressed with the gospel version of "I Still Haven't Found What I'm Looking For." However, to save time in class I typically cut the eight-minute version of "Bad," as we watched the Live Aid version a week before.

The final film, *From the Sky Down* (2011), is a documentary about the challenges of U2 post–*Joshua Tree* that led to making *Achtung Baby* (1991). After the incredible success of *The Joshua Tree* U2 was unsure about its musical direction, and tensions began to arise within the band. While at Hansa Studios in Berlin, Germany, trying to record their new album, U2 was seemingly on the verge of breaking up. However, U2 suddenly regained their confidence with the song "One," and soon after produced *Achtung Baby*, an album that redefined the band's sound and image for the 1990s. Unlike *Rattle and Hum*, critics were more positive about *From the Sky Down*, and it even received a 2013 Grammy nomination for Best Long Form Music Video. Watching *From the Sky Down* just a week after *Rattle and Hum* provides an interesting contrast of U2 in the late 1980s and early 1990s, showing their commercial highs and personal lows. The fact that U2 survived this difficult time and would continue to make music is a testament to their 40 years of friendship, brotherhood and dedication to their craft.

Writing Assignments

Students were required to write three short papers (3-pages minimum) over the first half of the semester, as well as a major research paper (10-pages minimum) due two weeks before finals. The first short paper required students to discuss their *Personal History with Popular Music*, answering questions such as: What types of music did you listen to growing up? Which artists are personally meaningful to you and why? What is your attitude toward U2's music, popularity and activism? This paper gave students a relatively easy first college writing assignment as the subject matter was their own experience with music and knowledge of U2. Interestingly, after reading these papers there were typically three different types of students: those who were familiar with U2 and their music, those who have heard of U2 but cannot name any of their songs, and those who have no idea who they are. Not surprisingly, some students commented that their parents were more excited about a U2 class than they were.

The second short paper offered two options for students: *U2 and Current Events* or *U2's Musical Influences*. The first option, *U2 and Current Events*, required the student to research and write about a person or event that inspired a U2 song. I provided a list of approximately 20 songs to choose from, with potential topics including South African anti-apartheid leader Nelson Mandela ("Ordinary Love"), 1980s U.S. policy in Central America ("Bullet the Blue Sky"), and the 1990s civil war in Yugoslavia ("Miss Sarajevo"). The second option, *U2's Musical Influences,* asked students to discuss the history and impact of an artist or group that inspired U2 such as the Ramones, the Clash, and David Bowie. I introduced this option during my third year teaching *Songs of Ascent*, but the majority of students still selected *U2 and Current Events*. I believe this was because it was generally easier to find sources and information about a song's inspiration and do a lyrical analysis than it was to find quotes from U2 about how an artist or group influenced their song writing and sound.

The third short paper, and arguably the most difficult, was the *U2 Concert Critique*. Students were required to watch an entire U2 concert (see Appendix), and then use one of two critical frameworks to analyze the music, themes and visual elements of the show. The first method of analysis was leitourgia, discussed by Beth Maynard in Calhoun's *Exploring U2: Is This Rock 'N' Roll: Essays on the Music, Work, and Influence of U2* (2012). According to Maynard, leitourgia is from the Greek meaning, "work taken on as a public service by private citizens" (p. 152). She explains that in Christianity leitourgia came to mean, "public, structured gatherings aimed at responding to and affecting both political and spiritual realities, presided over by leaders who in a spirit of public servanthood facilitated everyone's participation in the process" (p. 153). Maynard argues leitourgia is a way to understand how U2 attempts to engage the audience on a personal, spiritual and activist level by unifying the crowd though sing-alongs and coordinated gestures (e.g., raising hands in the air and clapping), calls to make change in the world (e.g., Bono advocating for the ONE campaign), and creating "ultimate fulfillment" (pp. 157–158) which is a feeling of justice or joy. By using the categories of leitourgia as a method of criticism students realize that a U2 concert is more than just an entertaining show, there are also carefully orchestrated moments designed to inspire, motivate and create a sense of community in the audience.

The second framework students could apply to analyzing a U2 concert was that of bricolage. Matthew Hamilton in Calhoun's *U2 Above, Across, and Beyond: Interdisciplinary Assessments* (2015) explains bricolage is a term used in art, music and literature, and is "the kind of art that is itself a unique piece but derived from individual pieces, objects, and other artwork" (p. 128). In other words, bricolage is the process of creating new art influenced by its older forms.

According to Hamilton, U2 has used bricolage throughout their career by experimenting with new technologies, patterns and styles to create music that is new, but still has the "U2 sound." In terms of the U2 concert experience Hamilton argues bricolage is evident in a variety of different ways. As a case study, Hamilton examines how U2 attempted to use bricolage to redefine the performer-audience relationship and create a feeling of intimacy during the record-setting *360° tour* (2009–2011), which was a challenge while playing in the round on a gigantic stage in massive stadiums packed with tens of thousands of fans. However, Hamilton believes U2 successfully achieved these ambitious goals based on his textual analysis of their 2010 concert DVD *U2360° at the Rose Bowl*. For example, during the opening notes of "Moment of Surrender" the stage lights were turned off, and many of the almost 100,000 attendees in the Rose Bowl turned on their cell phones, the glow of which created a spectacular pattern of stars in the darkened stadium, or what Bono called, "the Milky Way." Another example of bricolage was during "MLK/Walk On" dedicated to activist Aung San Suu Kyi. Before the song begins Bono explains that Suu Kyi has been under house arrest in Burma for almost 20 years, "peacefully campaigning for equality and freedom," and wants to send her a "message of love from the people of Los Angeles." Later in the song, members of Amnesty International and the ONE campaign appear onstage, each holding a mask of Suu Kyi's face (several had been distributed in the audience as well). Hamilton contends moments such as these, and others, produced performance art as the musical, visual and activist elements created a bricolage of new, personal and memorable experiences for both the band and audience each night during the *360° tour*.

The initial challenge of the *U2 Concert Critique* was for students to understand the concepts of leitourgia and bricolage before they apply either to a U2 concert. To help their comprehension, we spend a day in class discussing Maynard and Hamilton, discussing leitourgia and bricolage in relation to various U2 songs and concert moments. My hope was that by providing two different frameworks for analysis students would select the one they were more comfortable using, thereby making their critique easier to write. In terms of utilization, the majority of students selected Maynard as she provides five specific leitourgia categories which can be applied to the U2 concert experience (however, students only need to use 2–3 categories with examples of each), while Hamilton's description and application of bricolage is less prescriptive. The few students who used bricolage were, not surprisingly, theatre and music majors whose desire to study and create art made this framework a natural fit for their interests.

While writing assignments vary between AWS courses, the one requirement across all sections was the major research paper, which for my class was titled *U2 in 10*. Students had to select those U2 songs, albums, people and/or events they believe best define the band's career, but must do so in only 10 choices *total*. Consequently, student lists were typically very diverse including U2 albums, tours, manager Paul McGuinness, spirituality, activism, business relationship with Apple, and also deeply personal and transformative events like the death of Bono's and Larry's mothers. Because the research paper was a minimum of 10 pages, students needed to be concise describing each category, make an argument for why this category was important in U2's history, and include sources for support. Student reactions to this paper were incredibly positive, and I was encouraged to keep it each year as their major project. It probably helped that I told students not to think about writing a 10-page paper (which can seem intimidating for first-year students), but rather writing 10 one-page (or slightly longer) papers, which, taken as a whole, summarize U2's career.

Oral Presentations

In addition to written assignments, the AWS also requires a speaking component. For *Songs of Ascent* students gave an individual album introduction, and were part of a group project. The album introduction is exactly what it sounds like. Each student (sometimes two depending on class size) was assigned a U2 album to introduce to the class, providing information about its release date, where it was recorded, producers, and critical and commercial reception. Students then share stories from *U2 by U2*, and other sources, about challenges making the album, and play clips from 3–4 songs that best reflect the album's theme(s) (e.g., *Boy* [1980] theme of adolescence through the songs "I Will Follow," "Out of Control," and "Stories for Boys"), while also highlighting elements of its production (e.g., Edge's distinct guitar effects on *Boy* creating the "U2 sound"). Students included lyrics to selected songs on PowerPoint so the class could read along while listening (projecting song lyrics from websites like U2.com or atu2.com also works).

The album introductions were short, typically around 5–7 minutes, and followed by class discussion about the album's theme(s), interpretation of song lyrics, sound, and whatever else students wanted to discuss. Student opinions about listening to a U2 album for the first time were always interesting, but not without some challenges (discussed later). As someone who has followed U2 for decades I have definite, and sometimes quite strong, opinions about each album. However, for the novice U2 listener (most everyone in the class) their opinion was not influenced by history or expectations, and I valued their "fresh ears" perspective.

The other presentation, and more substantial in terms of preparation time, was a group project, which focused on an organization U2 supports. U2 history of activism can be traced back to Ireland in the late 1970s (e.g., Rock Against Sexism benefit show), but in the 1980s they shifted their focus to more global causes, supporting Greenpeace, playing Live Aid in 1985 and the Amnesty International: A Conspiracy of Hope tour in 1986. While Bono has received most of the attention for his philanthropic endeavors (the cover of the March 4, 2002, *Time* magazine had Bono's picture with the headline "Can Bono Save the World?"), other members of U2 have been active with various charities and non-profits. For example, Edge co-founded Music Rising (replacing instruments and preserving music culture in the Gulf states after Hurricanes Katrina and Rita in 2005) and Adam Clayton has been a longtime ally of MusiCares (supporting musicians in need of medical, personal and financial assistance), to name a few. After providing students with a list of organizations U2 supports, each selected their top five, and I created groups of 3–4 based on their preferences. These groups then researched and delivered a 20–25-minute presentation covering the history of the organization, their outreach and influence, and U2's involvement, citing sources and using visual aids for support.

One other unique speaking opportunity was U2 Radio. Later in the semester, after becoming more familiar with U2's history and music catalog, each student was required to develop a 1-hour radio program (or 2 hours if students pair up) of U2 music for the campus online radio station. The faculty sponsor for the station trained students to use the equipment, which was simply a matter of plugging their cell phone into the station's computer, pushing a few buttons on the radio console, and playing their set list. I encouraged students not to simply play an album from start to finish, but instead have a variety of singles, live tracks, rarities and even remixes. To ensure a level of professionalism, students were required to submit their playlist for my approval (a few U2 songs and live performances contain profanity, which were prohibited), along with a rough outline of any comments they wanted to make during their show. If my schedule allowed I listened to each show and was impressed with the detail some students included discussing a specific song, album, event or tour. While some students were initially reticent to be "on the air," most enjoyed the experience, and perhaps learned more about U2 through building and researching their set list than any other assignment.

Challenges and Student Reactions

There were three challenges teaching *Songs of Ascent*. The first was overcoming the perception that a class on U2 was a worthy area of study, justifying the high cost of college tuition. As one student wrote in their *Personal History of Popular Music* paper, "Before I enrolled in the U2 AWS, I wondered how a class could be based around a band that I'd never even truly heard of. My parents thought it sounded silly and questioned, 'Why U2?'" So, on the first day of semester I was already fighting a two-front battle against any skeptical students in the classroom, and their parents at home. Additionally, not everyone in the class selected *Songs of Ascent* as one of their top Archway Seminar choices. Some students reluctantly had to take the course as it was the only seminar that fit into their schedule. In this instance, I can only do my best and hope they eventually come around and enjoy the material.

The next, somewhat surprising challenge, was overcoming my disbelief at how many students had never heard of U2. Or, they heard of U2, but did not realize they sang popular songs like, "Pride (In the Name of Love)" or "Beautiful Day." On the second day of class I play brief snippets from several U2 songs, and almost immediately faces light up with a "Oh, that's U2? I've heard that song!" look. As one student wrote in their *Personal History with Popular Music* paper, "I have heard of Bono, but I had zero clue what band he was a part of. It's weird, I have heard songs by U2 that I really enjoy, but I never knew they were by U2." Looking back, their lack of familiarity with U2's music was more of a minor annoyance than a serious obstacle to learning. Still, it taught me an important lesson in patience, and that my knowledge and experience with music is not the same as my students.

The final challenge (and one mentioned by other authors in this volume about teaching their particular music topic), was how to encourage students to move beyond simply saying they "liked" or "didn't like" a U2 album, song or concert performance, to articulating exactly why. Newly minted high school graduates may not have had training in any type of textual analysis, which, for *Songs of Ascent*, would include the interpretation of song lyrics and visual imagery (e.g., album covers, music videos, concert performances, etc.). This is even more problematic for those first-year students trying to find their academic footing early in college, and who may lack the courage to express any opinions in class. However, as students became more familiar with U2 and their music catalog, class discussions about their albums, songs and concerts were more thoughtful and critical.

One possible solution to this problem was inspired by the music majors and musicians I had the last year teaching *Songs of Ascent*. I always appreciated during class discussions when these students would point out various musical elements of a U2 song, such as key changes, rhythms, and chord progressions. Because of their valuable insights, if I teach the course again I may ask a colleague in our music department to guest lecture and perhaps share some basics about music theory, analyze the various musical components of a U2 album or song, or even critique Bono's vocal style, Edge's guitar effects, Larry's drumming or Adam's bass playing. I could make the class even more interdisciplinary by asking someone in the art department to discuss how U2 uses visual imagery in their concerts (e.g., stage configuration, props, video, etc.). Having scholars from these disciplines share their knowledge and expertise would provide students a unique performance and composition perspective on U2, and even provide some rudimentary music and art vocabulary which they could draw upon for class discussions and writing assignments.

At the end of each semester course evaluations were conducted. Not surprisingly, some students enjoyed *Songs of Ascent*, while others did not. Those students who liked the class commented that by the end of 16 weeks they appreciated U2's music, respected their commitment to do "good in the world" through activism, and even considered themselves U2 fans. However, others thought the course was pointless, time consuming, and "hard to get into" not having much interest in U2's music. I can certainly appreciate the criticisms from those students who did not like the course. In response, I tried my best to improve *Songs of Ascent* each year with not just minor syllabus changes, but also different readings, activities and discussion topics. While the formula from 2015 to 2018 was never perfect, it hopefully got better with age.

Conclusion

Developing and teaching *Songs of Ascent: The Music and Meaning of U2* was definitely a labor of love. While I may not have always been successful getting every student to enjoy U2's music as much as I do, many walk away with at least some appreciation for their accomplishments as artists and activists. At the very least I hope students were inspired to think more critically about the history, music and influence of their own favorite singer or group. After teaching the course for four years I reluctantly decided to take a break to complete other projects (like this book). Someday, I may teach U2 once again, and introduce another generation of students to Ireland's most successful music export. Until then, I will look forward to hearing (hopefully soon) U2's next album, seeing them multiple times on tour, attending future U2 conventions, and most importantly, create new friendships with other U2 fans who share my passion for the "biggest band in the world."

Appendix

U2 Concerts on DVD
(as of November 2019)

- *Live at Red Rocks*: "*Under a Blood Red Sky*" (recorded 1983)
- Performance at *Live Aid* (recorded 1985) and excerpts from *A Conspiracy of Hope Concert* (recorded 1986)—Bonus DVD on *The Unforgettable Fire* Deluxe CD/DVD Box set released in 2009.
- *The Joshua Tree: Live in Paris* (recorded 1987)—Bonus DVD on *The Joshua Tree* Deluxe CD/DVD Box set released in 2007. *Live from Madison Square Garden* (recorded 1987) on the 30th Anniversary Super Deluxe CD/DVD Box set released in 2017.
- *ZooTV: Live from Sydney* (recorded 1993)
- *PopMart: Live from Mexico City* (recorded 1997)
- *Elevation: Live from Boston* (recorded 2001)
- *U2 Go Home: Live from Slane Castle* (recorded 2001)
- *Vertigo: Live from Chicago* (recorded 2005)
- *U2360° at the Rose Bowl* (recorded 2009)
- *Innocence + Experience: Live in Paris* (recorded 2015)

Full U2 Concerts on YouTube
(as of November 2019)

- *Elevation: Live from Boston* (recorded 2001)
- *U2 Go Home: Live from Slane Castle* (recorded 2001)
- *Vertigo: Live from Chicago* (recorded 2005)
- *Vertigo: Live from Milan* (recorded 2005)
- *Live at Glastonbury* (recorded 2011)
- *Innocence + Experience: Live in Paris* (recorded 2015)

Searching YouTube for *Live at Red Rocks, Live Aid, The Joshua Tree: Live in Paris, ZooTV: Live from Sydney, PopMart: Live from Mexico City*, and *360° at the Rose Bowl* you may find individual songs rather than the full concert. For *The Joshua Tree 2017, Experience + Innocence* 2018 and *The Joshua Tree 2019* there are numerous fan videos and even full multicam shows posted. Some look quite professional with excellent sound quality.

Other notable U2 performances found on YouTube include: the *US Festival* 1983, *America: A Tribute to Heroes* benefit concert 2001, Super Bowl halftime 2002, and Dreamforce 2016.

References

Calhoun, S. (2012). *Exploring U2: Is this rock 'n' roll: Essays on the music, work, and influence of U2*. Lanham, MD. The Scarecrow Press, Inc.

Calhoun, S. (2015). *U2 above, across, and beyond*. Lanham, MD: Lexington Books.

Cave, D. (2004, June 24). 50 moments that changed rock and roll: U2's gamble at Red Rocks. *Rolling Stone, 951*, 146.

Guggenheim, D. (Director). (2012). *From the sky down* [DVD]. United States: Universal Music Group.

Hamilton, M.J. (2015). The transformative fan: The bricolage of U2 life. In S. Calhoun (Ed.), *U2 above, across, and beyond* (pp. 123–136). Lanham, MD: Lexington Books.

Joanou, P. (Director). (1999). *Rattle and hum* [DVD]. United States: Paramount.

Maynard, B. (2012). Where leitourgia has no name: U2 live. In S. Calhoun (Ed.), *Exploring U2: Is this rock 'n' roll: Essays on the music, work, and influence of U2* (pp. 151–164). Lanham, MD: The Scarecrow Press, Inc.

Sutherland, J. (Director). (2005). *Live aid: Against all odds* [Television broadcast]. BBC: Brook Lapping. Accessed https://www.youtube.com/watch?v=WQWs23NtRas

Taylor, G. (Director). (2008). *U2 live at Red Rocks: Under a blood red sky* [DVD]. United States: Interscope.

U2 and McCormick, N. (2006). *U2 by U2*. New York: HarperCollins.

Part 3

Popular Music Analysis and Other Instructional Tools

Musical Identities
Teaching Race, Class and Gender Through Popular Music

JAMES L. DEYS *and* JACOB A. DICKERSON

Popular music is an important building block of identity. Particularly during adolescence, music helps us to understand ourselves and acts as a marker of our identity for others. It is more than the clichéd notion of a "soundtrack of our lives." In many cases, our music both reflects and shapes who we are. We use the term identity here to refer to an individual's understanding of their own subjectivity. It is a view of oneself as that self relates to those around it. Identity is always unstable and evolving. Therefore, by choosing to listen to a certain style of music, we perform our identity in order to establish a stable marker of who we are (Segal, 2008). Beyond the individual level, popular music can also represent a larger discourse about who we are on a cultural level. As with any element of popular culture, music is enveloped within competing values and ideologies. See, for instance, Elton John's statement requesting that Donald Trump cease using his music at rallies during the 2016 presidential campaign, suggesting that Trump use the music of Ted Nugent or a country star instead. John's statement explicitly positions music according to the perceived political values of those who make it. Music is, perhaps, the most pervasive outlet for expressions of cultural and political frustration, pride, excitement, and resentment. In short, music is the public performance of both our personal and cultural identities. The integrated relationship of identity and popular music makes for a rich exploration of identity-related questions of race, class, and gender from a music-centered perspective. In this essay, we explore an identity-based approach to teaching popular music as it relates to our respective courses.

Jacob teaches a course titled *Country Music and Issues of Difference* for his institution's general studies program. It is situated as one of many sections of a course on writing a research paper, each of which vary in their specific theme, and is taken in the second semester of the students' first year composition sequence. The course examines how identity issues, particularly those of race, class, and gender, have been dealt with throughout the history of country music from the genre's beginnings in nineteenth-century folk music and the "hillbilly records" of the early twentieth century through today. Since it is part of the general studies curriculum, not all students are fans of, or even familiar with, country music. As a result, many of the students may enter the course with either a bias against the genre, expectations informed by a stereotypical imagining of the music and its audience, or both. In a situation such as this, it is valuable in the early part of the class to provide students with the opportunity to engage with the music in a way that does not carry the baggage of the genre, but still introduces them to the primary themes of the class.

In addition to the potential problems with the genre, open discussions about race, class, and gender can be very uncomfortable for students, especially in their first year. Not only have most of them never been asked to discuss such sensitive issues in an academic setting, they are also struggling with being away from home for the first time and trying to define their own identity in a new setting. As a result, many students are already hesitant to participate in class discussions. This is particularly true of the population at Jacob's institution, which includes large percentages of economically disadvantaged students, many of whom are first-generation college students from the Appalachian mountain region. Add to this the sensitive nature of the course themes and it is imperative to create a non-threatening environment for student participation or the class could potentially face a long semester of difficult, slow-moving discussions.

Like Jacob, Jim has recently developed *Popular Music and Identity* as one option for students to fulfill a required writing-across-the-curriculum (WAC) course. Although housed in the General Education program and aimed at sophomores, the course often has a wide range of students from first-year to senior with varied interest in the course material. After previously teaching courses on popular music that emphasize its social history, Jim opted to adopt a more thematic approach with *Popular Music and Identity*. Though there is certainly value in the survey and expository courses that center on musical history or specific genres and their relationships, Jim has found that making identity the central theme emboldens students to analyze *why* they identify with certain popular music and artists, while also encouraging them to decode how artists create cultural meaning. It is important to ask students to reflect on music's personal impact on them because most students have passionate connections to particular artists and genres. Students learn to reflect on their own musical tastes as they critically examine the ways artists construct their musical and political identities. This process allows students a comfortable launching point from which they often realize their substantial knowledge about specific artists. As students build confidence, Jim encourages them to take ownership of their writing and scholarship and contribute to the infinite field of music criticism.

In this essay, we describe a number of assignments and activities that place identity in the center of our popular music classes. They are designed to increase student comfort with sensitive subjects, encourage students to explore their personal identities through music, and—perhaps most importantly—place identity at the front of students' minds as they consider the role popular music plays in the dominant cultural discourse, as well as their own lives.

Easing into the Genre and Encouraging Discussion

To help establish an environment in which students are comfortable engaging in a critical discussion of popular music, Jacob begins the course with activities designed to deal with challenges inherent in both the country genre and the delicate nature of his course's themes (race, class, and gender). One of those activities attempts to challenge typical conceptions of the genre, including the celebration of working class life, strong Christian values, and conservative political leanings. The goals for challenging the conceptions of the genre are twofold. First, this activity frees the students' analytical minds. By demonstrating that the genre is not necessarily what they perceive it to be, they are better able to offer more thoughtful interpretations of the music. Second, it introduces them to the genre by posing a "problem." The apparent contradiction of what a genre should be and what it can be frames their thinking in a way that suggests a question: what created my preconceived notions of what country music is? This is particularly useful as the course attempts to teach how to ask effective research questions. Songs for activities that challenge a genre can often be found in either the "alternative" threads of the genre or in its distant past. In the case of country music, "alternative" threads can often be found in the Americana subgenre (e.g., Margo Price or Jason Isbell) while the distant past might refer to country's folk origins (e.g., Stephen Foster, see below) or classic artists (e.g., Johnny Cash).

The activity is quite simple and takes place on the first day of class. Students are asked to look for references to race, class, or gender in a selection from the Americana form of country music. They listen to and are shown the lyrics for a different song for each theme (three songs in total) and discuss each of them separately. They are prompted by one question: Which aspects of this song make you think of race/class/gender? This question is intentionally broad. It allows students to pull from any line or aspect of the song that catches their ear. It allows them to be primarily descriptive (e.g., "This line mentions being poor.") or analytical (e.g., "The narrator is proud of being a member of the working class."). Finally, it also removes the pressure of needing to be correct since they are only asked to report their response to the song in general rather than analyze some specific portion of it.

One example of this is the use of Jason Isbell's "Cumberland Gap" (2017), a song with much more of a rock structure and sound than would typically be expected from a country song, despite that song's presence on an album nominated for the Country Music Association's Album of the Year award. The narrator in the song is openly critical of military service, admits to receiving government assistance, and expresses resentment at being trapped in a small town with limited economic opportunities. The setting of a town in Southern Appalachia (the titular Cumberland Gap) and references to the mining industry are both very familiar to the institution's population, as noted above. This makes it very easy for the students to spot and interpret the song's references to class, and move more comfortably into the academic discussion of both popular music and the course themes. Additionally, the song's sound and recognizable progressive politics expands the students' understanding of what country music is and can be. Introducing the genre in this way avoids many of the pitfalls associated with common stereotypes of country music that may hinder deeper discussions of course themes.

Jim eases his students into a critical examination of identity in popular music by encouraging them to turn inward. He begins his course by having students reflect and question why they identify with, admire, or simply "love" a particular artist/band. Doing so allows students to find value in rediscovering their own musical tastes and experiences, while also seeing beyond themselves. One propelling question he asks students is "what values and attitudes do we relate to and why?" Or, more interestingly, "why do we admire artists with contradictory values from our own?" To further the conversation, one assignment Jim has developed is the "Music Identity List Analysis." Briefly, it reads:

> For your first paper, you will explore music in relationship to your life. So, as an exercise, I want you to locate and list one song from every year since you were born until 2018 that resonates with you musically or lyrically and that you identify with. If you were born in 1998, you would list one song for that year and then every subsequent year up to 2018. After completing your list, select three songs from your list to analyze. These songs are your primary source material for your analysis. You do not need any outside research. You can use secondary material if you want, but you must cite this secondary source material accordingly. In analyzing the songs, consider the

lyrics and music and why it relates to you and holds meaning to you. Be thoughtful. (Approximately 4–5 double-spaced pages)

One goal of this essay is for students to analyze their three chosen songs in-depth and demonstrate how these songs connect to their experiences and identity. Often, students will have a story behind a significant song from their past, and Jim encourages them to articulate the story and reflect on its meaning. Since the assignment also asks students to locate and list a song for every year, they are required to look up songs from specific years that resonate with them. If they are 19-years-old, they most likely will have to do some light research into songs that coincide with each year, and they might even discover a new song in the process. Beyond hearing these songs as simply soundtracks to their lives, students think about the interrelationships between music, people, place, and memory.

Marginalization and Identity

When discussing identity-related issues, the discussion often turns to how those issues reflect cultural power relationships and dominant values (e.g., working-class resentment of the rich in country music or African American distrust of the police in rap music). These topics are regularly accompanied by questions of which ideologies are favored by cultural discourse and which are pushed to the margins. And, in many cases, that marginality is central to students' conceptions of identity for both themselves and others.

One activity Jacob uses to jumpstart student discussion early in the course is designed to address these questions of marginality through an accompanying reading. At the same, the activity helps students work together to better understand scholarly writing about music and introduce them to the critical analysis of a song's lyrics. The activity is a Chalk Talk (Brookfield, 2012) in which students, without speaking, write their responses to the reading and interpretations of the song on the chalkboard/whiteboard. In this way, students are able to formulate a group discussion of the material in a live, but essentially asynchronous, discussion. All students are given a marker or piece of chalk and asked to write their thoughts on the board at the same time as the rest of their classmates. Once they have contributed a thought, they can then read others' contributions and write responses to their peers. They are, therefore, able to take their time in responding to one another and may respond to any earlier comments that may interest them. Much like participation in an online forum, the asynchronous nature of the discussion allows for more considered contributions than may result from a real-time oral exchange of ideas (Brookfield & Preskill, 2005).

A silent discussion also allows students who may be hesitant to speak in class to participate on their own terms and in relative anonymity (students may be observed writing their responses, but they do not sign them). As Brookfield and Preskill (2005) point out, one way of encouraging introverted students to participate in discussion is to make it clear that talking aloud is not the only way to contribute to a discussion. And, according to Brookfield (2012), the Chalk Talk exercise can increase participation from 10 percent of students in traditional discussion to more than half of students in a silent discussion. This form of discussion also helps to encourage the creation of what Brookfield and Preskill (2005) refer to as a "democratic learning laboratory" (p. 263). This concept is rooted in the Habermasian notion that the "greater the freedom of discussion that people enjoy, the higher the chance that true critical reason … will emerge" (p. 264).

Jacob's Chalk Talk activity takes place during the second or third class meeting and helps to build students' confidence in their own ability to contribute to a scholarly discussion, encouraging future class participation. The activity focuses on Amy Lang's (1998) article "Jim Crow and the Pale Maiden," about Stephen Foster's 1854 parlor song, "Hard Times Come Again No More." While Foster's work is not typically classified within the country genre (let alone popular music), he is central to the traditional folk style that was foundational to the formation of country in the early twentieth century. The song has also been recorded in whole or in part by a number of prominent country artists, including Johnny Cash and Dolly Parton. Having already established that country is a broad genre, students are accepting of the song as an instance of it. The reading which accompanies the activity explores all of the course's relevant themes of race, class, and gender.

In this particular use of the chalk talk activity, the words "Race," "Class," and "Gender" (representing the course themes) are written on the board. Students are expected to have read the article about Stephen Foster's "Hard Times" prior to class. Any difficult concepts are explained, and students are given the opportunity to ask any questions to help with their understanding of the article. Special attention is drawn to Lang's (1998) claim that "social vocabularies of race and gender [in the song's lyrics] answer an overwhelming anxiety of class conflicts that afflicted white Americans" (p. 381), priming the students for a discussion of the intersection of the course themes. Discussion is then prompted by two questions: (1) What does the reading have to say about the above themes? and (2) Which parts of the song are relevant to each of the themes and in what ways? Students write answers to those questions and responses to one another's answers on the board. They then draw lines to link their responses to other relevant themes (see Image 1).

Students most easily recognize class differences in the song, as the lyrics explicitly refer to contrasts between the rich and poor (for instance, "Let us

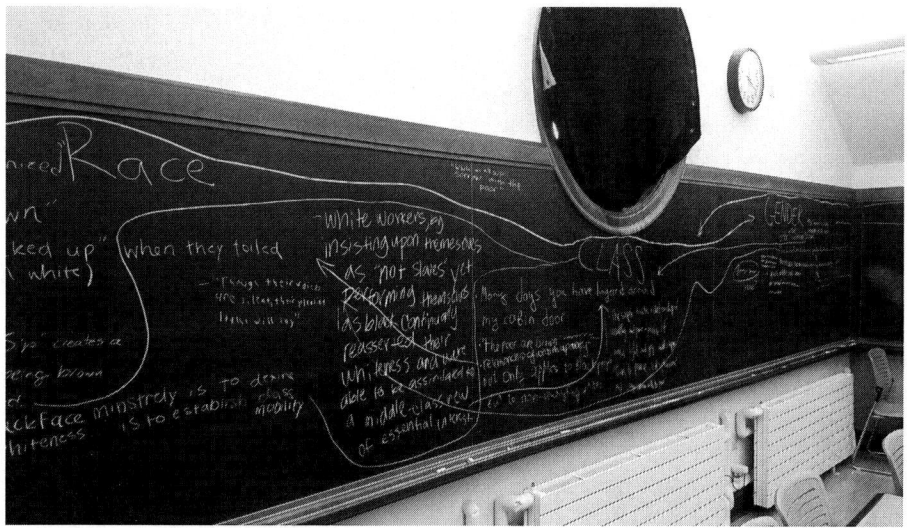

Image 1: Example of a chalk talk in Jacob's class.

pause in life's pleasures … while we all sup sorrow with the poor"). These contrasts often lead to comments about the responsibilities of society toward the poor, while at the same time encouraging them to question the rhetorical function of those comparisons (though they do not use that language). Some see the song as patronizing, as the rich are asked to pity the poor and be thankful that those same "hard times" have not befallen them. But others find themselves identifying instead with the poor—those with "frail forms" and whose "voices are silent." Allowing students to explore these questions with the protection of relative anonymity in this live/asynchronous format encourages greater exploration of these questions, which have likely been prompted by the accompanying reading. The reading's influence becomes more obvious in discussions of race and gender.

As with class, Foster's reference to gender is explicit in his reference to the "pale drooping maiden," something students quickly recognize. It is here that they most purposefully begin to integrate the reading into their co-analysis of the song. The reading suggests that the word "pale" refers to an assumed whiteness and "maiden" to the woman's purity. Students are often able to then make the leap of connecting white femininity to innocence, and contrast that to other contemporary images of femininity, which are described in the reading as "blacked up by their labors," even if they are not racially black (p. 384).

Students in Jim's class are also asked to explore artists that challenge and complicate common conceptions of race, class, and gender through readings and class discussions. For instance, class discussions consider how an artist has invented an identity and a brand via sound, lyrics, and image. Artists that Jim has found success with include: Screamin' Jay Hawkins, David Bowie, Nicki Minaj, and Laura Jane Grace. By examining both mainstream artists (e.g., Elvis Presley, Nirvana), and lesser-known or marginalized artists (e.g., Lee "Scratch" Perry, Bikini Kill), students gain historical context and forge connections between old and new artists in the conventional sense; yet, by placing identity at the center of the discussion, students are apt to think more critically about what the artists represent, how identities are invented/manufactured/sold, and what their larger cultural meaning may be. As Jim's class considers these artists, students analyze how disparate artists reflect, influence, and/or challenge societal values and cultural mores, and why musical artists hold this cultural sway. For example, analyzing Screamin' Jay Hawkins's sound and persona largely through his 1956 underground "hit," "I Put a Spell on You," is a complicated process, in that it was banned from commercial radio, yet became massively influential to the artists in the decades that followed, such as Creedence Clearwater Revival (in terms of singing style) and Alice Cooper (in terms of image). Hawkins was an R & B artist, but also became known as an early shock rocker who used images of death—caskets, skulls—and racialized imagery, such as the African American as the archetypal predator—apparent in the lyrics and menacing tone of the song—and his use of primitive and "exotic" outsider imagery—bones through his nose and middle-eastern headdresses—all complicate and add to fans' fascination with Hawkins. Hawkins challenged social mores back in the mid-1950s, and interestingly, still today his music and image challenge audiences, perhaps in diverse ways. This approach to the margins and artists that influenced the mainstream engages students in critical discussions and encourages debate and original inquiry.

Therefore, to help bolster students' original thinking and give their writing and research purpose, Jim asks them to look to the margins of popular music. The "Unsung Artist" paper utilizes this approach, while emphasizing the writing and research process. Adopting the term "unsung" from Nick Tosches's (1984) *Unsung Heroes of Rock 'n' Roll*, Jim frames the research paper around the concept of an unsung artist, or one who is underrepresented in the dominant history of popular music—by being commercially unsuccessful, by finding an audience too late, or for some other compelling reason. In Tosches's book, he argues for an alternative history of the birth of rock 'n' roll and profiles marginalized artists, such as Louis Jordan and Wanda Jackson. Tosches dispels many myths surrounding the origins of rock n' roll, including that "…Elvis Presley one day rose, dipped his comb in water, swept his hair into a duck's-ass. Bopped out into the world, and created—thank God, Alan Freed was there to give it a name—rock 'n' roll" (p. 1). Building upon this approach to rock 'n' roll, Jim asks students to become anthropologists of popular music, and bring insight to a marginalized artist/band. Importantly, they do not have to write about an artist from the rock n' roll era or rock genre, but can choose an artist/band/ghostwriter/producer from any genre, such as pop, reggae, punk, rap, metal, and beyond. After working with Tosches's book for a conceptual framework, students research and write about an artist or band that they believe is unsung and deserves greater recognition. Artists that students have profiled are as diverse as: Merry Clayton, David Ackles, The Last Poets, The Slits, Zolar X, and Mother Love Bone, to name a few. Jim communicates that the paper's purpose arrives through the writer's point-of-view and informed position. Thus, Jim underscores the importance of *argument* in such papers, as opposed to simple biographies or report-like papers. Students must develop a position as to why the artist is unsung, using sources to explore the artist's place in the canon of popular music. The more specific and compelling the reason why the artist is unsung, the more intriguing the paper will be; these reasons are the thrust of the paper—they are what give the paper a clear purpose. Then, the student argues for the artist's significance and merit, thus explaining why this artist has found little commercial success or has remained underground, overshadowed, or largely forgotten. The artist's influence, context, lyrics, and sound can all be synthesized and analyzed as source material to shape students' papers.

Pedagogically, Jim believes this assignment strikes a nice balance between allowing students choice, while also encouraging them out of their comfort zones. And, philosophically, asking students to look beyond the mainstream and toward the margins is also asking them to value the voices that have not been heard (as much), and to understand that our popular musical landscape runs deep and is more complex than at first glance. Furthermore, by digging into an artist that is "unsung," students find value in shaping an artist's musical history and story, and, subsequently, contribute to popular music criticism and ongoing dialogues in a more meaningful way. In part, the paper asks students to synthesize information and profile the band. But, it also asks students to develop an original point-of-view while paying close attention to lyrics and sound—even generating an artist's story and attention to an artist that he/she has yet to receive. This act of discovery and greater purpose resonates with most students.

However, this push outside of students' comfort zones does not come without its challenges. For example, sometimes Jim is met with resistance because students would prefer to write about a more famous or "sung" artist/band. Jim attempts to guide students, but he prefers them to pre-research, locate, and decide on the artist they want to write about because it offers them ownership of the research project. The premise of the assignment also allows for much debate about what qualifies as an "unsung" artist. Jim views this as a positive discussion to have with students. The very term "unsung" is rather slippery, and Jim is sometimes disappointed with students' initial choices, as he has had students ask if the Eagles were "unsung," for instance. Jim's response is always to ask them why they believe their chosen artist is unsung; they must support their argument. In the case of the Eagles, Jim says, "no," they are not unsung. But, other artists like Frank Zappa, Big Star, the Pixies, the Replacements, Big L., and the Dresden Dolls are debatable, with degrees of marginality. Often, Jim will direct the class to write a list of artists and bands that are clearly sung; this activity is fun (students like to list things), but also serves to eliminate sung artists. Only after the class pre-researches and brainstorms potential unsung artists does Jim share his working list of unsung artists. The "Unsung Artist" paper has several clear goals for writing, researching, and engaging with popular music. The assignment encourages students to stretch their ideas of what popular music means while they develop foundational writing and research skills. Furthermore, the assignment is rewarding for instructors, as well, because they do not have to read stacks of papers on mainstream artists that regurgitate the same information (e.g., Led Zeppelin, Nirvana, or Tupac Shakur).

Identity and Authenticity

Consideration of the roots of a genre—and what it means to produce "authentic" contributions to it—are important for developing students' understanding of how music and identity are intertwined. For example, students see how cultural and racial identities converge when they understand more about the complicated history of rock n' roll that fused together so many established genres, including jazz, early R & B, and country. Music influences its listeners' own identities and provides rhetorical evaluations of identity-related social issues, but it also possesses its own identity, typically thought of as authenticity. In any course that explores questions of identity, this is a central issue. It is particularly important in Jacob's country music class due to the music's connection to the Appalachian region in which many of his students were raised. As Hudson (2006) argues, "there are strong links between music and senses of place and identities" (p. 626). Therefore, examining authenticity is an important piece of understanding country music in this context. Questions of authenticity have plagued mainstream country music since its inception in the 1930s. As Peterson (1998) points out, the genre has oscillated between "soft-shell," pop-oriented styles (e.g., Glen Campbell or later artists like Taylor Swift) and "hard-core" country music (e.g., Merle Haggard or later artists like Chris Stapleton) viewed as more authentic, having been "made by and for those who remain faithful to the 'roots' of country" (p. 237). And, as Hubbs (2014) notes, "country is frequently condemned as phony, disingenuous, and inauthentic" (p. 39). Indeed, given the importance of all music in shaping cultural and individual identities, activities and assignments focusing on a genre's roots and authenticity would be helpful in any course dealing with popular music.

Nick Tosches's (1984) *Unsung Heroes of Rock 'n' Roll* serves as a launching point to discuss themes of identity and to initiate Jim's "Unsung Artist" paper (discussed above). But, it also introduces students to these unsung rock n' rollers—and the genre's roots. Later, the course builds upon these roots, asking students to make connections between the rise of rock n' roll and the emergence of hip-hop as a uniquely American, and later global, cultural phenomenon. Using Shea Serrano's (2015) book, *The Rap Yearbook*, has proven successful as a way of paralleling the roots of rock 'n' roll with the last 45 years of hip-hop. As the book's subtitle notes, it traces "the most important rap song every year since 1979, discussed, debated, and deconstructed." The text has a conversational but informative and insightful tone, filled with interviews and amusing visuals and charts. Jim begins the unit on *The Rap Yearbook* by presenting on two of its chapters, often choosing the years 1982 and 1983, which cover Grandmaster Flash and the Furious Five's "The Message" and Run DMC's "Sucker M.C.'s," respectively. After Jim presents on these years, student pairs or trios present on one or two chapters from the book in the weeks that follow. Jim attempts to give students their first choice in terms of chapter/year/artist, but not everyone can get N.W.A. or Tupac Shakur—often the most popular artists. Allowing students to select the content and to direct the discussions affords them a unique ownership of the course. One challenge Jim has found during these presentations is that he does have to redirect the conversation back to critical discussions of artists, their music, and notions of identity because the class does easily fall into informative trivia and entertainment—using PowerPoint and Kahoot! is a favorite for students. Yet, the book and students' engagement with rap has encouraged him to gain greater appreciation and understanding for contemporary hip-hop, which is the premier musical genre in his students' lives. Thus, Jim has decided to devote more time to hip-hop and rap, specifically in regards to identity, as well as its social history and controversies.

Hip-hop culture, and rap music specifically, has much to offer instructors and students, especially those interested in ideas of identity building and notions of race and gender. Jim admits that he has been most confident discussing the origins of hip-hop, and the often-described golden period of the late 1970s to early 1990s. But, to shy away from contemporary rap artists such as Kendrick Lamar and Lil Dicky is a disservice to our students, especially since rap has become more lyrically complex in recent years. Jim discusses blues and heavy metal—genres that generate discussions about race and misogyny—so why not rap? A challenge for some instructors might be that they have to listen to explicit words and watch disturbing images with their students. So, instructors must face some of the material head on and be willing to confront sensitive issues and maybe even learn from students, who, in Jim's experience, have a great knowledge of rap. Furthermore, students often tell Jim that this is the first time a teacher has taken the rap genre seriously; students will say, "Oh, I took a class in high-school on pop or rock music, and we just talked about the Beatles and the 1960s, but no one ever discussed rap as an art form or taken it seriously." Thus, examining rap in an academic setting validates the genre and demonstrates to students that their music is culturally significant.

By refocusing popular music courses toward themes of identity, instructors and students can heighten their critical discussions. The emphasis on identity construction, first from the students themselves, and secondly, to the artists both past and present, resonates with many students. Beginning with why students identify with particular artists and developing this approach outward toward interpreting disparate artists' identities is a logical and successful approach. This way, at the forefront of discussions are the complicated but fascinating issues surrounding identity, such as race, class, gender, and sexuality. Jacob attempts to address these issues in a slightly different way, encouraging students to examine their own identity as well as the identity of the music itself.

One approach to creating a free and open environment for discussion related to identity involves allowing students "to talk about themselves as members of cultural groups or social classes" (Brookfield & Preskill, 2005, p. 128). In other words, allow students to define their own identity. With this in mind, and given the centrality of music to identity formation and relevant debates about authenticity, Jacob encourages his students to both define their own identity and the authentic form of the country genre through an activity he refers to as a Video Sharing Discussion. In this activity, students work in small groups to discuss the characteristics of "authentic" country music and to choose a video (usually a music video) that represents that authenticity. The activity is primed by a short lecture about music and identity of people and place. We also watch a video of a 2016 parody song by comedian Bo Burnham ("Country Song [Pandering]") that criticizes the supposed inauthentic nature of mainstream country music. Burnham's song includes lines about the wealthy pretending to be working class and country artists writing songs about lives they would never want to live. After a short discussion of the video, students are then prompted by the following questions: (1) What does it mean to be from the Appalachian region? (2) Which aspects of country music reflect that understanding? and (3) What characterizes authentic country music? The first of these questions is easily adaptable to other contexts—

it is primarily intended to get them thinking about and defining their own identity. The second two, in which any genre could substitute for country, help them approach the question of authenticity in music from their own subject position. In other words, what is authentic *for them*?

Students then meet in groups of two or three to discuss the prompt questions and to find a music video that reflects both their own sense of identity (as loosely defined by the first question) as well as the characteristics of authentic country music. After their group discussions, they present their videos to the rest of the class and explain how the song's lyrics or other content of the video reflects how they understand themselves and the question of authenticity. For example, one group chose "The Coal Miner Song" (1993) by Jimmy Joe Lee. This song describes the life of a Kentucky coal miner, and the video features historical images of coal miners in the early twentieth century. The group explained that they chose this song because it most accurately depicted either their lives, or the lives of people they knew. They also felt that the video was authentic because it used actual photographs of those who had lived that life rather than featuring a musician singing or re-created scenes. Often, the question of authenticity mirrors their own understanding of their identity. In the example above, students were most drawn to the "truth" of the lyrics and the images, suggesting that what makes country music authentic is whether or not it honestly reflects the lives of its listeners. This helps the students to connect their own self-concept to its expression in popular music, but it also helps them to recognize the slippery nature of the concept of authenticity and the fact that it is more a question of congruence with the listener's identity. Indeed, Hubbs (2014) points out that musical style, and country's presumed rusticity in particular, can serve as a proxy for class standing. Students are able to better understand this concept by looking for evidence of identity congruence in music videos.

An important aspect of this activity is that students are approaching the issue from their own standpoint—using their own understanding of who they are in order to build an appreciation for what they believe country music is or should be. Following the activity, students have exercised their ability to locate their own objects for analysis (the music videos) and tie them directly to who they view themselves to be, providing them with insight they do not typically receive from the guided analysis of an instructor-chosen artifact. And, by having groups present their videos to one another, they are also able to see how others view the same issue and potentially make comparisons or reconcile differences either individually or through responding in discussion. And therein lies the central purpose of the activity: to engage students in an active process of defining both themselves *and* the country genre through an examination of the music itself.

Conclusion

Identity is a rich field to explore in relation to popular music. Focusing on identity helps students and instructors listen to music differently, perhaps more intimately, as it draws attention to the music's creators and the musical expression of one's identity. By beginning with students' exploration of how and why they identify with popular music, students examine their own musical catalogue. Yet, this identity-based approach to music generates discussions beyond mere identity politics. In both Jacob's and Jim's courses, the often-sensitive issues of race, class, and gender are examined through various activities and assignments. Students and instructors also consider the music business, notions of authenticity, and contexts of the music to better understand the music itself. Additional activities that ask students to discover artists that construct and deconstruct notions of identity within musical genres facilitate learning beyond oneself. Examining artists that reinstate genre stereotypes, and artists that challenge stereotypes, proves helpful in getting students to examine popular music. These practices allow students to connect their personal tastes with the complex public sphere, opening them up to critically explore music, identity, and culture.

By thinking about, listening to, and writing about music with attention to its context and its relation to issues of identity, students more capably understand the cultural role of music and their relationship with music. Furthermore, this approach to popular music encourages student ownership of ideas. Centralizing identity in its various forms explicitly asks students to recognize themselves and their perspectives in the dialogue about music. Both Jacob's Chalk Talk and Jim's Identity List Analysis assignments/activities encourage students to participate in the creation of knowledge. Rather than seeming static and untouchable (as many academic disciplines do to students), the study of identity and popular music invites students to participate. Through this process, students can rethink both music and their role as students and academics.

REFERENCES

Brookfield, S.D. (2012). *Teaching for critical thinking: Tools and techniques to help students question their assumptions.* San Francisco: Jossey-Bass.

Brookfield, S.D., & Preskill, S. (2005). *Discussion as a way of teaching: Tools and techniques for democratic classrooms.* San Francisco: Jossey-Bass.

Hubbs, N. (2014). *Rednecks, queers, and country music.* Berkeley: University of California Press.

Hudson, R. (2006). Regions and place: Music, identity, and place. *Progress in Human Geography, 30*(5), 626–634.

Lang, A.S. (1998). Jim Crow and the pale maiden: Gender, color, and class in Stephen Foster's "Hard Times." In C. Tichi (Ed.), *Reading country music: Steel guitars, opry stars, and honky-tonk bars* (pp. 378–388). Durham, NC: Duke University Press.

Peterson, R.A. (1998). The dialectic of hard-core and soft-shell country music. In C. Tichi (Ed.), *Reading country music: Steel guitars, opry stars, and honky-tonk bars* (pp. 234–255). Durham, NC: Duke University Press.

Segal, L. (2008). After Judith Butler: Identities, who needs them? *Subjectivity, 25*, 381–394.

Serrano, S., & Torres, A. (2015). *The rap yearbook: The most important rap song from every year since 1979, discussed, debated, and deconstructed.* New York: Abrams Image.

Tosches, N. (1984). *Unsung heroes of rock-n-roll: The birth of rock-n-roll in the wild years before Elvis.* New York: Scribner's.

Patriarchy, Cross-Dressing, Agency and Violence

Women and the Pedagogical Opportunities in Heavy Metal

Daniel Guberman

On the surface, heavy metal appears to be a music genre dominated by cisgender straight white men. Band titles, artwork, videos, and lyrics have a long tradition of explicit misogyny, seeming to celebrate a culture that ranges from objectification of women to explicit sexual violence (racism and other forms of oppression or hatred also exist throughout the genre). It may be difficult to imagine how courses focusing on heavy metal music and its surrounding culture can promote the development of more accepting and inclusive mindsets among students. I have found that the task of encouraging students to appreciate the value of diversity, which underlies much of my pedagogical philosophy, may be accomplished quite effectively within heavy metal's flexible and surprisingly diverse framework. Furthermore, the explicit nature and lack of nuance in some of the genre's sounds, lyrics, and imagery may facilitate discussions about students' own perspectives and assumptions with regard to heavy metal musicians, audiences, and community members. In this essay, I offer background on my own teaching philosophy and aims, grounding my goals in feminist pedagogical work, as well as how it connects with scholarship on heavy metal music and its culture. I then share examples of bands, musicians, and songs that form the basis of robust discussions on a variety of topics related to gender issues within the genre and society at large.

My Teaching Aims

I have taught courses on heavy metal music four times across multiple departments (music, honors, and global studies), moving from a survey of the genre to three iterations focused on global heavy metal music. The two most recent iterations involved live video-conference discussions with college students around the world (e.g., Japan, Pakistan, Egypt, Argentina). While these discussions were interesting, they were also unpredictable because many of our partners were learning English and had limited familiarity with local or global heavy metal scenes. Considering that this situation is rarely transferable to other potential teaching situations, I will focus my discussion here around the other elements of the course, which stand alone without the need for these partnerships.

In all of these iterations of the class, we take an expansive view of the heavy metal. In a genre noted for fans who serve as adamant gatekeepers, I share with my students that we are not interested in whether a particular group is or is not sufficiently heavy metal. Instead, we focus on what these debates tell us about particular fans, critics, and musicians, as well as their view of the genre. For example, I have no qualms discussing Led Zeppelin as an important pioneering heavy metal band, or AC/DC and the glam metal/hard rock bands of the 1980s (e.g., Poison, Cinderella, and Bon Jovi), all of which have fit into reasonable definitions of the genre used by fan communities and critics. Recognizing that the definitions of the genre have always been fluid, we can interrogate the motivations of those who would seek to include or exclude certain people, bands, sounds, or ideas from their definition of the genre.

Heavy metal music classes have never been part of a core major in music, and even within recent discussions about expanding music curricula, the genre receives little attention (e.g., Moore, 2017). When I taught in a relatively traditional school of music, no courses on rock or other forms of popular music contributed toward a student's music degree. This meant that my courses on heavy metal music fulfilled broader institutional aims common to many arts and humanities electives, including promoting critical thinking, intercultural competence, and diversity/inclusion. Nevertheless, my aim was not just to get through a university curriculum committee. As when I design classes on classical music for non-majors, I want my students to leave the class as more engaged listeners to whatever music they hear around them—aware of and able to articulate their own tastes, and comfortable engaging in discussions about what a piece of music means to them, and why that might be different for others. In heavy metal classes, I do not care if they remember the members of Slayer, or the differences between doom metal and sludge metal, but I do want them to be aware of their own tastes, be open to diverse styles and others' tastes, as well as have meaningful discussions about the music that they hear. In most cases, less than a third of my students are already familiar with the genre, and often only one or two enter the class fans of the growls or squeals of death and black metal.

All of these goals aim higher—I want to contribute toward the development of justice-oriented citizens, who can engage in meaningful and respectful dialogue about complex issues (Westheimer & Kahne, 2004). I frame this aim within the critical pedagogy writings of bell hooks and Paolo Freire, who highlight the classroom as a space for the co-construction of knowledge, and as a forum for student empowerment (hooks, 1994; Freire, 2000). Studying cultural issues through heavy metal music from this perspective has been particularly effective in relatively small classes (20 students or fewer), because I can place an emphasis on students directing our path. I do not feel bound by a particular heavy metal canon. Instead, I ask students to explore our topic for the week and choose a song to write about and share. This means that I often encounter music for the first time through my students, and I can participate in our discussions as a new listener as well (a memorable example of this was a student presentation on Hatebeak, a band that relies on a Congo grey parrot named Waldo as its vocalist). Additionally, because I push students to search for bands and songs around the world, they often encounter and deal with music that has little readily available information. They cannot go to Wikipedia and try to put it into their own words because there is not anything there. This forces students to develop and share their own interpretation of a particular band or song, which we can then discuss. Often, they come up with ideas that I may have never considered.

At the start of each semester, I remind myself that for many students, deriving and sharing their own interpretation can be uncomfortable. Students have mostly experienced learning environments designed in a controlled manner (Reeve, 2009), and many have internalized a desire for controlled teaching environments. As part of an effort to create an autonomy-supportive environment, I emphasize throughout the course that we are not studying this music to determine a certain truth, but to explore what this music and the people involved in various scenes (musicians, critics, fans etc.) can reveal about society, both local and global, and what we can learn about ourselves as learners, cultural consumers, and scholars.

I did not always view this class and its goals along these lines. The first course I taught, titled simply *Heavy Metal Music and Culture*, followed the structure of many traditional histories of Western Classical Music. I focused on students' ability to trace the history of the genre and identify the ways "important" bands adapted and innovated stylistically. I focused almost entirely on listening and stylistic analysis, with the musicians and people providing interesting context and stories to make the class more engaging.

In doing so, the class progressed from precursor blues musicians like Howlin' Wolf, through distinct stylistic periods, and I expected students to recognize the developments from Black Sabbath to Judas Priest and later Metallica (focusing almost entirely on each band's early stylistic innovations and ignoring their ongoing music). Heavy metal, in this class, formed a nice linear progression of increasing complexity, volume, and intensity, with a few offshoots for popular hair bands. In this teaching experience, I found the most interesting and sophisticated discussions did not center around musical style, but around the social elements of this music, which could include everything from artwork and clothing to fan interviews on discussion forums (note: this is not to say that there are not incredibly sophisticated scholarly discussions of musical structure and style in the genre; see, for example Pieslak, 2007). The importance of social issues became most apparent when I taught the second iteration of the class, through an honors program. I asked students to choose topics for research papers, and through consultations, the most interesting projects used music as an entryway for students to explore topics ranging from white supremacy in North America to cross-dressing in Japan. These projects also enhanced my own engagement with the genre.

In response to these experiences, I changed my approach to designing the course and the outcomes I wanted for my students. We began to pay particular attention to how individual critics or publications may present events, music, or bands that we considered interesting (in an effort to move away from canonization and expand what music we studied, I asked students to think about why music was interesting to us, rather than measuring the impact it may have had on others). Over time, I also became much more transparent. In initial changes, I continued to describe the course as one focused on style with some discussion of social and political issues, such as gender, class, race, and religion. After further revisions, I began to forefront awareness and analysis of these social and political issues as primary outcomes (on transparency see Palmer, Bach, & Streifer, 2016). This transition to a focus on the people, cultural, and political contexts aligns with recent discussions on future directions for music study more broadly (Robin, 2017).

Patriarchy as a Threshold Concept

One of the core challenges in courses dealing with gender and contemporary culture involves students understanding patriarchy as a social system. Or, that a subculture "is patriarchal to the degree that it promotes male privilege by being male-dominated, male-identified, and male-centered" (Johnson, 2007, p. 5). To some degree, it is easy to demonstrate this mindset through a study of heavy metal music and musicians, who are often assumed to be male. A large number of scholars and critics have written about the male-centricity of heavy metal scenes. Deena Weinstein, a sociologist who wrote one of the first and seminal scholarly texts on the genre, discusses the male-centeredness of the music from multiple angles. For example, in discussing lyrics and themes, she explains that in songs about sex "women are rarely given personal names" (Weinstein, 2000, p. 36). In another early seminal work on the genre, Robert Walser (2014) takes his description of heavy metal's male-centeredness even further by describing a complete erasure of women in some contexts explaining:

> metal's enactments of masculinity include varieties of misogyny as well as "exscription" [Walser's term] of the feminine—that is, total denial of gender anxieties through the articulation of fantastic worlds without women—supported by male, sometimes homoerotic bonding [p. 110].

This may be most evident in the heavy metal scenes emerging in the late 1970s and early 1980s, featuring tight leather clothing, long sometimes teased hair, and occasionally large amounts of makeup. This look, often credited to Judas Priest, quickly spread in multiple directions, including the American subgenre "glam" metal and the Japanese subgenre "visual kei." In many cases, glam metal bands featured all-male performers singing slow ballads while adopting androgynous appearances. Many such songs lamented failed relationships as in Cinderella's 1988 hit "Don't Know What You Got (Till It's Gone)." In imagery, these all-male bands often presented themselves as a close knit group, which Weinstein (2000) compares to a family unit, exemplified by Led Zeppelin's dissolution after John Bonham's death and Def Leppard's determination to keep Rick Allen as their drummer after he lost his left arm in 1984. The idea of band as a family eliminates roles for women. Even in troubling times, such as after traumatic accidents (e.g., Def Leppard), when we often turn to family, the band provides an alternative. In these cases, the band mourns the loss of life, or reorganizes itself in response to loss of limb. In other cases, bands can have traumatic separations, leading to ongoing attempts to find peace mixed with extreme anger, as exemplified by Guns N' Roses approximately two-decade break starting in the mid–1990s. This suggests a form of patriarchy in which women are not just secondary, but entirely unrecognized.

Examining Women's Experiences in Mixed-Gender Bands

We can explore how patriarchal structures have become embedded within the genre when comparing the "family-unit" experiences of these all-male groups with the experiences of women in mixed-gender groups. Doing so, suggests that many male band-members see women in the bands as replaceable. Similarly, when women do leave, or are dismissed, the discussion rarely focuses on artistic reasons, but instead personal reasons. In this context, I often ask students to explore the Finnish symphonic death metal band Nightwish. Symphonic metal, one of the most prominent subgenres over the past decade, combines loud distorted guitar and heavy drumming from heavy metal music with an operatic female vocalist (operatic is a term used relatively). This subgenre relies on participation by a female vocalist, and this woman is often presented centrally throughout marketing and videos. As a subgenre dependent upon participation by women vocalists, these bands rarely include other women as instrumentalists, reinforcing a patriarchal structure that defines women's work in a very limited context for a role that cannot be fulfilled by a male performer.

Nightwish, one of the most prominent bands in this genre, now has its third female lead vocalist, while the male band members (everyone else) have remained largely consistent. Even percussionist Jukka Nevalainen, upon determining that he could not continue due to insomnia in 2014, has remained part of the band as a manager (suggesting a family-like concern for everyone's well-being). In our study of the band, I ask students to explore the events and interpret the situation around their change in vocalists, particularly the dismissal of their original vocalist, Tarja Turunen, comparing her treatment to what they read about male members' dismissals from bands. Additionally, I ask students to explore fan responses, to think about the many ways gender plays into discussions of the band, performers and genre.

Many of the band's fans believed that the dismissal of Tarja Turunen stemmed from the bandleader, Tuomas Holopainen's, jealousy after she married businessman Marcelo Cabuli. We can consider interpreting the band's songs through the lens of Holopainen's desire. One example is the 2004 song "I Wish I Had an Angel," which contrasts Turunen's voice with bass player Marco Hietala, suggesting that the song specifically depicts a man's lust for a woman who has chosen someone else. Other, broader interpretations are certainly possible, such as a commentary on Western, or specifically Christian notions of sexuality, with references to angels, the Virgin Mary, and the 13th disciple. I ask students to consider how they might interpret the song, as well as to look at how fans have interpreted the song, and to consider the position of a woman performing this song, written for her in light of a recent marriage (Turunen and Cabuli married the previous year, in 2003). Adding another dimension to the narrative, one of the first hits with new singer Anette Olzon, the 2007 song "Bye Bye Beautiful," specifically dealt with Holopainen's response to Turunen leaving the band, including lyrics asking whether she had read the lyrics to the previous songs. When examining this song, I ask students to consider not only what this tells us about the relationship between Turunen and Holopainen as band members, but also what does this mean for Olzon, as a new member entering the band, again, as the only woman.

The classroom becomes a place to examine this interpersonal conflict from multiple perspectives, considering how different people, including band members, fans, and media, may have interpreted Nightwish's music in light of changing narratives and details. In this way, I seek to model musicological ways of thinking by combining songs with primary sources and considering varying perspectives. Marco Cabuli, Turunen's husband, created a particularly interesting primary source for examination, when he responded to 157 questions submitted by fans, now preserved in archival form (Cabuli, 2007). The further addition of extensive media coverage and fan reactions adds to a rich collection of documents ripe for interpretation and comparison with other bands' treatment, inclusion, and exclusion of women. Students can also examine the dismissal of Turunen's replacement, Anette Olzon, a few years later, possibly due to her pregnancy.

As an example of the ways in which women involved in the genre are often treated differently than men, this Nightwish saga poses fascinating questions. First, does the "family unit" feeling of heavy metal bands remain today, or is it a remnant of the period when Weinstein was writing? Does the dismissal of Turunen differ from male members leaving bands, for example when Ozzy Osbourne left Black Sabbath? The relationships within Nightwish also bring up questions of creativity and authorship in the "family unit." One component of the "family" narrative is that many band members share in the creative process. Interviews abound in which members discuss the spontaneity of creativity stemming from a guitarist experimenting with short riffs and a vocalist finding immediate inspiration. But, Nightwish seems to treat its vocalists as performers, who may be interchangeable. Because the band has developed such a large following, students are able to explore these questions through multiple types of sources, including official marketing, media, and interviews, press coverage, and fan engagement. They might consider if a writer's background affects how they view these events. They can also compare the experiences of other female performers across the genre, in order to gain a broader perspective on their roles and relative positions throughout different metal scenes (similar bands include: Epica, Within Temptation, and Theatre of Tragedy).

Walser's notion of "exscription," or apparent elimination of women, found in many heavy metal scenes may have given rise to a significant number of all-female bands. Often, these groups received very different responses from media and fans than all-male groups, and I ask students to examine these differences. For example, we can compare the music and stories of bands like Girlschool and Vixen. While many band names suggest that the members are women, the music and lyrics vary in how explicitly they deal with gender issues, offering another fruitful path for discussion and analysis. Some songs, like Girlschool's "Demolition Boys," do not have particularly detailed narratives, and instead seem to focus on conveying an attitude about life using generic male pronouns (comparable to Judas Priest's "Exciter" or Motörhead's "Ace of Spades"). In other cases, we can identify patriarchy, or even exscription, in music and imagery by women heavy metal performers. For example, in The Great Kat's (guitarist and violinist Katherine Thomas) video for "Metal Messiah," a group of all-male fans follows and worships her. In the lyrics, she also uses masculine terms (i.e., god and master, as opposed to goddess and mistress). In another song on the same album, "Kat Possessed," she refers to herself as a goddess, among lyrics that are more sexually explicit, suggesting strategic deployment of her gender.

Whenever we discuss the meaning of a song, I ask students to consider whose perspective is taken, both in songs by male and female musicians. I also ask them to look at fan responses, who seems to identify with the meaning of particular songs, and how meanings change for different people (gender being only one of many ways we may answer this question). I also ask students to think about their own perspectives, and what these songs mean to them. Especially when we listen to older songs, it is important to examine them both in historical context, and their potential for relevance in contemporary life. We can then explore if and how these ideas are reflected in contemporary commentary (e.g., in comments on YouTube videos).

The mistreatment of female band members, as part of misogyny in the heavy metal genre, also comes to the forefront in the story of the band Cerebral Bore, which began in 2006 as an all-male Scottish death metal band, slowly achieving recognition through radio play and by opening for a variety of bands' European tours. They were thrust into the international spotlight in 2010, when Simone Pluijmers (aka: Som), a female Dutch singer, joined the band. Som, who was only 18 years old at the time, had developed a small following by posting videos on YouTube in which she covered moderately obscure death metal songs. Som's addition to Cerebral Bore led to international media attention, pushing them to record and release their first full album, produce videos, sign a recording contract with Earache Records, and headline major international tours. Two years later, in November 2012, the band announced that Som had left, just 24 hours before the start of a United States tour. While the remaining band members presented themselves as shocked and abandoned, Som ultimately shared that she left because she did not feel safe around her bandmates (both male).

As in the Nightwish situation, a woman was likely forced out of a band due to the actions and attitudes of male bandmates. In the case of Som and Cerebral Bore, we do not have as much information, but the remaining two band members also did little to contest that their actions led to her quitting the band. This situation is also particularly notable because, after a male vocalist replaced Som, the band's popularity fizzled out over the next two years and they never produced another album. We can discuss why this might be. Was Som's voice the difference between success and failure of a band, or does the novelty of a female who can effectively perform the growls of death metal provide enough marketing and attention that it enables otherwise obscure bands to gain notoriety? If so, what does this say about the genre and its fans?

Meanwhile, Som returned to her YouTube channel, and posted a new cover in which she growled to the lyrics of Aqua's 1997 song "Barbie Girl." She provided no explanation, titling the video "Unexpected Cover" signifying its out-of-place spot on her channel (Pluijmers, 2012). This opens numerous interpretive possibilities: First, we can explore what it means to record a cover of a song on YouTube, and how this reflects a changing industry, providing opportunities previously unavailable. We can also compare the cover of "Barbie Girl" to her earlier covers. The previous covers largely sought to recreate and practice certain vocal styles, while "Barbie Girl" adapted a well-known song to the sounds of a seemingly contrasting genre and style. Students can also look at responses to the song in the media and among fans. This example can also lead to other instances in which heavy metal bands cover a range of non-heavy metal songs, potentially generating new meanings. Some examples leading to fruitful discussions include Megadeth's "The Boots" (a cover of "These Boots Are Made for Walking," which most students today know through Jessica Simpson in 2005, but first gained popularity with Nancy Sinatra in 1966), and A Perfect Circle's cover of John Lennon's "Imagine."

Cross-Dressing in Heavy Metal Music

Another significant component of heavy metal, connecting discussions about gender and visual imagery, involves the role of clothing in the genre. A notable element of Som's story with Cerebral Bore is the notion that she could be "perceived" as "one of the guys." In the band's most prominent video on YouTube, "The Bald Cadaver," Som wears the same type of loose-fitting black clothing as her band-mates, as well as a brimmed hat, which obscures much of her face. This image, combined with her growling voice, suggests that a casual viewer may have no idea that she is not another male band member. Of course, the band's notoriety and publicity, focused on her gender, means that the likelihood of this happening is slim, and, as such there has been little room for women to play with gender identities and appearances. For men, on the other hand, gender became a fluid construct fairly early in the development of the genre. In particular, Rob Halford of Judas Priest adopted a widely emulated leather and studs look in the late 1970s. For Halford, this served as an expression of his closeted homosexuality, drawing inspiration from the gay S&M scene (Petridis, 2014). As other bands adopted similar looks (e.g., Iron Maiden, Motörhead, and Saxon), it became expressions of both masculinity and a path to adopt, or perhaps more accurately colonize, feminine imagery. Throughout the 1980s male musicians, in bands like Van Halen and Twisted Sister, increasingly added long teased hair and makeup to their tight leather pants, which were sometimes traded in for spandex. While adopting women's fashion styles, often these men were also displaying their toned athletic bodies. Weinstein describes the ways in which music often depicted lives filled with partying and drugs, but in reality musicians spent significant time exercising and staying healthy (pp. 64–65).

The development of gender-bending dress codes aligned with a period of metal's globalization, including a particularly large scene in Japan. After initial bands like Loudness, Earthshaker, and Anthem, in the mold of Judas Priest or Black Sabbath, the Japanese scene quickly adopted increasingly elaborate costumes. By the end of the 1980s, the visual appearance took on such central importance that it spun out into its own subgenre, termed Visual Kei (or "visual style"). The subgenre's pioneers, X Japan, embraced the androgynous and ostentatious styles of glam artists like David Bowie. By the mid–2000s, groups like Versailles had male performers cross-dressing in elaborate gothic costumes both on stage and in music videos acting out grand narratives in gothic mansions (e.g., the video for "Aristocrat's Symphony"). The performers in Versailles have maintained these characters through numerous acts, and some are rarely seen, or nearly unrecognizable when not in costume.

The contrast between Som's adoption of gender-neutral or assumed-male clothing and Versailles feminine costumes has resulted in interesting contrasts between student approaches to presentations. Students often discuss Cerebral Bore by highlighting Som's gender before playing any music, often in an attempt to share some background about an artist before listening (a standard approach to class presentations). For Versailles, this tends to change. Without prompting from me, multiple students have chosen to offer very little background information about the band before playing a video. This leads to interesting discussions and confusion as students try to identify the gender of individuals and discuss how their impressions of the music, video, and band change when the learn more. For those interested, it can also open up avenues for comparing cross-dressed performances in the United States and Japan over history, to see how this act may have entirely different meanings based on our cultural roots.

Are Female Performers Objectified or in Control?

Students often struggle to examine the same material from multiple perspectives, and this struggle comes to the forefront in discussions of gender in heavy metal music. Many students initially see the vast majority of female performers as victims or objects within a patriarchal or sexist society, an idea found in some scholarship as well. In their ethnographic study of the heavy metal scene in an Australian music club, Krenske and McKay (2000) highlight the position of some women, who described the music's appeal as an "escape," by explaining that "Women drawn to the HM [heavy metal] scene to escape one oppressive context merely inserted themselves into another" (p. 302). Within their interviews, we find a wide range of reasons for participating in the heavy metal scene, and multiple social subcultures within a single heavy metal concert venue. As such, these women's experiences of sexism and misogyny varied, and in many cases their concerns differed from the presumed concerns of male participants (e.g., men described the negative effects of groping while stage diving, and women generally did not). For this reason, it seems essential to find opportunities to give voice to individual women participants as often as possible.

In my classes, I encourage students to seek out interviews with female performers, noting how frequently their gender is a central question in the interviews. Additionally, with my focus on global scenes and bands, often gender intersects with other identities, leading to fruitful discussions regarding how people view their own identity in different contexts. For example, Massive Scar Era became a central figure in an emerging Egyptian heavy metal scene as one of the few female-led bands from the Islamic Middle East. Their song "My Ground" expresses frustration with the policies of the Muslim Brotherhood, focusing on their religious and gender-based persecution. In interviews, bandleader Cherine Amr discusses this multi-faceted persecution. When focusing on the heavy metal scene in Egypt, she points to the band's struggles to find performance venues, which were often shut down by the government, and depictions of her as a Satanist in Egyptian media. Meanwhile, when discussing her international recognition and responses from others in the Egyptian heavy metal scene, she highlights their objectification of her as a woman and their dismissal of her musical abilities and commitment. She states in an interview with Donald Maguire, "we are talking to the metal scene, because whatever we achieve they say 'Ah, they do it because they are girls and they show some skin.' As if we show skin! They neglect all of the effort" (Maguire, 2013). In examining Massive Scar Era's song "My Ground," I ask students to think about how it may be read as a response to both the government and other musicians in terms of politics, religion, and gender (Guberman, 2018).

While many women in metal bands, like Som and Amr, do not wear elaborate and revealing costumes, others do by choice, and students can struggle to recognize this decision as a reflection of individual agency, which can be empowering. I theorize that there are class issues at play here. Perhaps, the historical association of heavy metal music with working class musicians and audiences may lead to a distrust of women's agency. This association has never been articulated clearly in my classes, perhaps because American students are often reluctant to speak about class issues. I became aware of this potential discomfort with discussions around class and metal music when we were studying the Japanese band Sigh. First formed in 1989, Sigh has experimented with a variety of styles under the extreme metal umbrella (thrash, death, black, etc.). Their saxophonist and backup vocalist, Dr. Mikannibal, embraces her position as a sexual icon—she appears on magazine lists of "sexiest women in metal" (Scuderi, 2015). When asked how she views this attention, she explains:

> I do wear sexy costumes, and I wear less clothes than other metal chicks in other bands. It's not intentional. I don't do it to try to get attention from men. I just wear what I wear because I like it. I love myself, my looks and my body, and I like to show it off on stage. That's the whole idea [Simms, 2009].

Initially, I found that many students dismissed these statements, especially from a performer who often drips hot wax on her body or covers herself in fake blood during performances. However, these impressions changed when they learned that she calls herself Dr. Mikannibal because she has a Ph.D. in physics from the University of Tokyo, and speaks about the lack of women in heavy metal bands as comparable to the lack of women in the sciences. I suspect that for my undergraduate students, this type of academic credentialing, and the class differences projected by her degree, gave weight and legitimacy to her claims of agency over her body and image.

Based on the numerous examples I provide and that students find on their own, I encourage students to find interviews and other sources in which performers speak for themselves about issues related to patriarchy, misogyny, and agency while considering how performers present specific images in different venues and forums. We often discuss why performers may project a certain image on social media platforms like Facebook and Twitter, and how that image may or may not align with interviews in a variety of sources. Throughout all of these discussions, I try to frame questions and discussions around how our knowledge and experience with performers can inform our engagement with and interpretation of their music, recognizing that our opinions are formed by our own biases, as demonstrated in the case of Dr.

Mikannibal. The additional course emphasis on valuing the voices of fans reinforces the idea that our interpretations are valuable tools for learning about ourselves and the world, but not do not impart a singular "truth" about a performer.

Violence

Violence serves as a common theme in heavy metal. Many of the genre's detractors declare that the genre is filled with horrific imagery, including sexual violence. Certainly, violence against women is present in the genre, but its degree of prominence compared to other forms of violence is difficult to determine. Most early songs by the American band Death, a forerunner in the death metal subgenre, involve relatively generic depictions of brutality (e.g., "Mutilation" from the 1987 album *Scream Bloody Gore*). This focus may trace back to a long trend of horror film-inspired lyrics and sounds beginning with Black Sabbath's 1970 song "Black Sabbath." But this is complicated by bands like Cannibal Corpse, another American death metal band, whose lyrics quickly shift between generic violence, as in "Hammer Smashed Face," and explicit sexual assault found throughout most of the remainder of the 1992 album *Tomb of the Mutilated*. This type of sexual brutality appears on Cannibal Corpse's album covers as well. Even Metallica, a band whose violent imagery often deals with personal struggles (e.g., drug addiction in "Master of Puppets" or suicide in "Fade to Black"), suggests the possibility of sexual assault through the blindfolded, bound, and bare-chested image of Lady Justice on the cover of ...*And Justice for All* (1988).

Class discussions can connect this aspect of heavy metal imagery with other cultural forms and trends (e.g., films). First, we explore the seeming constant escalation of violence in metal through the 1980s and early '90s. And, how the over-the-top nature of songs by bands like Cannibal Corpse compare to the seemingly serious discussions about internal psychological struggles, such as Metallica's "Master of Puppets." In many cases fans and bands transition easily between these two types of violence, for example comparing the random violence of Death's "Mutilation" (1987) with their exploration of the human psyche in "Trapped in a Corner" (1993). Similarly, how does violence in music compare to how we perceive it in other forms of media? In films and television, we justify violent imagery, including sexual violence, through the need to tell specific narratives that have emotional ties for the viewer. With musical sound offering something much more abstract, is this violence necessary, and does the type of violence matter? Unlike popular television shows, like NBC's *Law and Order: Special Victims Unit*, which depict scenes from contemporary society, many metal bands provide little context that would suggest a connection with people's lived realities. Additionally, the victims in most of these heavy metal songs are entirely anonymous, another way in which women are erased.

Another central question when it comes to violence within death and/or black metal involves our ability to comprehend lyrics. In many cases, especially songs depicting the most extreme violent situations, the average listener will be unable to decipher the lyrics through listening—often even through multiple close, focused hearings. In class, we often study the Canadian-based Mares of Thrace's song "General Sherman" with its accompanying video. The video alternates imagery of the two-woman duo, Stefani Mickichan (drums) and Therese Lanz (guitars, vocals, and electronics), performing and enacting a narrative in which they torture and murder a seemingly innocent man. The unintelligible lyrics are not accessible online, meaning as a class we could only theorize whether some imagined lyrics might justify the brutality of the imagery, which is shockingly realistic. Eventually, I did read the lyrics (available in the album insert), and they depict exacting revenge after being the subject of prior torture. Because of the value of the more abstract discussions, I hesitate to share these lyrics with the students, and when I have (after watching the video), they seem to feel that the violence remains unjustified.

Conclusion

Throughout my courses examining heavy metal music, I seek to accomplish several goals with my students. First, I ask them to examine their own assumptions about music, society, culture, and gender. Certain modes of experiencing songs (just listening, videos with music, lyrics or not, background information first or later), enable us to explore our own reactions and approaches to interpretation. Second, I ask students to think about how these assumptions derive from broader cultural forces. What do interviews and primary sources tell us about heavy metal subcultures and broader culture structures, and how do they relate and inform each other? Finally, I always try to connect back to the music, recognizing how music serves many roles in our lives, and we can all derive very different, yet valid interpretations of the same music.

These lessons, developed while teaching about heavy metal music, led me to rethink teaching other classes as well. Some of these dealt specifically with globalization and the diversity of global music scenes. In classes about rock and popular music more broadly, I often found that students would assume that whatever was popular in America would be popular elsewhere (which can be true in many cases), and that other music was limited to "national" styles (e.g., K-Pop in South Korea or Bollywood in India). By introducing these students to examples from the heavy metal class, I challenged them to think about other nations' music scenes as complex entities, and to consider the ways that popular music can cross international boundaries, even before the expansion of the internet.

I have even brought examples from my experience teaching courses on heavy metal into discussions of western classical music, another area that has traditionally been dominated by white men in the classroom. As part of my interest in breaking down the barriers between classical music and popular music, I try to make connections with a variety of other forms, including heavy metal. For example, when exploring the historical use of male performers to depict women in opera, initially performed by castrati and today by countertenors, I also employ examples from Som's singing with Cerebral Bore. This serves two purposes, first to challenge assumptions about the connection between gender and voice, demonstrating that women are capable of producing equally varied and wide-ranging pitches and timbres. Second, I use this as an example to expand students' conceptions of virtuosity beyond traditional notions in classical music, which are often associated with certain types of technical playing or singing (fast, high, loud, etc.). Instead, I present this as an exemplar of virtuosity based in timbre, or the quality of a musical sound, which later in the semester becomes a central theme in the classical repertoire, with the music of contemporary composers like Krystof Penderecki and Caroline Shaw.

Do all of these discussions of heavy metal music actually make my students more accepting of difference, and aware of the ways in which society's structures and institutions perpetuate unequal access and treatment of not just women, but other traditionally marginalized communities? It is difficult to know definitively. I can observe how students change the ways they engage with music. They recognize that it has the potential to be more than entertainment, and that our fruitful discussions about a wide range of music do not need to rely on technical terminology. I also know that many students expand their tastes, and acceptance of diverse styles of music. My hope is that readers of this essay will find opportunities in their classes to have music serve these diverse educational aims, whether through the concrete examples I have shared, or through a re-examination of whatever music they regularly engage with.

REFERENCES

Cabuli, M. (2007). Dear fans of Nightwish and Tarja. Retrieved January 28, 2018, from http://web.archive.org/web/20070703211904/http://www.tarjaturunen.com/fans.html.

Freire, P. (2000). *Pedagogy of the oppressed* (30th anniversary edition). New York: Bloomsbury.

Guberman, D. (2017). Massive Scar Era, heavy metal, and two tyrannies. In J. Morgan, and G. Reish, G. (Eds.), *Tyranny and music* (pp.183–198). Lanham, MD: Lexington Books.

hooks, b. (1994). *Teaching to transgress*. New York: Routledge.

Johnson, A.G. (2014). *The gender knot: Unraveling our patriarchal legacy*. Philadelphia: Temple University Press.

Krenske, L., & McKay, J. (2000). "Hard and heavy": Gender and power in a heavy metal music subculture. *Gender, Place and Culture: A Journal of Feminist Geography, 7*(3), 287–304.

Maguire, D. (2013). Massive Scar Era. *Twisted Hillbilly Magazine*. Retrieved January 28, 2018, from http://www.thmag.us/massivescarera.html.

Moore, R.D. (2017). *College music curricula for a new century*. New York: Oxford University Press.

Palmer, M.S., Bach, D.J., & Streifer, A.C. (2014). Measuring the promise: A learning-focused syllabus rubric. *To Improve the Academy: A Journal of Educational Development, 33*(1), 14–36.

Petridis, A. (2014, July 3). Judas Priest's Rob Halford: I've become the stately homo of heavy metal. *The Guardian*. Retrieved April 10, 2018, from https://www.theguardian.com/music/2014/jul/03/judas-priest-rob-halford-quentin-crispinterview-redeemer-of-souls.

Pieslak, J. (2007). Re-casting metal: Rhythm and meter in the music of Meshuggah. *Music Theory Spectrum, 29*(2), 219–245.

Pluijmers, S. (2012, December 14). Unexpected cover: Aqua—Barbie girl. YouTube. Retrieved January 28, 2018, from https://www.youtube.com/watch?v=A7mRKJdWSbY.

Reeve, J. (2009). Why teachers adopt a controlling motivating style toward students and how they can become more autonomy supportive. *Educational Psychologist, 44*(3), 159–175.

Robin, W. (2017, April 24). What controversial changes at Harvard mean for music in the university. Retrieved January 28, 2018, from https://nationalsawdust.org/thelog/2017/04/25/what-controversial-changes-at-harvard-means-for-music-in-the-university/.

Scuderi, G. (2015, December 1). Metal chick of the month—Dr. Mikannibal. The Headbanging moose. Retrieved January 28, 2018, from https://theheadbangingmoose.wordpress.com/2015/12/01/metal-chick-of-the-month-dr-mikannibal.

Simms, K. (2009, December 29). Sigh-Dr. Mikannibal (vocals/saxophone). SMN News. Retrieved January 28, 2018, from http://www.smnnews.com/2009/12/29/dr-mikannibal-sigh-vocalssaxaphone.

Walser, R. (2013). *Running with the devil: Power, gender, and madness in heavy metal music*. Middletown, CT: Wesleyan University Press.

Weinstein, D. (2000). *Heavy metal: The music and its culture*. Boston: Da Capo Press.

Westheimer, J., & Kahne, J. (2004). What kind of citizen? the politics of educating for democracy. *American Educational Research Journal, 41*(2), 237–269.

Music and Protest
Dissecting and Creating Social and Political Music

Michael W. McFarland

> Movements begin when some pivotal individual or group—suffering attitudes of alienation in a given social system and drawn (consciously or unconsciously) by the impious dream of mythic Order—enacts and gives voice to a No.
> —Leland M. Griffin (1969)

In the spring of 2012, my family and I attended a Bruce Springsteen and the E Street Band concert in Tampa, Florida, as part of their "Wrecking Ball" tour. The concert was at the Tampa Bay Times Forum, the home of the Tampa Bay Lightning hockey team. I confess we did not have great seats, especially considering the venue. The forum is a site where the seats are significantly raked. There is a good and a bad to that set-up. The good is that even if you are in what is often called the "nose bleed" section, you are not, in one sense, significantly far from the stage. On the other hand, the angle of the stands means you are high up and the rows are necessarily close together. There is not a lot of room to stand, and the drop-off to the floor is always present in a person's mind. There is a lot of standing at a Springsteen show and I felt almost as I had to hold on to keep from tumbling down to the arena floor.

The lack of room to stand became very noticeable when Springsteen played his eighth song of the night, "Jack of All Trades." It is a song about the economic downturn crisis of 2008. In the song, a man out of work is desperate to provide for his family. It is a quiet song—not an anthem. However, when Springsteen got to a line in the final verse that suggests that if the narrator had a gun, he would shoot bankers on sight, the crowd stood and roared its approval. We found ourselves standing as well. This was quite awkward. First, because of the lack of leg space and our high position in the hall, we felt wobbly and a bit disoriented. But, in addition, I began to wonder exactly what we were standing and cheering for. I thought to myself, this is an interesting moment, where the political and social power of the song is connecting with the audience and garnering support for an act that no one (surely) there understood or agreed with. Nor did the performer presumably—he was singing in the voice of the song's protagonist. Springsteen was in his stance as the working man's voice, and the crowd probably did feel a sense of alienation with the elite. The line in the song was noted as being received positively during the tour. An anonymous commenter (SameOldShawn, 2012) on genius.com wrote on the line in the song that seems to call for violence toward bankers, "As a measure of peoples' feelings towards the 1% these days, note that this line in particular has been getting thunderous response in performances on Springsteen's spring 2012 American tour" (comment on lyrical line). The power of the moment was both disconcerting and overwhelming. In that instant, I thought about both the force of a crowd and the mythic quality of music. I went back to campus and began creating a new course.

My class at Stetson University is called *Music and Protest* and is an outgrowth of classes I have taught over the years on protest, rhetoric, and social movements. The class, with a cap of 18, is a 300-level course in the Communication and Media Studies Department, and is mostly populated by communication students who do not come from a music background. In other words, "regular" students. Students generally enter the course enthusiastically, primarily because it is about music and, perhaps, sounds fun. Most students, however, do not have a particularly good understanding of music from an academic or musical perspective. They like music, and want to discuss music, but they are not necessarily inclined toward careful consideration of the sounds, rhythms and melodies of music and lyrical interpretation of a song. In addition, they like what they like, and are not always ready to listen and discuss music of different eras and genres.

In *Music and Protest*, we look at music, protest, and their interrelationship. The class focuses primarily on American protest and music of the last one hundred years—but mostly beginning in the 1930s. This is primarily a choice of convenience and time as a 15-week semester does not allow for much more breadth than that. But, we do examine the beginning of blues, jazz, popular music, rock, folk, country, and hip-hop. The consideration of music used as protest becomes increasingly packed as we move through the last century to today—economics, civil rights, anti-war, immigration all become fuel for the creation of social movements and songs with rhetorical content. Our purpose is to critically investigate and analyze significant public discourse as it takes musical form, and relates to protests of varying kinds.

We look at the topic theoretically to a degree, but our chief focus is on the critical view of the subject.

Music and Protest has become one of my favorite classes to teach. It is not, however, without trial. The academic and analytical response required of the student who shows up in the class without significant practice or background in the topic is daunting. The class requires that I teach some level of rhetorical criticism, social history, musical history, and musical theory. I am not a musical historian or theorist. What I am is a longtime gigging musician and a trained rhetorical social critic. I suspect some combination of the above is necessary to lead students down this particular road. In this essay, I will explore the issues related to teaching about music to non-music students, and the ways in which music can be created and performed in the service of attempting to change the world. I will first briefly look at the rhetoric of social movements, the rhetoric of music, and then look at the way the class is structured to reach those goals.

Rhetoric and the Rhetoric of Protest

Music and Protest is centered around the concept of rhetoric. A full discussion of rhetoric is not warranted or possible in this essay. Nor, in the class itself. My main goal at the beginning of the semester is to acquaint students with the basic underpinnings of the field. What is rhetoric? What does it do? How do we understand the world rhetorically? Those enquiries could be an entire semester (and in fact are). In the perfect world we dream about, all students enter our classes with full background knowledge of the subject matter in preparation for what they will learn in the course, but naturally, this does not occur. A semester does not allow me the luxury to review the history of rhetoric, or the many applications and benefits of understanding rhetoric and rhetorical criticism before beginning a discussion of protest music. What I do is attempt to open the door to this knowledge and give them a platform upon which to build.

I begin with a definition of what I mean by the term rhetoric. My blended understanding is that rhetoric is symbolic persuasion that occurs when a communicator presents a message to create an effect in an audience. In other words, the rhetor (speaker, leader, singer) attempts to move the audience from one position to another, or to solidify a position and move to action. Rhetorical acts may therefore have instrumental, symbolic and symbolic action goals. Examples of such rhetoric include advertisements, political speeches and campaigns, cultural and social movements, with symbolic acts that range from holding signs at a protest march to acts of destruction such as war and terrorism.

There are three basic goals of student understanding during the beginning section of the course. My first goal is for students to understand what rhetoric means and see it as part of our human condition. Then, my goal is to help them understand how rhetoric fits within the framework of changing people's minds and changing the world, or portions of it. Because this is a communication course, it needs to address how rhetoric works in a general way before understanding how it works more specifically with music.

I begin with the notion of the varying degrees, or a scale, of rhetoric that starts with pure logic where reason is enough to get people to change their minds. The scale then moves through the idea of what Richard Weaver (2009) terms "truth plus artful presentation" (p. 15). By that he means the clever or artistic packaging of a truthful claim. What is truth is a question for a different time. However, here the idea is that this type of rhetoric does not attempt to change reality by embellishing it, but instead creates art out of that truth. This makes the claim more likely to be listened to, while still maintaining an ethics of rhetoric. A clear example of argument that is skillful with such artistic flourish is Martin Luther King's "I Have a Dream" speech in 1963. In it, he argues for a redefinition of the American Dream. The speech transcends the particular logical discourse of the moment and moves into a mythic, almost musical quality, especially as the speech reaches its apotheosis. Controlled repetition, word choice, metaphor, and soaring delivery create not only an emotional release for the audience, but serves to help the listener make sense of King's overall social and political message.

After exploring Weaver's notion of rhetoric as "truth plus artful presentation," we move to emotional appeals (for example, animal rescue fundraising), manipulation (deceptive advertisements), propaganda (Nazi and Soviet posters), threats (terrorists' demands), and finally to direct force (bombings and such). Finally, I would like students to see how the above applies to areas outside of the traditional—either as symbolic action (for example, environmental activists chaining themselves to a tree) or, in the case of this course, music. I also make it clear that by music I mean both the music and the lyrics. I want to make sure that they know that the course is not just lyric analysis.

Once we have established a framework for understanding the basic principles of rhetoric, the course turns to social movements and social protest. We discuss questions such as, what is a social movement, how do they function, and how do they live and die? Leland Griffin's (1952) seminal work on rhetorical movements is our guide to that understanding.

In Griffin's first work on movements, he points out that movements go through the stages of inception, precipitating event/crisis, and consummation (p. 186). Movements come and go. There may be a natural feel to them at times, but they are constructed. Constructed often out of a felt necessity, but constructed nonetheless. Since this course focuses on protest, the types of movements might be mostly categorized as resistance movements. A resistance social movement seeks to block changes, or to fight back against the status quo. Examples of such movements include the battle for equal rights, anti-war movements, the fight against abortion rights, and so forth.

What Griffin calls inception is the pre-period of a movement when the stew of history cooks, and waits. Out of that inception period, a crisis either occurs or is sometimes orchestrated. A well-known and tragic example occurred on May 4, 1970, when four students were shot and killed during an anti-war protest at Kent State University. There were many protests and counter protests that came from that event, but in class we discuss the writing and recording of Neil Young's "Ohio." Recorded by Crosby, Stills, Nash and Young, and released as a single in 1970, a live version was then included on their 1971 album *4 Way Street*. The song represented a musical pushback to what was seen by some as violent government overreach and it helped push the anti-war movement forward (Lynskey, 2011). As people begin to react to, and say no to the status quo, a discourse or an act is called for. Music can function here as a call to change within an existing order. The consummation of a movement occurs either when the movement cannot hold together because its desires are met, or perhaps more often, discouragement and complacency returns. Not everything can be solved by discourse, and certainly not everything can be solved by protest music. Sometimes, as the students say, a song is just a song,

Protest music, however, can linger far longer than the context it was built upon, and the nature of the discourse moves from a call for action into nostalgia. Or, they are reformed and reconstructed. For instance, Bob Dylan's 1964 anthem "The Times They Are a-Changin'," with its call to make way for a new generation, was recently performed live by Jennifer Hudson at the anti-gun rally March for Our Lives in Washington, D.C. (Kreps, 2018).

Protest and the Form of Music

When we reach the point in the semester where we are comfortable talking about the rhetorical nature of protest, we turn our attention to music. As a musician and songwriter myself, and a rhetorical critic, I focus regularly on the power of music in my own life and the life of my students. The first substantive questions on music I ask the class are, "Why do we care about music?" and "Why is music powerful to you?" It will surprise no one reading this essay that these are difficult questions to answer. Additionally, it is no surprise that we do not satisfactorily answer them during the course.

In his book *33 Revolutions Per Minute*, writer Dorian Lynskey (2011)

opens his book with a quotation from folk singer Phil Ochs, "As bad as it may sound, I'd rather listen to a good song on the side of segregation than a bad song on the side of integration" (p. vii). It is a pithy statement, but a good warning. Music is powerful on its own decoupled from its place as political discourse. Students admit that they often do not even know what a song they like is about, even though they have listened to it countless times. For a song to work as a social force and protest, it needs to work well as popular music of the day, as well as present a message that is dynamically connected to the argument. Ochs' statement is a warning that though music might be used in service to an idea, it must bring its own quality as a song if it is to have worth.

Neil Young has a similar, though somewhat different, take on the musical quality behind the message. Discussing political songs in a 2008 interview, *Don't Be Denied—A Documentary*, he said:

> A melody that everybody already knows, that's how you get in their head. They've got the melody and you've got the words. You put the words to the melody and they start whistling along, and they go "Oh, I know that!" and they start singing the words.... It makes it easy for people to sing the same thing over again [Whaley, 2008].

Of course, not all protest songs use simple known melodies. He admits that sometimes he uses difficult melodies in order to make the listener a bit angry. And then, some songs use beauty and gentle melodies to surround their ideas.

In my class, I like to use the example of the song "What's Going On," the 1971 release from Motown recording artist Marvin Gaye. The song was a radio hit and functions artistically in that era as a commentary about the Vietnam War, civil rights, and a call for civility and understanding. Decades later the song's meaning transcends the 1970s as "What's Going On" can be listened to as a tune, or a social plea for justice, or both. Of course, quality is a value whose meaning is not necessarily shared by all, and commercial jingles have taught us that staying power is not always correlated with quality. That said, the music should generally have some musical worth for it to capture the minds and hearts of the listeners.

If the particular music has that musical worth to the listener (or seems to), however, it might escalate and transcend traditional political and social rhetoric. Music often has different meanings to different people, and is not necessarily as easily verified as other types of discourse. In "Religious and Poetical Speaking" Hans-Georg Gadamer (1980) compares religious language and music stating, "In music we find a similar hovering feeling of vagueness and significance" (p. 94). It is Gadamer's understanding that we know that music has certain laws and rules, "but at the same time music retains a certain floating wordlessness" (p. 94). In other words, music has a certain "liberty of interpretation" (p. 94).

An example of this power is the song by Mathangi "Maya" Arulpragasam, who goes by the stage name of M.I.A. (Ray, 2010). The song "Paper Planes" was a hit in 2007 through 2009, and a Grammy nominee for Record of the Year for 2008. My students know the song, but mostly as a dance track, and not the critique/commentary on immigration the lyrics convey. The importance of this example is the way the song is used in the immigration debate. M.I.A. argues against anti-immigration by seemingly arguing against immigration. There are a variety of points here, but the song seems to be suggesting that all immigrants want is "your" money. But, M.I.A. is a British-born Sri Lankan, an activist, and her lyrics are ridicule. *Rolling Stone* called the song "a shot at immigrant-fearing Westerners" (Goodman, 2016, par. 8). However, there is no developed argument, and removed from its musical context it makes almost no point at all. "Paper Planes" can be read in a variety of ways, but its power comes from a combination of its lyrics, beat, tone, and projected authenticity of its rhetor, M.I.A. As Michael Drewett (2007) points out, "Songs are an interwoven combination of lyrics, voice, music, style, and other factors too, such as social and political context and perhaps dynamics of stage performance where this is relevant" (p. 41). And, this is especially true for the protest song.

As the semester progresses, I give some mini-histories and explanations of the varying types of music that inform the protest song. This is not a history of popular music course, but I have found that I need to incorporate some history so that the students begin to understand where musical styles come from, and how interconnected they are with social issues in the United States. For instance, we look at the genre of jazz. Jazz is examined because it sets up and flows as a stream into the popular music of the day, from the 1920s through the 1950s and onward. I want students to understand the role of jazz in creating much of popular music as the century progresses.

With some exceptions, jazz is not typically discussed as a type of protest music. There is a clear reason for this lack of examination. It is often non-lyrical, and even when there are words they were rarely political. When lyrics were present, they were generally of a traditional kind, love songs primarily. There are exceptions. A song such as Billie Holiday's 1939 recording of "Strange Fruit," which mournfully comments on the lynching of African Americans, is a clear protest song, and would certainly fit the genre (Meeropol, 1937). Most jazz songs, though, do not have lyrical content, and thus seem less enticing to rhetorical critics drawn to dissect discourse. However, I point to non-lyrical examples, such as jazz drummer Art Blakey's move in the late 1940s to a more tribal or African drumming style in the 1950s and 1960s as a way of reclaiming an African history and a heightened social position. Tribal drumming generally has a stronger use of the toms (and fewer cymbals and snare use) and more polyrhythms in the beat than standard Western popular music. Some examples of Blakey's more African style would include "A Night in Tunisia" (1961), "Afrique" (1961), and "Ayiko Ayiko" (1962) (McFarland, 2018). This music occasionally had a more direct rhetorical message such as "A Message from Kenya" (1955), recorded in the aftermath of the Mau Mau uprising in Kenya, but often it was simply the presentation of African influenced American music in a style that projected strength and virtuosity by African American musicians. The Modern Jazz Quartet, formed in the early 1950s, had a dignified approach to the art and as such is another example of music and presentation that could be seen as symbolic arguments of equality (Rupp, 2011). And, if the idea of protest is expanded to include such ideas as social standing, the elevation of African American musicians to virtuoso status in the post-war era is a significant moment of protest against the status quo. John Squinobal, in his dissertation, *West African Music in the Music of Art Blakey, Yusef Lateef, and Randy Weston* (2009) explains:

> For too long African Americans had been subverted into the lower social caste and were unable to elevate themselves in white America's social system. By rejecting white American cultural traits for their own African traditional cultural roots, they hoped to gain equality. Though it may have been considered primitive and savage, in the eyes of white America, it was their own identity and it set them apart and imparted them with pride and individuality [p. 92].

In *Music and Protest*, we also cover genres such as blues, rhythm and blues, country, folk, rock, punk and hip-hop. Performers include people such as the aforementioned Billie Holiday, Woody Guthrie, Pete Seeger, Bob Dylan, Sam Cooke, Nina Simone, Marvin Gaye, Gil Scott-Heron, the Clash, Sex Pistols, NWA, Public Enemy, and many others. Specific songs will generally include: Woody Guthrie's "This Land Is Your Land" (1940, recorded 1944), Billie Holiday's "Strange Fruit" (1937, recorded in 1939), Bob Dylan's "Masters of War" (1963), Barry McGuire's "Eve of Destruction" (1964), NWA's "F** tha Police" (1988), and Green Day's "American Idiot" (2004), to name a few.

My usual method is to work through a type of music and highlight various protest songs from the genre. Then we move to a representative song of the category outlining the political and social context to which the song is a rhetorical answer. Before we listen to the song the lyrics are handed out and the students mark up the sheet in the same manner that they would be instructed to attack any piece of political discourse. They account for the message, the style—word choice, repetition, phrasing, and overall content—and what problem the song is trying to address. An example here is the Woody Guthrie song mentioned above, "This Land is Your Land" (1940) as a representative folk protest song. The class session consists of information on Guthrie, a little on the era (the Great Depression, the war years), how the song functions as folk music, and its creation as a direct counterpoint to Kate Smith's recording of Irving Berlin's "God Bless America" (1938).

At this point, I ask them if they know the Woody Guthrie song. They often do not recognize the earlier songs I choose, but in this particular case, they usually do because they sang it in elementary school. With "This Land Is Your Land" even though they have heard the song they often have not heard all the words, or realized its social context. They think of it simply as another patriotic school song, and not as a damning critique of capitalistic America. For those songs they do not know, I ask them to imagine what the song might sound like—tempo, instrumentation, melody. Students next brainstorm what they would imagine the most effective presentation of the particular message would be. What would the music sound like? How would they think it would be performed? The discussion that follows is designed for the students to create an understanding of discourse construction in the form of art and music.

Finally, we listen to the recording (in this case "This Land Is Your Land") to see the creative result of the writer and performer. Here we talk on effectiveness of presentation and effectiveness of the message. What happened to the problem, to the movement? Did the song have any lasting impact as a song and/or as rhetoric? What could be reasonably expected?

Assignments

The specific goals at this point of the course are to bring to the surface the power of music in the student's life in a social context, to become aware of some of the rich history of popular music in America, and to explore some examples of the use of music to further a protest agenda. Indirectly, I want to further students' research, organization, and presentation skills. Since this is a communication class, students should have a direct communication experience. In addition, I want students to individually delve deeply into subject matter and learn about a particular song(s) and movement as a case study. Each student chooses a song that has a protest/social movement function centered in a point in time. Lynskey (2011) is helpful in guiding students to possible protest songs, but students are encouraged to find their own topics, songs and examples. The assignment here is to research the song as music, and the events that called the song(s), the discourse, into being. The report must include the song description, the context/event, the writer, the performer(s), and the result(s). Paul Friedlander in *Rock & Roll: A Social History* (2006) guides students in breaking down the music. His categories for understanding are: music, lyrics, artist history, and societal context. For instance, under the category of music he asks the critic to look for instrumentation, rhythm, vocal style, and the like. Some of these questions are beyond most of my students' current understanding (such as identifying harmonic structure), but even if they are unable to completely recognize the intricacies of the category it helps them hone in on the various elements of the song. The students slow down their experience, and begin to listen more closely to the music to hear the layers of complexity (or the lack thereof) in what they are examining. And, they begin to ask questions about what makes it music, what it makes it art.

For their final paper, students are asked to extend their case study and examine/analyze a particular performer, writer, or movement. It is meant to be a social movement critique of the musical rhetoric of a moment of protest. In a recent class, students examined a range of material including musical responses to events surrounding Black Lives Matter and police brutality, the musical response to the war in Iraq, late 1960s anti-war songs, songs dealing with Irish independence, gender equality, liberals in country music, just to name a few.

Moving from Critique to Creation

The final part of the semester deals with a creative response to social and political issues and is actualized in group work. The final project where students create their own protest music might be the most interesting part of the course. As a reminder, this course is in the Communication and Media Studies department, not the School of Music. Therefore, most students are not likely to be musicians.

The goals for this long assignment are to open students up creatively to a type of discourse in which they are generally not conversant (protest music), to help them not to be stuck in infinite critique, and to understand the subject matter from the inside of the creative endeavor as opposed to breaking things apart from an outsider's view. When this assignment is discussed on the first day of class, the fear is palpable (tinged with some cool excitement). Over the years I have given this type of assignment in different kinds of courses on a semi-regular basis (for instance, having non-production students create short films in a course that is essentially film criticism). Teaching criticism is a pleasure, as it opens the student's mind to a new world of understanding. But, it is not without some peril. Students can become so fixated on criticism that they cannot simply enjoy the art. Their critical training might reduce their ability to do anything else. And so, I want them to be able to connect with the creative process in themselves, as well as experiencing an attempt to create within the type of discourse they are being asked to critique.

We return to the problem of musicianship. What can we do when, almost assuredly, the members of the class do not have that talent in abundance? I spend some time reassuring students that the grade for the assignment is not based on the quality of their finished product, but on their attention to detail, in their ability to use available technology, and their clarity of purpose in creating a discourse (i.e., protest song) that furthers their group's political and social agenda. So first, I conduct a survey of students to find out their musical abilities, experience and desires. For instance, a student might have low experience in recording, but might have a strong desire to learn and participate in the activity. Explicit in the instructions is the warning for the students to not over- or understate their abilities. I attempt to separate the students with musical or recording ability into separate groups so that one group is not favored. Group size is kept to four or five, depending the size of the class.

The assignment is given at the beginning of the semester and the groups are created by the second week. They then have the rest of the term to write and produce a protest song that tackles a current social or political idea that the group wants to counter. I would prefer for them to tackle issues of importance, but some gravitate to more local campus issues, for instance campus dining options. And while I am sometimes disappointed in their reach, I believe it is important for the group to find what they are comfortable in protesting. Students have tackled topics such as campus parking, gender identification, the environment, and the election of Donald Trump.

After selecting an issue to address, they then research and consolidate their idea on the problem they are tackling. At this point, students begin the process of song writing, song preparation, recording, and creating a simple video accompaniment. As they begin the process, I give some explanation of rhythm, chord progressions and rhyming schemes.

The great equalizer for the musical ability necessary for this assignment is technology. This is what makes this assignment work for these types of students. Many if not most students have, or can easily acquire, GarageBand or something similar on their phones, tablets, or computers, or by using the software installed on the computers in our departmental lab (Android has similar types of applications). By using this software, they can create music. In other words, instead of playing the guitar, they program the computer to play the guitar. The software also has beats, loops and chord progressions. It works quite well. There are more complete digital audio workstations (DAW) available, and students may use them if they are comfortable doing so. With any type of music software, however, there is obviously a learning curve. Consequently, we spend a class session learning the basics of the software and as a class, we write a simple song together.

Although it is not a requirement, I suggest that students create their music first because it is generally easier to write words to match music than vice versa. During this period, I encourage them to try to pick music that fits with the song's message and find a style (e.g., country, folk, hip-hop) they believe reflects the persuasive intent and appeals to the intended audience. At the end of the semester, we have a mini-music festival where the students screen their song with accompanying simple videos, and we discuss and evaluate them as both music and protest rhetorical discourse. You can sense the pride in their creations.

Conclusion

As mentioned, *Music and Protest* has become one of my favorite classes to teach. I remain convinced that the blending of the creative and the critical helps students from sinking into a nitpicky, overly critical mindset. At the same time, the tools of critique they learn are powerful and useful in all manner of applications. Naturally, all of my many goals are not met by every student (perhaps no student). I do believe, however, that students leave with a solid foundation of rhetoric, and what it means to critique alternative forms of discourse. In addition, they have been exposed to the history and social significance of music, and specifically protest music, and given the chance to create rhetorical artifacts (i.e., songs, designed to say no to power [great and small] when appropriate).

Along the way, students learn about the power that music has on the world, and on them. In civil society, we hope that such actions as Springsteen's protagonist in "Jack of All Trades" contemplates remain metaphorical. However, we also hope that our students are willing to rise up to say no to the existing order when the hurricane blows.

REFERENCES

Armstrong, B.J. (2004). American idiot. On *American idiot*. Reprise Records.
Arulpragasam, M. (2007). Paper planes. On *Kayla*. XL Interscope.
Berlin, I. (1918). *God bless America*. Performed by Kate Smith (1938).
Bitzer, L. (1968). The rhetorical situation. *Philosophy of Rhetoric, 1*(1), 1–14.
Blakey, A. (1955). A message from Kenya. On *Horace Silver Trio and Art Blakey—Sabu*. Blue Note Records.
Brigance, L.C. (2002). Persuasion and protest music, *Communication Teacher, 16*(3), 7–9
Burke, K.B. (1954). *Permanence and change: An anatomy of purpose*. Berkeley, CA: University of California Press.
Crosby, Stills, Nash & Young. (1971). *4 way street*. Atlantic Records.
Drewett, M. (2003). The eyes of the world are watching now: The political effectiveness of "Biko" by Peter Gabriel. *Popular Music and Society, 30*(1), 39–51.
Dylan, B. (1963). Masters of War. On *The freewheelin' Bob Dylan*. Columbia Records.
Dylan, B. (1964). The times they are a-changin'. On *The times they are a-changin'*. Columbia Records.
Friedlander, P. (2006). *Rock and roll: A social history* (2nd Ed.). Cambridge, MA: Routledge.

Gadamer, H-G. (1980). Religious and poetical speaking. In A. Olson (Ed.), *Myth, symbol and reality 1* (pp. 86–98). Notre Dame, IN: University of Notre Dame Press.

Gaye, M. (1971). What's Going On. On *What's going on*. Tamia Records.

Gillespie, D., & F. Paparelli (1942). Night in Tunisia. [Recorded by Art Blakey and the Jazz Messengers, 1961. On *Night in Tunisia*. Blue Note Records.]

Goodman, L. (2016) M.I.A.: The permanent revolution of pop's most fascinating radical. *Rolling Stone*. Retrieved from https://www.rollingstone.com/music/music-features/m-i-a-the-permanent-revolution-of-pops-most-fascinating-radical-248355/.

Griffin, L.M. (1952). The rhetoric of social movements. *Quarterly Journal of Speech*, 38(2), 184–188.

Griffin, L.M. (1969). A dramatistic theory of the rhetoric of movements. In W.H. Rueckert (Ed.), *Critical responses to Kenneth Burke 1924–1966* (pp. 456–478). Minneapolis: University of Minnesota Press.

Guthrie, W. (1940). This Land Is Your Land. Recorded (1944).

Ice Cube and MC Ren. (1988). F**k tha Police. On *Straight Outta Compton*. Ruthless Records.

King, M.L., Jr. I have a dream. August 28, 1963 [Speech transcript]. Retrieved from https://www.archives.gov/files/press/exhibits/dream-speech.pdf.

Kreps, D. (2018). See Jennifer Hudson's powerful Bob Dylan cover at March for Our Lives Rally. Retrieved from https://www.rollingstone.com/music/music-news/see-jennifer-hudsons-powerful-bob-dylan-cover-at-march-for-our-lives-rally-202446/.

Llori. (1962). Ayiko, ayiko (Welcome, welcome, my darling). On *The African beat*. [Recorded by Art Blakey and The Afro-Drum Ensemble]. Blue Note Records.

Lynskey, D. (2011). *33 Revolutions per minute: A history of protest songs, from Billie Holiday to Green Day*. New York: HarperCollins Publishers.

McFarland, M.W. (2018). Beats as rhetoric: Art Blakey, tribal rhythms, and the use of jazz as political and social protest in the 1950s and 60s. Southern Communication Association Convention, Nashville, TN.

Meeropol, A. (1937). Strange Fruit. [Recorded by Billie Holiday, 1939]. Commodore Records.

Morgan, L. (1961). Afrique. On *The witch doctor*. [Recorded by Art Blakey and the Jazz Messengers]. Blue Note Records.

Ray, M. (2010). M.I.A. British-born Sri Lankan rapper. In *Encyclopedia Britannica*. Retrieved from https://www.britannica.com/biography/MIA#ref1085090

Rupp, C.M. (2011). Respectability and the Modern Jazz Quartet; Some cultural aspects of its image and legacy as seen through the press. (Master's thesis). The City College of New York. Retrieved from http://academicworks.cuny.edu/cc_etds_theses/74?utm_source=academicworks.cuny.edu%2Fcc_etds_theses%2F74&utm_medium=PDF&utm_campaign=PDFCoverPages

SameOldShawn. (2012, April 6). Re: Jack of all trades lyrics [annotation]. Retrieved from https://genius.com/684425.

Sloan, P.F. (1964). Eve of destruction. [Recorded by Barry McGuire. 1965.] Dunhill Records.

Springsteen, B. (2012). Jack of all trades. On *Wrecking Ball*. Columbia Records.

Squinobal, J.J. (2009). African music in the music of Art Blakey, Yusef Lateef, and Randy Weston. (Doctoral dissertation). University of Pittsburgh. OCLC Number: 775369305.

Weaver, R. (2009). *The ethics of rhetoric*. New York: Routledge.

Weismann, D. (2010). *Talkin' bout a revolution: Music and social change in America*. Milwaukee, WI: Blackbear Books.

Whaley, B. (Producer & Director). (2008). *Don't be denied*. United Kingdom: BBC Four. Retrieved from https://youtu.be/l_tkfK-uKyE.

Young, N. (1970). Ohio. [Recorded 1970]. Atlantic Records.

Can Bro-Country Kill Your Parents?

Using Shifting Musical Taste to Explore the Relationship of Youth and Parent Cultures

CHARLES R. WARNER

Now that I am painfully aware that I occupy a position in that occupational category known as "senior faculty member," I find that one of the few joys in that reality is the opportunity to observe and compare multiple generations of young people engaged in the business of figuring out how to become adult. However, that joy is tempered in an interactive classroom setting by difficulties inherent to age difference. The students are always youthful. I, and my storehouse of cultural references, continue to age. Overcoming this student-professor age gap is a constant pedagogical concern when teaching coursework dealing with popular culture, an academic discipline in which relevant reference points seem to have the shelf life of whole milk.

At one level, combating this problem is simply a matter of maintaining currency, which should be considered a professional responsibility each time one prepares to teach such coursework. Yet, focusing exclusively on being informationally up-to-date runs the risk of turning the course into little more than a time-sensitive trivia contest—one which the comparatively ancient professor is destined to lose. In order to avoid this fate and to preserve some sense of disciplinary standards and historical continuity, I have found maintaining a classroom focus on conceptual knowledge to be an absolute necessity. Concepts endure, and any fleeting repository of experiential knowledge gleaned from the current cultural moment can be used to exemplify a concept, thereby allowing even the hippest student in the room to view that concept as relevant to their own lived experience.

Killing Your Parents: What a Concept!

As a case study of this method, I will discuss a concept I have introduced to students for more than 20 years in a course titled *Popular Music as Cultural Text*, which explores the use of popular music as a signifying practice for youth culture. When discussing the emergence of rock and roll in the 1950s, I invariably refer to this music as a means of distancing the relatively new sociological phenomenon of youth culture from the traditional cultural realm of the parent. Stated more provocatively, as a music genre that contradicted the cultural status quo both aesthetically and thematically, rock and roll established itself as a vehicle through which youth might metaphorically "kill their parents," thereby opening a space for exploring alternative cultural models. As someone who entered their own adolescence in the late 1960s, I find this topic fascinating, in no small part because I lived a version of it and it played a major role in my own personal development. I understand how my students might not fully share my enthusiasm, since for them it bears the taint of that boring thing called history that is all about stuff before they were born and the world began. Still, my course is about music, something that plays a major role in a young person's life regardless of generation, so my students always managed to find a good deal of relevance in the discussion of this concept. Until recently.

Over the last ten years or so, I have noticed a rapid decline in the number of my students who identify as fans of anything that might be labeled rock and roll, even in the broadest, most genre-inclusive sense of the term. Of course, there are always a few metalheads or Jack White enthusiasts, but every year, they are fewer and farther between. The ascent of hip-hop to mainstream cultural status surely accounts for the bulk of this attrition. The notion that coolness somehow originated in African American cultural expression before being appropriated at-large is itself a fascinating and time-honored concept in American popular culture. So, while the increasing dominance of hip-hop should come as little surprise, what is surprising is the genre that seems to account for the remainder of this shift in musical taste away from rock—country music. A decade ago, I could barely get a single student to admit they listened to it—there may have been some closeted country fans in there, but declaring it publicly in class would have been tantamount to a form of social suicide reserved for only the most tragically uncool. Now, it stands as a significant genre preference—and this at a university in eastern Pennsylvania, which features a student body heavily drawn from the seemingly un-country Philadelphia and New York metro areas. As a result, I now have a somewhat different issue to discuss with these students: what accounts for this shift in youth culture musical taste and, perhaps more importantly, is country music capable of performing the cultural work that rock and roll has performed for youth culture since its inception? In other words, can country music kill your parents?

Not Country, Bro—Bro-Country

To simply state that my students have developed a preference for country music would be painting with too broad a brush. As an indigenous American music with a history as deep as America itself, country music's evolutionary complexity is something my students seem relatively uninterested in. Rather, their taste runs to a subgenre minted within the last decade often referred to as bro-country. Featuring relative newcomers including Blake Shelton, Jason Aldean, and Luke Bryan, bro-country quickly became a cash cow for the Nashville establishment. At first blush, this bro-country variant might seem to share much in common with traditional mainstream country music. Like the culture of the American South from which it springs, traditional mainstream country has always reflected conservatism, a working-class sensibility, and an operational connection between human goodness and dedication to "the land."

But as a music largely made by and for Southern white males, traditional mainstream country contained fatal limitations that were unmasked by profound and rapid changes in American society in the late-twentieth and twenty-first centuries. Its central focus, the opposition of urban v. rural value systems, was easily and often mapped onto narratives of racial difference which not only chafed against a rising tide of racial equality, but also served to limit the music's audience and commercial viability. As a result, attempts have been made to minimize this opposition for some time now—the bland and suburb-friendly countrypolitan variant of the 1970s is an early example, featuring tales of love, work, and nuclear family bliss that attempted to transcend geography and enable nationwide radio airplay.

Culture critic Joshua Clover (2014a) sees bro-country burying this urban/rural opposition differently, by establishing an all-inclusive party zone where everyone is welcome, regardless of zip code. A newfound multicultural and multiracial acceptance becomes a natural consequence of this open invitation for a good time, mirroring the demographic realities of twenty-first century America, and allowing musical inflections borrowed from hip-hop and other urban genres to pepper the country music foundation of many bro-country songs. And it can't be a party without some chicks! Female artists have thrived in tandem with this bro-country environment with explorations of realities unheard of in traditional country—consider Kasey Musgraves' "Follow Your Arrow," a song that stands as something of a country companion piece to "I Kissed a Girl," Katy Perry's pop ode to same-sex experimentation. It might be called bro-country, but bros today are down with that sort of thing.

Class Discussion I: Regional Culture and Regional Music

Classroom discussion of bro-country as a new means of burying the urban/rural opposition of traditional country music has revealed a rather surprising perception common to my students: any significant difference between urban and rural culture as a distinction informing country music is simply not on their radar. When I refer to country music as "Southern music," students are routinely confused by the regional reference—"What do you mean by 'Southern music?' I live in New Jersey, and I've been listening to country all my life." Of course, they understand the physical difference between the city, the suburbs, and the sticks. Still, any attempt I might make to map the urban/rural distinction on top of historical developmental differences of North and South in American culture always seems to result in lots of head-scratching and confused looks. Attempts at discussing country music as an additional extension of this geographical and cultural difference has only resulted in additional confusion.

While having this discussion is, at times, uncomfortable, I find it to be an essential starting point for examining the appeal of bro-country among my students. Confusion quickly turns into comprehension as students reveal that they do not view country music as "Southern" music at all. To do so would chafe against their perception of living in one modern, unified American culture. Indeed, this discussion reveals that virtually all my students, regardless of personal musical preference, regard all popular music as simply "American" music, transcending any outdated notion of regional specificity. I have come to consider this class discussion a starting point for a brief but necessary review of cultural distinctions between North and South in American history, which can then lead to a better understanding of corresponding musical differences.

For example, discussing the music of Alabama-born Hank Williams had always been problematic. A central figure in country music's history, Williams recorded over 30 top ten country hits in a remarkably brief career as a national recording artist from 1947 to 1952. Despite his prodigious popularity, he had always been dismissed by my students as a somewhat irrelevant, twangy relic of the past. However, dedicating a bit of class time to discussing this urban/rural, North/South, historical/cultural complex has allowed my students to view Williams' tragic personal life as an analog of the decay of Southern culture, poignantly expressed through his music. Much like the South and its twin legacies of agrarian poverty and slavery, Williams was burdened at birth with the seeds of his own personal tragedy—spina bifida, leading to a lifetime of crippling back pain, leading to self-medication with the drink and drugs that would end his life at age 29. And, much like the South, Williams approached such horrid curses with an ambivalent resilience and an inexplicable, fatalistic irony. Indeed, who but Williams could make "Move It On Over"—his first national hit in 1947 about being forced to sleep with his dog after his wife kicks him out of the house—into an up-tempo celebration? And, after producing a songbook chronicling a life of failed relationships and personal torment, is it at all surprising that the last single he gave us before his death was titled "I'll Never Get Out of This World Alive?" In addition to introducing my students to an artist as fascinating and troubling as Southern culture itself, this discussion has also allowed them to view the bro-country they love through a different contextual lens, one that acknowledges it as an index of an increasingly nationalized culture, and not just music that sonically resonates with their more modern tastes. From that point, the class is primed to deal with bro-country not just as music, but as a rich and meaningful cultural text.

Bro-Country's Drinking Problem

The bro-country ethic of inclusive free expression in service to a no-holds-barred good time goes a long way toward explaining why bro-country is a growing musical preference for college students. It is country music that deemphasizes dreary laments about that job at the factory in favor of an endless fraternity party. As long as that red Solo cup is full, it is easy to look past differences of gender, sexual orientation, race, and class. However, that full red Solo cup also portends an uncomfortable hangover for bro-country.

Throughout much of the music's brief history, it has been something of an open secret that bro-country has a drinking problem. Forcing that problem into the public consciousness in the summer of 2011 was an incident at a Tim McGraw concert in Mansfield, Massachusetts, in which 19-year-old Michael Skehill was beaten so badly by a fellow concertgoer that he had to have his spleen surgically removed. Reflecting on the incident, the Mansfield Police Chief remarked that "country used to be an easy night for us. Now it is anything but. Country's just changed. I'm a country fan, but the music and the singers have a party motif about them now. It's all about drinking" (Trigger, 2011, para. 3). Demonstrating that this was no isolated incident, a Kenny Chesney concert in June 2013 at Pittsburgh's Heinz Field resulted in 73 arrests—49 during the performance and 24 during a post-concert brawl. Alcohol-fueled anarchy became so common on the tour that a roadie for supporting act Eric Church renamed it the "Fucking and Fighting Tour" in reference to the almost ritual occurrence of brawling and public sexual behavior among fans (Trigger, 2013). One year later, a replay of that mayhem occurred at the same venue, this time at a concert headlined by bro-country stars Luke Bryan and Dierks Bentley, resulting in public safety officials issuing 20 citations for underage drinking, breaking up 15 fights, escorting 34 people to area hospitals, and responding to at least 150 emergency calls (Trigger, 2014a). One month later, providing more evidence that this may be less a random crowd phenomenon than a possible emergent local tradition, a replay of the 2011 Mansfield, Massachusetts, debacle during a Keith Urban concert resulted in 55 arrests, 46 medical incidents, and 22 fans transported to hospitals, many for treatment due to excessive alcohol consumption. So overwhelming was the situation that the Mansfield Fire Department declared the concert to be a "mass casualty event" in order to solicit the help of first responders from at least five surrounding communities and a number of private ambulance contractors (Trigger, 2014b). While Urban's music tends to deemphasize heavy drinking and the fighting it often fuels, the majority of bro-country artists frequently portray alcohol-soaked aggressive behavior as the default mode of social interaction in their lyrics. It is, inarguably, one of the music's defining themes.

Of course, lyrical themes of drinking and fighting are nothing new in country music, but the bro-country attitude of gleeful approval of such behaviors might be. When Hank Williams or Johnny Cash sang of drunkenness and the violence it can lead to, they often did so in the context of cautionary tales of sorrow and remorse over the tragically scarred lives they lived as a result of those indiscretions. By contrast, bro-country lyrics and the fan behavior modeled on them arrive as a celebration of the thoughtless youthful emergence of the pre-socialized Id. No wonder so many of my students use it as a soundtrack for their lives! However, caution must be exercised so as not to alienate those bro-country fans in class by blaming such antisocial behavior on the music they love. Citing an equivalence with past complaints about rock and roll and hip-hop, country music historian Don Cusic insists, "it's not the music that creates the problem. It might be the soundtrack while the problem is happening, but really, it's young people who tend to get a little wild and crazy" (Yahr, 2014, para. 19). Still, it is worth noting that when youth-oriented genres like hip-hop work this type of hardline machismo, parental advisory warnings invariably follow. Not so with bro-country. So, while bro-country's public excesses seem to provide a sheen of naughty, transgressive danger capable of violating the norms of a safe and secure cultural status quo, it is just not the same thing I experienced in my rock and roll youth. There just seems to be something different at work here.

Class Discussion II: Bro-Country, Binge Drinking and Rape Culture

It is not difficult to detect some intersection of this aspect of bro-country with current debates regarding binge drinking and rape culture so common on college campuses today, and that connection routinely results in the most lively class discussion of the semester. Students are quite eager to proudly express their opinions regarding the centrality of alcohol to their collegiate lifestyles. However, that pride is not so much rooted in their individual experience with inebriation, but rather in their sense of carrying on a cultural tradition that they perceive as quintessentially American. What remains unspoken is the obvious clash between their amusing tales of drunken American debauchery, and their current experience with mandatory university indoctrination focused on preventing such behavior. Highlighting this source of potential cognitive dissonance becomes the professor's responsibility, and it often leads to any number of fascinating revelations regarding campus life, student attitudes, and how bro-country might inform them. For instance, when asked if the causal relationship between drinking and sexual assault, so central to educational efforts to curb both conflicts with the bro-country ethic, fans of the music roundly deny any connection. As one student with a fondness for self-disclosure put it, "Please, catching a buzz at a concert doesn't make me a rapist!" The implication, expressed by both male and female students in similar numbers, is that sexual assault is simply intolerable but has virtually nothing to do with alcohol consumption.

Invariably, this classroom discussion allows for a number of probing questions to emerge from my side of the podium that might reveal the impact of bro-country on youth culture:

> In light of your resistance to university efforts to temper your alcohol use, has bro-country and its celebration of drinking become your generation's transgressive music? If so, is that similar to how drug references informed your parents' transgressive rock music back in the day? As marijuana becomes more socially acceptable, has your parents' rock music lost its transgressive power? Since a rough equivalence of acceptance for both alcohol and marijuana is emerging for both youth culture and your parents' culture, do you even want to kill the cultural authority of your parents anymore? Is the educational emphasis on alcohol as the forbidden problematic substance shifting the youth culture target from your parents to a new iteration of the university as an alternative parental authority?

These are fascinating questions that my students love to grapple with. They frame a class discussion that invariably leads to a deeper understanding of bro-country's cultural position, while allowing students to more thoughtfully consider their attraction to the music. Perhaps most importantly, they are questions that can be applied to any genre of music that might emerge as a student preference in the future.

Love, Work and Bro-Country Conservatism

As modern and hedonistically liberating as bro-country's no-limits party zone might appear, a passing familiarity with country music history teaches us that tradition rules. To jettison the urban/rural opposition in service to remaining relevant in twenty-first century American culture does not necessarily mean that all country music tradition has been abandoned. Clover (2014b) suggests one such tradition that continues to inform country music even as the tradition of urban/rural antagonism dissolves: the themes of love and work. More specifically, Clover posits that the ethos of country music is structured by the interplay of two cycles—the cycle of life, and the cycle of money. The former features a long arc, from childhood innocence, to sexual awakening, to marriage, to childbirth, to death. The latter cycle charts a shorter course, from the start of the working week on Monday morning, to payday on Friday, to a weekend of alcohol-fueled release occasioned by a few moments of flirtatious or fraternal pleasure, to the eventual hangover and purging of guilt at church on Sunday morning, which prepares us to start all over again on Monday. Clover reminds us that country music has forever mined these two cycles for its narrative content, but it has always done so in a heavily gendered manner, the cycle of life expressed largely through a female voice, with the cycle of money generally handled by men.

This arrangement has proven more enduring than the urban/rural opposition for good reason—while the latter eventually became unwanted cultural baggage due to the march of social progress, the cycles of life and money seem like the inescapable stuff of nature. As coded by country music, they present as almost biological imperatives—maintaining the cycle of life through love is the site of female labor, while the cycle of money is maintained by the labor of the hard-working man. Unlike the outdated urban/rural dichotomy which required rural values to triumph, love and work don't really present an opposition that can be resolved. They are locked into a gendered, mutual dependency. As Clover explains it, "the money cycle needs the life cycle's product. The life cycle needs money from labor to make more life, more love and weddings and babies" (Clover, 2014b, p. 43). Of course, as hardwired as this appears, it is really just another cultural construct; a reflection of our material and social relations. Still, masking it behind a screen of biologically distinct gender makes it appear as inescapable as nature itself. Each gender has its own prison—separate but interdependent forced labor camps, really—which must always be affirmed and never transcended lest a predictable future be jeopardized. Pretty conservative stuff, this. It is a conservatism that bro-country—a realm of hard-drinking, hard-fighting, hard-working men and the hot women who love them—shows few signs of abandoning.

So, again, how can music this committed to the replication of preexisting cultural categories be used by my students to resist parental cultural authority? How can it possibly be the weapon that can kill their parents? Perhaps an examination of the nature of their parents' cultural model can provide some clues. One immutable truth of parental cultural authority would seem to be that it must be a reflection of the concerns of adulthood. Regardless of chronological age, once you have a kid, you can't really be a kid anymore. You now have an investment in the future that demands a new, more responsible, cultural position—that of the grown-up. Or does it?

New York Times media critic A.O. Scott (2014) has considered this question in a piece titled "The Death of Adulthood in American Culture," which featured the opening premise that recent television and film indicates that no one knows how to be a grown-up anymore. The troubled existence and eventual fall of traditionally grown-up, patriarchal television characters like Don Draper of *Mad Men*, Tony Soprano of *The Sopranos*, and Walter White of *Breaking Bad* provide the empirical data for this assertion, as does the ascent of the "man-boy" character type in the films of Judd Apatow. However, Scott softens his complaint with some historical context, admitting that American culture has always had a problem with adulthood—founding father Ben Franklin was, after all, just a horny adolescent rebelling against an abusive parent figure in King George, and Mark Twain's *Huckleberry Finn* (1885) became great American literature by being a simple adventure story of a boy refusing to grow up in the standard way. In other words, the American project has long been one of preserving the cultural freedom of youth into the chronological category of adulthood. Within that framework, it seems reasonable to wonder if America's post–Elvis generations—including the generation that eventually became the parents of my current students—came of age in a time when this project had finally succeeded. Is the culture of these chronologically adult parents a tradition they grew into and inherited, or is it something they brought with them on their journey from adolescence? Did they step out of childhood into a preexisting adult world, or did they replace that world with one of their own creation? If the answer is the latter, have these parents failed to provide a fully adult parental culture for their own kids to kick against?

Class Discussion III: Are Students More Adult Than Their Parents?

Examining the inherent conservativism of the mutually dependent country music theme cycles of life and money, along with the possible death of adulthood always seems to yield the most thorny, complex classroom discussion of the semester. I broach the discussion with an observation that often surprises and flatters the students in the room—they work too much. They are acutely aware of faculty complaints regarding the short shrift given to their academic pursuits, their unwillingness to read, deficits in their intellectual curiosity, and so on. I suggest to them that these perceived shortcomings are not really the product of their failure to properly prioritize academics, but rather a function of the fact that they are working several minimum-wage jobs in order to pay their tuition. When the time crunch hits, they know it is easier and less risky to get an extension on that assignment than it is to call in sick at work.

Once I empathize with this plight, the expressive floodgates are truly opened as personal accounts of being stretched too thin fill the classroom. It becomes evident to many that they are trapped within the cycle of money that Clover describes, and that hypothetical concept becomes a rather obvious description of their lived reality. A more complex understanding is often expressed by female students who consider themselves feminists, for they feel the need to adhere to both the cycle of money and the cycle of life in order to achieve a modern sense of fulfillment. Regardless of gender, students always seem to realize something through this discussion that explains at least part of the appeal of bro-country to a student cohort—at a very young age, they are already locked in to those inescapable cycles of life and money. They intellectually acknowledge that these cycles are merely cultural constructs, but they feel like the stuff of nature. That bro-country provides a playlist that honors this, while simultaneously offering a path to momentary hedonistic pleasure, becomes something these students can now relate to personally, not just objectively. As a result of this discussion, a new perspective on bro-country's youth culture popularity is quickly and easily established.

Within this class discussion, a window of understanding as to why the rock music of their parents does not quite speak to their existential condition can be opened, as well. In discussing their parents' rock music, students quickly reveal it to be something of a musical legacy passed down from parent to child as some sort of heirloom. Indeed, for the parents of most of my students, "classic rock" is truly their classical music—music that enjoys a high degree of enduring cultural credibility, deserving of respect as historically significant art, and worthy of preservation as a valuable cultural tradition. Of course, there is a problem with this use of rock music—it does not exactly coincide with its traditional youth culture function as a vehicle for questioning the cultural status quo. When a young person grows up and can bring the music of their youth with them into adulthood, rather than be forced to cultivate new musical tastes and accept an extant cannon of "adult" music, that music must then serve a different, more conservative, cultural mission. In a way, rock has become a victim of its own cultural success. No longer can it be a weapon used for killing one's parents. The firing pin has been removed and is now safely kept in a museum in Cleveland.

At the same time, the content of that rock music remains unchanged, and it contradicts this newfound conservative cultural use. Focused on the values of an earlier iteration of youth culture, rock music trades in themes of turning on and dropping out—themes that clearly do not resonate with my overworked, stressed-out students. As a result, these students seem to simultaneously view rock music as something too conservative AND too irresponsibly free to occupy any meaningful place in their hectic, overscheduled lives. I am reminded of one student's comment that exemplifies this conundrum—"I appreciate the significance of the Grateful Dead in music history, and I respect how important they were to my dad growing up. But I could never afford to just quit my job and follow them!"

One recent classroom experience nicely encapsulates this generational disconnect. It involves my advice to a student regarding his completion of one of the assignments in my class, a comparative analysis of two live music events, grounded in ethnographic observation and analysis—"Who are the performers and who are the audience members in terms of age, gender, ethnicity, or other relevant metrics? Why are people gathered to hear these performances? How spontaneous are they? How routine? In what ways has the composition of the audience affected the nature of the performance? How and what do these musical events communicate?" I had managed to generate some interest for the student in the music of Sturgill Simpson—by no means a purveyor of bro-country, but an upscale, highly regarded critic's darling loosely associated with the outlaw country genre. Waxing poetic about his flirtations with Buddhism, psychedelics, and out-of-body experiences, Simpson presents an interesting mix—the sound is very country, but the sensibility is very much "sex and drugs and rock and roll." Since he was booked for a concert in Brooklyn a few weeks prior to the due date for the assignment, I suggested the student might attend. He declined, citing his inability to deal with "all those Brooklyn hipster assholes." For him, and many other students in the class who nodded in agreement, it appears that the latte-sipping, microbrew-loving hipster of today has become an analog of the lazy, jobless, barefoot hippie of the past. Then, as now, we have a negative youth culture archetype of low productivity and irresponsibility derided as a self-appointed cultural elite. However, it was parental culture complaining in the past. Now, it is my 20-year-old students rolling their eyes at the rebirth of the hippie that lies inside mom and dad. In that brief classroom exchange, a possible key to the appeal of bro-country for my students became apparent to everyone in the room—music with a thematic focus on the inescapable cycles of life and money, featuring momentary alcohol-fueled good times as a coping device, speaks more effectively to current youth culture realities than the drug-fueled permanent escape embodied by the rock music of their parents.

Dedicating class time to wrestling with these issues has clearly led to a deeper understanding of the appeal of bro-country for my students, allowing them to discover a conceptually informed historical context to what had simply been their private lived experience. At times, I have toyed with the idea of assigning some of the writings referenced here in order to attempt a more formalized and lengthy consideration of this material. I have also encouraged some bro-country fans to elaborate on that fandom in yet another class assignment—a proposal for a chapter in a future edition of *The Rolling Stone Illustrated History of Rock and Roll* which makes an argument for inclusion of a significant genre or artist that has emerged since the 1992 publication of the current edition. While none have taken me up on the suggestion to date, I continue to push for it. However, I am beginning to think that this material works best as a more spontaneous, parenthetical item; one which leaves the student fans of this music with unresolved issues which they might work through more privately and personally in their still unresolved journeys toward adulthood. In any case, this sort of discussion seems essential for achieving the goal of teaching the popular to students who bask in it every day—the realization that it is not about celebrating your tastes, but about understanding where those tastes come from and how they function culturally.

As described here, bro-country presents my students with a curious blend; a vision of a socially liberal party zone of hedonistic freedom wrapped around a core of very traditional, conservative values that have always formed the basis of country music. Even alcohol—the intoxicant of choice featured in bro-country which enables the loss of inhibition that fuels the party—adheres to the standards of traditional, conservative Southern culture while downplaying the countercultural psychoactive preferences that informed their parents' early years. By contrast, the content of the rock music that informs the adult culture of their parents presents itself as too playfully subversive to be accepted as wisdom handed down from an elder. It is too purely expressive of youthful irresponsibility, lacking the ambivalent blend of momentary fun and hardwired duty featured in bro-country. At the same time, rock will be forever too old, always more the province of their parents than a music capable of articulating their non-parental impulses. Ultimately, a classroom discussion spurred by vague student expressions of a taste preference for bro-country might lead to those students being confronted with a disquieting perception that is metaphorically supported by their musical preference: in their embodiment of a higher degree of strict, conformist responsibility, they may be more grown-up than their own parents.

Yet, in the end, this perception might itself be a youthful indiscretion. Perhaps American culture is not abandoning adulthood after all. Maybe it is just deconstructing it. In other words, maybe we are finally examining adulthood in terms of what it has always been—a facade, one carefully engineered into a useful cultural construct of authority. Maybe adults have always been uncertain about their role and are forever just trying to figure things out on the fly. But if that is actually the case, it is probably tactically wise to conceal this truth from the kids lest they conclude that their parents don't know best after all. Ultimately, perhaps the most adult thing we can do is just admit to ourselves that the wisdom conferred by age is always incomplete, we will never have all the answers, and we are just patching it together the best we can. Perhaps honestly sharing that secret with the young adult bro-country fans in my class is essential to an objective examination and demystification of their puzzling attraction to the genre. The conservative core that bro-country shares with traditional mainstream country music continues to provide these students with simple, reliable myths that make simplistic sense of a complex and confusing existence, while enabling the temporary avoidance of life's more thorny issues in its all-inclusive party zone. It is actually quite easy to see how this reductionist mix might be very attractive to young adult students. It promises a future full of reliable answers instead of troubling questions—answers that their forever-young rock and roll parents could not pass down to them because they are still struggling with the questions.

At the beginning of this essay, I emphasized my preference for a focus on conceptual knowledge when teaching the popular. I find it the best means of preventing students from becoming enthralled by their own experiential moment and reminding them that popular culture is something we are born into. In other words, a little historical context goes a long way in preserving some sense of continuity across generations. So, in pursuing this classroom discussion dealing with the metaphorical killing of my students' parents through music, I have found it helpful to temper such a provocative, potentially disturbing concept by cautioning students not to assume too great a difference between their path to adulthood and that of their parents. In a response to Scott's article on the death of adulthood, Andrew O'Hehir (2014) observes that anyone's path might be less about personal choice and individual will than it is about historical developments beyond anyone's control. O'Hehir sees the undermining of the concept of adulthood as an unavoidable consequence of late capitalism, which has shifted our adult identities from being serious producers of material goods to being passive consumers of pleasurable things. The parents of today may be one of the first generations to fully experience this shift, which could help explain the absence of more traditional modes of adulthood in their lives.

However, my students seem to indicate that it is they who feel this shift more strongly—chronic fears that they will never have a truly meaningful career, that they will produce nothing of enduring worth, that all they ever do is work so they can buy stuff that they do not even like, and so on. Why not just find solace in an adulthood of video games and action figures? This level of cynical self-loathing among what should be optimistic young people with their futures ahead of them is troubling, indeed. Yet, it is not surprising. Current members of youth culture cannot be seriously asked to give up youth culture values and assume traditional adult cultural roles, for late capitalism has effectively eliminated those roles. Nor can they simply embark on a project of constructing new conceptions of adulthood through reacting against the traditional adult standards of their parents—those parents are still celebrating the cultural standards of their youth as they near retirement age.

The Future, for Students and Faculty

So, what is left for my students moving forward? A starting point would seem to involve finding something that can re-establish the tradition of adulthood that their own parents never managed to achieve and that late capitalism has now obliterated. Could that something be found in the meld of fading tradition and youthful fun offered by bro-country? Could the simple mythic facades of a party-hearty yet responsible adulthood in that music provide the prospect of serious meaning for those students who already feel they are looking at a pretty meaningless existence?

Again, can bro-country kill your parents, ushering in a more highly evolved conception of what adulthood can be? We may never know, for a number of reasons. First, answering this question may depend on this generation of young adults being able to identify a parental culture worth killing. As suggested above, that may not be in the cards. Second, the moment in the sun for the bro-country variant of country music favored by my students has already begun to fade. With turns toward more serious and substantive material by bro-country stars like Dierks Bentley and Chase Rice, what was once viewed as a culturally troubling musical impulse too difficult to refuse due to its commercial viability seems to be showing signs of moderation as it becomes more fully absorbed into the institutional mainstream of country music's Nashville establishment. Compare the bro-country hits—Bentley's "Somewhere on a Beach" and Rice's "Whisper"—to the more complex, less commercial remainder of each album, and the shift appears obvious. Who knows if the future of country music will even resonate with our future students? Lastly and, at least for me, most sadly, perhaps the concept of youth culture killing its parents is simply losing relevance. Considering the retro allure of vinyl, maybe my students are actually looking forward to inheriting their parents' moldy album collection. Perhaps, for the first time since Elvis, both the parents and the kids are all right. If so, preparation for teaching courses dealing with popular music will require far more than simply updating the download list. Popular music as a vehicle through which youth culture metaphorically kills the parent may now become a period piece lecture. In order to make all that history somehow speak to the lives of students and the music they love, it is back to the conceptual drawing board.

In sum, the case study of bro-country offered here represents just one attempt to achieve the enabling condition for senior faculty effectively teaching the popular—personal credibility. I am not referring here to academic credibility, the relevance of which is somehow vaguely sensed even by first-year students as something that will offer some benefit post-graduation. I am referring to a sort of "street cred," which can only be based in an understanding of a young person's inarticulate and unexamined impulse to identify with some music of the moment. As spontaneous and ahistorical as such identification might appear, it may be the only portal through which my students might access the rich historical connections and conceptual frameworks that can more fully reveal the nature and meaning of their musical taste. We as teaching faculty may possess a wealth of useful knowledge, but that knowledge will simply remain our own if we do not meet the student on his or her own musical turf. This does suggest a pedagogy that must be completely retooled each time a new set of students strolls into the classroom with something new blaring from their earbuds. Still, I find that effort essential for the task of cultivating analysis and understanding in students where only consumption and celebration initially exist.

References

Clover, J. (2014a, May 19). Pop and circumstance. *The Nation, 298*(20), 45.
Clover, J. (2014b, July 7). Pop and circumstance. *The Nation, 299*(1/2), 43.
O'Hehir, A. (2014, September 12). *The death of adulthood is really just capitalism at work.* Retrieved from http://www.salon.com/2014/09/12/the_death_of_adulthood_is_really_just_capitalism_at_work/.
Scott, A. (2014, September 11). *The death of adulthood in American culture.* Retrieved from https://www.nytimes.com/2014/09/14/magazine/the-death-of-adulthood-in-american-culture.html/.
Trigger. (2011, August 7). *Country checklist songs causing an erosion of values.* Retrieved from http://www.savingcountrymusic.com/country-checklist-songs-causing-an-erosion-of-values/.
Trigger. (2013, June 24). *Big mess and fights left in Kenny Chesney/Eric Church concert wake.* Retrieved from http://www.savingcountrymusic.com/big-mess-fights-left-in-kenny-chesney-eric-church-concert-wake/.
Trigger. (2014a, June 22). *Huge mess left in wake of Luke Bryan Pittsburgh concert.* Retrieved from http://www.savingcountrymusic.com/it/happened/again/huge/mess/left/in/wake/of/luke/bryan/pittsburgh/concert/.
Trigger. (2014b, July 27). *55 people arrested, 22 hospitalized at Keith Urban concert.* Retrieved from http://www.savingcountrymusic.com/55-people-arrested-22-hospitalized-in-mass-casuality-event-at-keith-urban-concert/.
Yahr, E. (2014, August 7). *Violence, tragedy, mass arrests: What is going on with country music concerts this summer?* Retrieved from https://www.washingtonpost.com/news/arts-and-entertainment/wp/2014/08/07/violence-tragedy-mass-arrests-what-is-going-on-with-coountry-music-concerts-this-summer/.

Game-Based Learning in the Popular Music Classroom

BRIAN ROBISON

In this essay, I describe instructional games I have used in *Popular Music Since 1945*, a historical survey course which I taught at Northeastern University for three semesters. The course material comprises a wide variety of pop styles from the early postwar era up to the mid-aughts, including ambient, boogie-woogie, blues, country, disco, doo-wop, electronica, funk, grunge, hip-hop, honky-tonk, post-rock, punk, reggae, rockabilly, soul, and urban folk, with attention to how changes in technology and social contexts shaped the music's sounds and influenced how audiences received it. Given most students' intrinsic interest in the subject matter, a course on popular music would not seem to need games as a respite from conventional lectures and classroom discussion. But although students may start the course with a strong interest and deep familiarity with some popular music, they typically know only a limited selection of styles, usually with only a shallow sense (if any) of their historical contexts. Well-designed games draw on students' competitive instincts to motivate them to listen more closely and think more carefully about music that they might previously have thought of as a break from study, rather than a serious subject for it. In this way, games can support and deepen learning about popular music, by transforming the potentially stressful work of study and assessment into a more emotionally relaxed (but intellectually engaged) state of play (Gareau & Guo, 2009). Although the games I describe were implemented in a college course, they could be adapted to the content of any course on popular music, at any level.

Game-based learning enhances students' understanding by directly incorporating course material, rather than distracting from it, as typically occurs in games generated at websites such as ContentGenerator (http://www.contentgenerator.net/), ClassTools (http://www.classtools.net/), and

EdCreate (http://www.edcreate.com/). For example, a game created on such a site might interleave quiz questions written by the instructor with a conventional video game. Student players must answer each question correctly to play a round of a video game that bears no relation to the course material. The video game ultimately interrupts students' learning, rather than supporting it.

Perhaps the most successful, sustained, and thoroughgoing implementation of game-based learning is the set of historical simulations Reacting to the Past (RttP), in which students may spend an entire month poring over primary texts and enacting the roles of major figures at a turning point in history, albeit with no obligation to arrive at the same resolution as their real-world historical counterparts. For instance, students playing the French Revolution game study foundational texts including Jean-Jacques Rousseau's *Social Contract* and Edmund Burke's *Reflections on the Revolution in France*, as they take on the roles of King Louis XVI, the Marquis de Lafayette, the Catholic Church, and various political factions in the National Assembly (Feuillants, Jacobins, "Friends of the King"), enacting the effort "to create a constitution amidst internal chaos and threats of foreign invasion" (descriptive summary at https://reacting.barnard.edu/node/3166). As they perform these roles, students are individually required to act consistently with their role's political thought and interests, preferably by citing primary sources, and thus remain true to the historical context. Collectively, though, they are not bound to arrive at all of the same decisions, leaving many aspects of the scenario as open questions, contingent on student interactions such as:

> Will the king retain power? Will the priests of the Catholic Church obey the "general will" of the National Assembly or the dictates of the Pope in Rome? Do traditional institutions and values constitute restraints on freedom and individual dignity or are they its essential bulwarks? Are slaves, women, and Jews entitled to the "rights of man"? Is violence a legitimate means of changing society or of purging it of dangerous enemies? [https://reacting.barnard.edu/node/3166].

Through immersion and detailed argumentation, students acquire a deep understanding of the material, despite the subversive atmosphere of "play" in the classroom. (Carnes, 2014). However, as of this writing, no RttP games exist for popular-music curricula, so interested instructors face a long development process.

Here I will describe much smaller, simpler games that can be played in brief rounds of just 15 minutes, making them easy to incorporate in an existing curriculum. Each presumes organizing the students into teams, as individual play would take too long, and would become too complex for the instructor to monitor if more than a handful of students were to compete. Beyond simple expedience, team participation leverages social engagement as motivation for learning, and fosters corrective feedback among students. For example, extroverted students of limited, inaccurate knowledge learn to value and solicit the contributions of introverted students with more detailed, accurate knowledge. To prevent any one team from dominating the competition, the instructor should choose the team rosters, based on students' responses to a questionnaire about prior coursework and musical experience. This allows the instructor to balance competencies, making sure there is no team consisting exclusively of seniors competing with another team consisting exclusively of sophomores, or a team of guitarists competing with a team of drummers, and so on. These and many other details of the games that follow approximate some of the best practices of Team-Based Learning (Michaelson, Knight, & Fink, 2004).

For each game, my description follows the model of "backward" course design (Wiggins & McTighe, 1998), diagrammed in Figure 1: The instructor begins by identifying specific course goals ("What should students know, understand, and be able to do?"), then identifies suitable assessment evidence toward those goals ("What will we accept as evidence of student understanding and proficiency?"), and then plans classroom instruction accordingly ("What activities will equip students with the needed knowledge and skills?"). In each case, I will first outline the game mechanics in a general way, and suggest ways to adapt the game to other popular-music subject matter. Then I will supply an example of the specific implementation I used in my course, with notes on what worked well and what I could do better next time.

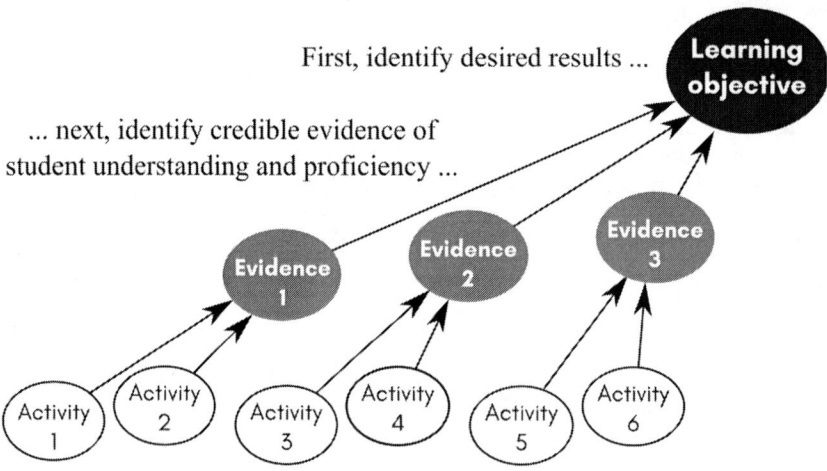

Figure 1. Diagram of "backward" course design (after Wiggins & McTighe, 1998).

Before I delve into details, the frequent blurring between the terms "game-based learning" and "gamification" obliges me to clarify: strictly speaking, game-based learning utilizes game mechanics to achieve specific pedagogic goals. For example, each of the games I describe hinges on either of two specific pedagogic principles: developing mastery and knowledge organization (Ambrose, Bridges, DiPietro, Lovett, & Norman, 2010). In contrast, the term gamification refers to structuring a course like a game (with students accumulating points, "leveling up," etc.), but not necessarily incorporating actual gameplay. Thus, an instructor could incorporate any of the learning games described in this article without necessarily "gamifying" the course syllabus, or vice versa.

Games to Develop Mastery

In *How Learning Works* (Ambrose et al., 2010), the authors identify developing mastery as one of seven research-based principles of learning. They state, "To develop mastery, students must acquire component skills, practice integrating them, and know when to apply what they have learned" (p. 95). The following two game frameworks represent opportunities for focused practice and, via game scoring, low-stakes assessment, with instant, formative feedback from the instructor. The first is built around helping students pay closer attention to information that can be ranked unambiguously along a single dimension (for example, "Which of the following selections features the most intense [or least intense] vocal delivery?"), and the second helps them integrate observations along more than one dimension (such as music, lyrics, and production values) to distinguish between two closely-related categories.

Game #1: High-Low Split

Framework: Card players will recognize how the following game derives from poker variants such as Omaha, Dakota, and Pyramid, in which the pot for each round is split between the highest-ranking and the lowest-ranking hands of cards. Rather than try to parallel the entire complex system of poker hands, this framework reduces winning to holding either the highest card or the lowest card. The sharing of points helps to maintain motivation, as a team that is dealt a hand of only low-scoring items can still reasonably hope to win points in that round.

The specific implementation I will present below was designed to hone students' skills in the aural analysis of popular music, but any aspect of the course material that lends itself to unambiguous ranking could be adapted to the same framework. For example, an instructor could focus on songs' lyric content or cultural background ("Which of these songs projects the most/least conventional social role for women?," "Which of these songs offers the strongest/weakest connection to the civil rights movement of the 1960s?," or "Which of these songs represents the strongest/weakest example of globalism in the popular music market?"). Also, in lieu of song selections, each card could instead present a salient quotation from a songwriter, performer, producer, critic, or historian. (So, in each of the alternative criteria above, substitute "quotations" for "songs.")

Gameplay: The instructor deals to each team a hand of "cards," each specifying a separate item from the course material, all from the same category and without any duplicates. (Card stock is ideal, but plain paper will suffice and is easier to cut apart; I formatted each sheet of "cards" as a table in Microsoft Word.) During a fixed period of time, each team evaluates their cards, and then advances one selection as an explicit candidate for "Most" or "Least" (that is, a team cannot blindly put a selection forward and hope to score points either way). The instructor may solicit brief statements that summarize a team's "case" for their candidate selection, but ultimately must serve as the final arbiter of "Most" and "Least," and should explain judgments. Points are then distributed to the teams that advance the "Most" and "Least" selections.

Sample Implementation: At Northeastern, many of my students (especially those with an interest in music recording) are more apt to notice immediate, moment-to-moment features of production (timbral qualities, including those from guitar effects pedals, levels of distortion in a guitar part, different amounts of echo or reverberation, etc.) rather than larger-scale structures and patterns of melody, harmony, rhythm, texture, and form. I wanted to broaden and deepen my students' listening, to get them to engage consciously with these latter aspects of curricular repertoire. With this learning goal in mind, I sought to simplify the task of aural analysis by requiring conscious focus on only one specific musical parameter at a time, such as recognizing harmonic contrasts among verses, chorus, and bridge, or considering changes in rhythmic activity among song sections, or assessing the extent and depth of syncopation. So, the deck of cards comprises selections of music from the curricular repertoire, and in each round, teams are instructed to focus on a specific parameter of music.

For the round illustrated in Figure 2, the selections are all drawn from the unit on African American popular music in the 1960s, and the evaluation criterion is, "Which selection features the most (or least) persistent melisma?" For those unfamiliar with the term, melisma refers to singing a single syllable on more than one note; for a quick example, listen to the beginning of the refrain in the Beatles' "I Want to Hold Your Hand." All six words are one syllable apiece; the first five words are correspondingly set to one note apiece, but the word "ha-a-a-a-a-a-and" stretches over seven notes (for those of you keeping score at home, they are D-C-B-A-B-A-G). So, the first five words are set syllabically, but the word "hand" is set melismatically.

In the illustrated round, each team evaluates the selections they have been dealt, looking for one that they believe might represent the most or least persistent vocal melisma. For each team, there is an element of uncertainty, as they do not know any of the other teams' cards, with the exception of anything they might overhear as another team consults a recording. Teams then hear the four chosen selections side-by-side; with luck, the "Most" and "Least" selections are self-evident; in some cases, the instructor may need to intervene: perhaps to declare a tie between two selections, or to clarify why two selections that the students believe to be tied are not, in fact, equivalent (for example, "Yes, there are some passages of striking melisma in selection X, but they are brief and few and far between. Selection Y may not include such florid melisma, but there is melisma in every phrase throughout; recall the criteria 'most' and 'least.'")

Personal Notes. I found this game extremely useful in gauging how carefully students listened to the music, as opposed to making an educated guess based on general knowledge of the genre or artist. Figure 2 almost reflects something that happened in actual gameplay, except in that case a team advanced James Brown's "Papa's Got a Brand New Bag" as the selection with the "Most" persistent melisma. This decision clearly was not based on the music, in which Brown applies melisma sparingly; rather, it seems to have resulted from a faulty syllogism along the lines of: "Melisma is a characteristic feature of much African-American music" (correct) and "James Brown was an icon of African-American music" (correct), therefore "James Brown's music must feature lots of melisma" (incorrect). Similarly, another team advanced Aretha Franklin's "I Never Loved a Man (The Way I Loved You)" as the selection with persistent melisma, which may have resulted from a more subtly flawed line of reasoning such as: "Melisma is a characteristic feature of African-American gospel singing" (correct) and "When Aretha Franklin started her career in popular music, she already had years of gospel singing under her belt" (correct), therefore "Any selection by Aretha Franklin must exhibit the most persistent melisma" (close, but not necessarily true in all cases: different selections by Aretha Franklin exhibit different degrees of melismatic singing). Thus, a single round of the game demonstrated to students the need to move beyond a simple binary division (either syllabic or melismatic) to recognize different degrees along a continuum (ranging from purely syllabic to purely melismatic, with many intermediate levels).

Poker aficionados might wonder about the absence of betting: should not the students be putting something on the line with each play? I started

a. Instructor deals cards, and announces criterion for evaluation

Team W Team X Team Y Team Z

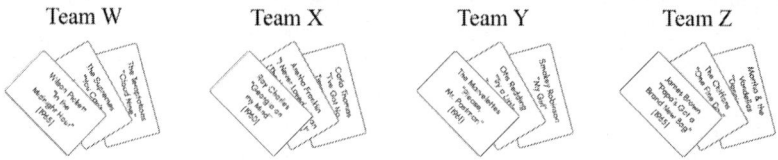

"Which selection features the most (or least) persistent melisma?"

b. Teams confer

c. Instructor calls time; teams advance candidates

Team W	Team X	Team Y	Team Z
LEAST	MOST	MOST	LEAST
The Supremes "You Can't Hurry Love" (1966)	Carla Thomas "I've Got No Time to Lose" (1964)	Otis Redding "Try a Little Tenderness" (1966)	James Brown "Papa's Got a Brand New Bag" (1965)

d. Class discusses selections; instructor judges and awards points

Team W	Team X	Team Y	Team Z
~~LEAST~~	MOST	~~MOST~~	LEAST
The Supremes "You Can't Hurry Love" (1966)	Carla Thomas "I've Got No Time to Lose" (1964)	Otis Redding "Try a Little Tenderness" (1966)	James Brown "Papa's Got a Brand New Bag" (1965)
	25 pts		25 pts

Figure 2. Sample round of "High-Low Split," here implemented for aural analysis: (a) Instructor deals repertoire cards and announces parameter (in this case, persistent melisma); (b) Teams are given a few minutes to confer, consult audio, etc.; (c) Instructor calls time, and teams put forward their candidate selections, as either "Most" or "Least" along that parameter; (d) After discussion of candidates, Instructor adjudicates "Most" and "Least," and distributes points accordingly.

from this perspective, and learned the hard way that on the whole, it is a mistake to incorporate poker-style betting, as it slows gameplay significantly while teams confer to decide on how much to bet. Worse yet, it might become some students' primary focus; in one course evaluation, a student referred to the game not as "The High-Low Game" or even as "The Analysis Game," but rather as "The Betting Game." The other common pitfall is the ease with which the combined atmosphere of play and the component of debate among selections could lead some students to shift from genuine argumentation into jokes and lighthearted trash-talking; in one cohort of students, I repeatedly needed to tighten the reins on classroom behavior to keep the game focused on the course content. At the very least, the instructor must prevent opposing teams from interrupting whichever team has the floor at that moment; in extreme cases, you might need to deduct points to penalize a team for counterproductive commentary.

Despite these stumbles, my students generally enjoyed playing this game. I heard lively discussion within the groups; students listened carefully, and usually supplied sophisticated observations when debating the merits of competing candidates for "Most" or "Least." On the occasions when I needed to point them toward subtler aspects of the selections under discussion, I was gratified to see and hear their "aha" reactions as they deepened their understanding of material they were actively engaging.

Game #2: X or Y?

Framework: The next game is designed to help students better distinguish between two superficially similar categories, which they might otherwise confuse. While it could be applied to categories with a single criterion for membership ("Is SZA a drummer or a singer?"), it provides a much richer learning experience if the categories involve multiple criteria, with less crisp yes-or-no values, and thus require the students to integrate observations along multiple dimensions (for example, distinguishing whether a quotation represents a perspective of "Sociology or Ethnography?," "Postcolonial Studies or Postmodernism?," or "Semiotics or Hermeneutics?").

Gameplay: Prior to the class meeting, the instructor curates a list of ten brief excerpts from the course material, each of which belongs to one of two categories (here labeled with the placeholders "X" and "Y"). These could be audio excerpts from assigned listening, or representative quotations from assigned reading. During class, the instructor announces the two categories, and if there are multiple distinguishing characteristics and criteria, names them explicitly and reminds the students to attend to all of them. The game then proceeds in ten rounds: On each round, the teams hear a selection, with no identifying labels beyond "Selection #1," "Selection #2," etc., and then have one minute to confer and reach consensus on which category it belongs to. Teams submit their answers simultaneously, and the instructor highlights the selection's salient characteristics that mark whether it belongs to category X, or category Y. Scoring is a simple matter of tallying correct identifications.

Sample Implementation. I used this game to refine my students' ability to distinguish between similar styles of music. For example, in the first iteration of our survey course at Northeastern, during the 1970s unit, students easily distinguished punk music from other styles. However, during the 1990s unit, few students could consistently distinguish punk from grunge; that is, they attended to few details beyond a general impression of "rough guitar sounds" or "shouted vocals," without noting telltale aspects of harmony, melody, and lyrical content.

To address this gap, in the next iteration of the course, I introduced a game called "Punk or Grunge?" I curated a playlist of brief excerpts from five punk songs and five grunge songs, shown in Figure 3. For the sake of lively gameplay, each excerpt lasts only 30 to 45 seconds, so the playlist includes time indices for the most characteristic passages. In compiling the list, I avoided the most familiar hits and any selections named in the textbook, because I did not want students to base their identifications on purely declarative knowledge such as, "Oh, that's 'Smells like Teen Spirit,' which was a hit

	Artist	Title	Year	Start
1	Ramones	"Rock and Roll High School"	1979	0:30
2	Alice in Chains	"Grind"	1995	0:55
3	Richard Hell & the Voidoids	"Blank Generation"	1977	0:45
4	Sex Pistols	"Pretty Vacant"	1977	0:25
5	Hole	"Violet"	1994	1:00
6	Patti Smith	"Kimberly"	1977	1:00
7	Nirvana	"Heart-Shaped Box"	1993	1:00
8	Bikini Kill	"Rebel Girl"	1993	0:30
9	Melvins	"Honey Bucket"	1993	1:30
10	Dictators	"Master Race Rock"	1975	1:00

Figure 3. Sample round of "X or Y?," here implemented as "Punk or Grunge?" Teams hear each item in turn, without any identifying information. Here, the items are excerpts from musical selections; alternatively, each item could be a quotation from assigned reading. For musical selections, time indices enable the instructor to play representative 30-second excerpts, rather than entire songs.

for Nirvana, and Nirvana was a prominent grunge band, so this must be a grunge song."

Personal Notes. The first time I implemented this game, I inadvertently structured it as a summative assessment, because we listened to all ten selections before I revealed any answers and explained how each selection exhibited characteristics of its category. This approach did not develop students' knowledge over the course of the game, because I was not giving them feedback to hone their skills; indeed, some students became visibly frustrated, as they felt trapped in a loop of not knowing and not learning. It also used time less efficiently than the gameplay outlined above, because I had to replay each excerpt to refresh the students' memory, and so the entire exercise took up much more class time than I had planned. So, from perspectives of both pedagogy and time management, it is much more effective to reveal each answer in turn and discuss it immediately, so that students can improve significantly over the course of hearing the ten selections (or, for a shorter segment of class time, only five or six).

Games to Develop Knowledge Organization

Another research-based principle of learning is "The important way experts' and novices' knowledge organizations differ," namely, "in the number or density of connections among the concepts, facts, and skills they know" (Ambrose et al., 2010, p. 49). That is, beginners' connections are sparse, leaving significant gaps that make it harder for them to retrieve past knowledge and relate new information to what they have learned previously. Alternatively, they may remember the sequence in which they learned course material, but without a clear sense of hierarchy or connections across categories. The following two games represent opportunities for integrating information which students might learn in different course units, and thus might not connect properly. For example, students might learn in a unit on 1950s pop music that Les Paul experimented with extensive multitrack recording, and then after studying the 1960s, learn in a unit on 1970s rock music that Queen experimented with extensive multitrack recording; but unless the instructor specifically highlights this parallel, students might not connect the two pieces of information.

Game #3: Ordering

Framework: The next game focuses on any single parameter that allows unambiguous ordering: least-to-most, smallest-to-largest, worst-selling-to-best-selling, earliest-to-most-recent. When items in any such series are studied in different course units, students need to revisit the material periodically and observe relationships between items they previously learned separately. The need for strict ordering complicates attempts to translate this game to the social aspects of popular music, such as race, class, and gender, unless highlighting the historical organization of material studied: for example, a round focusing on feminist movements (as part of music's social context) could check and clarify students' understanding that Betty Friedan's *The Feminine Mystique* (1963) was published after Virginia Woolf's *A Room of One's Own* (1929), but before Naomi Klein's *The Beauty Myth* (1990).

Gameplay: In each round, all teams see the same five items, presented in quasi-random order. The teams have a minute or two to confer, and then all teams simultaneously submit their orderings of the events. The instructor then reveals the correct ordering, and explicitly reviews the relationships among events; ideally, students move past simply learning the correct ordering to understand the structure that underlies it, such that if they were to forget the actual ordering they could easily reconstruct it. A team earns a point for each correct pairwise relation. For example, if five events are presented out of order with sequential labels VWXYZ, and if their correct ordering is ZXYWV, then there are ten correctly ordered pairs of events (ZX, ZY, ZW, ZV, XY, XW, XV, YW, YV, and WV), and hence ten available points. While this system is more work than an overall right-or-wrong determination, it provides proportionate partial credit to orderings that are mostly correct, versus only half-correct, versus mostly wrong (see the example below). As a practical matter, if the instructor prepares a complete list of these pairs before class, it greatly speeds scoring, especially if there is a separate copy for scoring each team. This way, the instructor can simply cross off each missed pair, and then tally the correct pairs.

Sample Implementation. The following game applies the above framework to the parameter of chronology. With the Internet's explosion of access to music, students today encounter a broad selection of genres, artists, and songs, but too often devoid of any historical context. While any historical survey would ostensibly remedy this gap in knowledge, in practice students are prone to forget material from prior weeks in the course, unless periodically prodded to integrate new knowledge with the old. I have found this true whether the course is organized chronologically (in which case, students tend to miss connections across different decades) or by styles (in which case, students tend to miss contemporaneous similarities and differences across different styles). This game helps students to situate individual musical selections in a broader historical sequence, including non-musical events such as the civil rights movement, the Vietnam War, and the conservative backlash to the hippie counterculture. Importantly, the game does not require students to memorize dates, but rather, to learn the overall sequence of events.

So, in each round, all teams see the same set of five historical/cultural events, presented in quasi-random order. In the simplest cases, each set can include events that strongly mark a particular decade or portion of a decade (for example, the Beatles' first performance on *The Ed Sullivan Show* as an event of the mid–1960s, vs. the Woodstock Festival as an event of the late 1960s). More strongly, each set can include events that are causally or sequentially linked (such as: the rise of disco culture in the early 1970s necessarily preceded the release of the film *Saturday Night Fever* [1977], which brought disco to the cultural mainstream and helped to launch the late 1970s disco craze, which sparked a backlash that culminated in the 1979 Disco Demolition Night event at Comiskey Park in Chicago).

Figure 4 illustrates a typical round and its scoring. In this case, Team 1 supplies the correct ordering, and scores 10 points. Team 2 supplies an ordering which is almost entirely correct, in that only one item is out of order, and it is only one place out of order; the other nine out of ten pairs are correct, so the team scores 9 out of 10 points. Team 3's ordering puts one item only one place out of order, but another item two places out of order, such that three ordered pairs are wrong, so the team scores 7 out of 10 points. Lastly, Team 4's ordering is wildly wrong, and yet it still correctly identifies three pairwise orderings, so the team scores 3 out of 10 points. The only way for a team to score zero points would be to put all five items in reverse chronological order; in practice; I have yet to see this happen.

Personal Notes. In addition to checking student's understanding, a round of this game can emphasize changes in lyrical content across the decades (and thus, indirectly, changes in societal attitudes). For example, in the 1960s, the Chiffons submissively look forward to "One Fine Day" of requited affection; in the 1970s, Carole King takes the lead in asserting to her partner that "It's Too Late" to salvage their romance. In the 1980s, Madonna highlights her excitement with the expression (previously unthinkable in the Top 40) "Like a Virgin"; in the 1990s, PJ Harvey uses even stronger, more aggressive language to warn her ex-lover that he is not "Rid of Me"; and in the early naughts, Lady Gaga tosses conventional morality entirely aside, opting to "Just Dance" rather than moderate her hedonistic behaviors.

Alternatively, recurrent words or phrases can function as unifying themes, or as red herrings, or even as both within the same set (again, presented here in its correct order):

Teen idol Frank Sinatra sparks the "Columbus Day Riot"
Teen idols the Beatles first perform on *The Ed Sullivan Show*
Teen pop Svengali Phil Spector launches the Crystals and the
    Ronettes
Teen Spirit (and its fragrance) launches Seattle's alt-rock nationwide

234 Part 3: Popular Music Analysis and Other Instructional Tools

a. Instructor presents five items, listed out of order

V	Coastal gangsta rap rivalry culminates in the shootings of Christopher Wallace (Notorious B.I.G.) and Tupac Shakur
W	MC Hammer achieves unprecedented R&B & hip-hop success with "U Can't Touch This"
X	MC Melle Mel warns us not to push him, because of how close he is to the edge
Y	Public Enemy takes on the socially conscious role of "Black CNN"
Z	"Rapper's Delight" by the Sugar Hill Gang achieves unprecedented mainstream market success for hip-hop

b. Teams confer, then submit their orderings

c. Teams discuss discrepancies, then instructor reveals correct sequence

Team 1	Team 2	Team 3	Team 4
ZXYWV	XZYWV	XYZVW	YVXWZ

Correct sequence = ZXYWV

d. Scoring: Each correctly ordered pair earns one point

Team 1	Team 2	Team 3	Team 4
ZX ZY ZW ZV	(X̶)̶ ZY ZW ZV	(X̶)̶(Y̶)̶ ZW ZV	(X̶)̶(Y̶)̶(W̶)̶(V̶)̶
XY XW XV	XY XW XV	XY XW XV	(X̶)̶ XW (X̶)̶
YW YV	YW YV	YW YV	YW YV
WV	WV	(V̶)̶	(V̶)̶
= 10 pts	= 9 pts	= 7 pts	= 3 pts

Figure 4. Sample round of Ordering, here implemented as Chronology. (a) Teams see five items in a series, but presented out of their proper order; (b) Teams confer, then submit their orderings; (c) Teams discuss discrepancies, and the instructor reveals the correct sequence; (d) Each correct pairwise ordering earns a point; this system proportionately rewards answers that are partially correct (the closer to the proper sequence, the more points are earned).

Teen pop Svengali Lou Pearlman launches the Backstreet Boys and *NSYNC

Note how the fourth item obliquely checks whether students can recognize Nirvana's breakthrough grunge hit without explicit reference to either "Nirvana" or "grunge." Each set can be constructed as narrowly (say, focusing only on actual teen idols across the decades) or as broadly (say, referring to events in five different musical style across five different decades) as the instructor desires, depending on which relationships need additional emphasis.

The only hitch I have encountered with this game is the instinctive narrow focus of some students: the misconception that because it is a class about popular music, it is therefore inappropriate to ask them to learn about anything other than popular music (such as the civil rights movement, the Vietnam War, or the 2003 invasion of Iraq). This is not a problem with the game per se, but the occasional complaint along these lines in course evaluations highlights the need to draw explicit connections between a given social context and the music produced within it. Overall, my students enjoyed playing, and as in the High-Low split game, I was pleased to hear substantive discussion within teams as students sorted out what they knew definitely and what they were not sure of, and tried to determine logically how to fit the latter into the overall sequence.

Game #4: Only Connect

Framework: Readers of a certain age may recognize the following game as an earnest incarnation of the old parlor game "Analogies," in which players try to construct completely nonsensical analogies (such as, "A grapefruit is to a backpack as Chaka Khan is to a seashore"). That game's challenge lies in the flexibility of the human imagination: confronted with such outlandish juxtapositions, our brains nonetheless find connections ("Well, you could fit multiple grapefruits inside a backpack, and if you had multiple Chaka Khans, you could likewise fit them onto a seashore," or "A grapefruit would supply a contrasting touch of acidity in the otherwise bland taste of a backpack, and Chaka Khan likewise would supply a contrasting touch of funk in the otherwise serene setting of a seashore.") Given how well we can connect utter nonsense when prodded to do so, why not harness that propensity toward the goal of organizing disparate course material?

Exercising these conceptual muscles is particularly valuable because students, as novices, naturally tend to compartmentalize their knowledge about music genres; information about rock is information about rock, information about country is information about country, and never the twain shall meet, unless the instructor specifically directs the class to think about how they overlap. To develop a rich network of conceptual connections, the following game arbitrarily pairs disparate curricular categories, and requires students to identify a connection between them, whether via low-level, concrete details, or by higher-level, abstract relationships.

Gameplay: Before class, the instructor prepares a grid of topics, as illustrated in Figure 5. Because I was teaching a music history course, my game boards focused on entire decades and broad musical styles, but the nature of grid topics is entirely flexible. Instructors teaching other material could list more narrowly defined items (say, on specific curricular selections of music), or more broadly defined ones, such as different extramusical contexts (for example, theoretical perspectives such as gender studies. globalism, postmodernism, etc.), in which case one might rename the game "Theory Twister."

During class, the instructor shares the board with the students. On each turn, the instructor selects two topics, preferably at random (I roll dice in full view of the class). Teams have a minute to confer, and then each team writes down their proposed connection. The latter could be narrowly focused (perhaps citing two comparable musical selections) or broadly defined (perhaps comparing the social contexts of different times and different places). The instructor awards points for drawing conceptual connections, the stronger and more distinctive, the better; conversely, any proposition that could be applied to any pair of the topics is vacuously true and accrues no points. For example, if the selected topics were "1960s Countrypolitan" and "1970s Progressive Rock," then the statements "Both styles represent an attempt to 'elevate' a comparatively simple musical style and make it sound more 'sophisticated'" would represent a stronger connection than "Both styles layer vocals with sounds of keyboards, guitars, and strings" (which is true of many, but not all other styles), which in turn would represent a stronger connection than "Both styles feature lyrics that often tell a story" (which is true about virtually any style).

Sample Implementation. In my survey course, I found that despite my frequent reminders that all tests were cumulative, students tended to focus exclusively on the new material of each week, and thus neglected to revisit material they had already learned, and to think about relationships more complex than "X happened before Y, and both happened before Z." I wanted them to think more broadly about musical features and social contexts, to identify parallelisms that cut across course units based on specific time periods or specific musical styles (for example, recalling parental concern over the societal transgressions of rock 'n' roll in the 1950s, and noting its echoes in parental concern over the societal transgressions of gangsta rap in the 1990s). Hence, my grids closely tracked subtopics (specifically, decades)

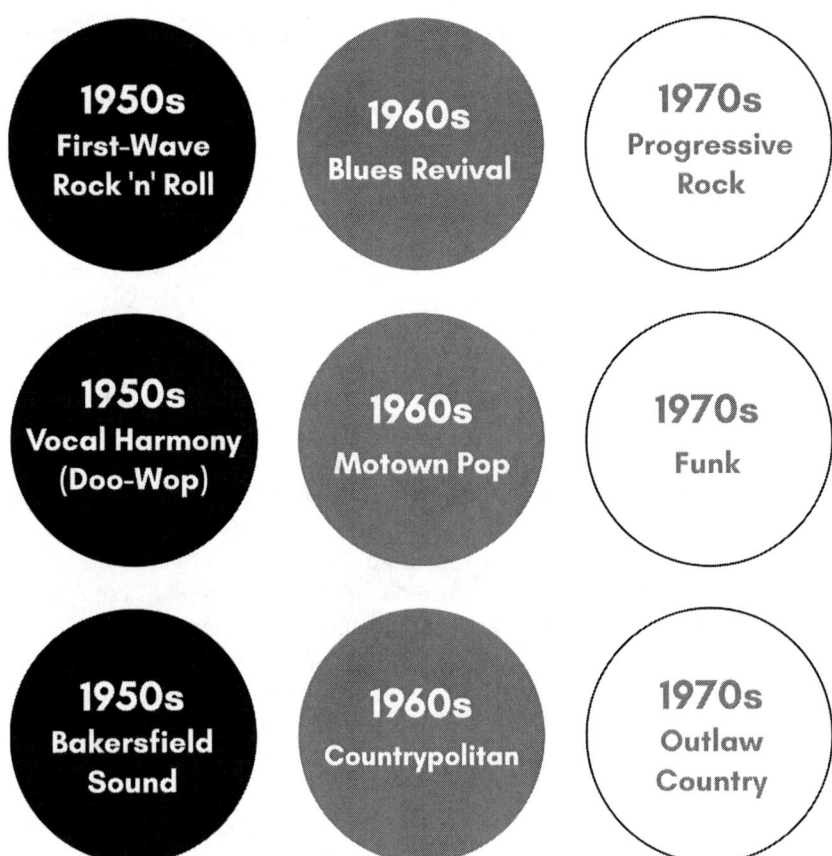

Figure 5. Sample categories for "Only Connect," here implemented as "Twistory" for a survey course that has reached the early 1970s. Teams must find connections between randomly paired categories: for example, if the two categories are "1950s Bakersfield Sound" and "1970s Funk," one valid answer is: "Both can be heard as infusing a non-rock genre with elements of rock." Likewise, for "1960s Countrypolitan" and "1970s Progressive Rock," one valid answer is: "Both can be heard as attempts to 'elevate' a genre associated with a lower social class." Statements such as "both are in the same overall genre" and "both are in the same decade" are considered vacuously true and thus accrue no points.

within the three larger course units (rock and pop, African American styles, and country and folk).

Personal Notes. I originally devised this game to enliven an end-of-semester review session, with an eye on the final exam, and especially its possible essay questions which would certainly require students to draw connections across different decades and different musical styles. In a classic demonstration of an expert blind spot, I was surprised to see how often my students would miss a connection that seemed obvious to me (for example, from Figure 5, both the 1950s "Bakersfield Sound" and 1970s "Funk" represent fusions of rock and non-rock styles). The ability to draw a dense network of connections among pieces of information is a specific intellectual skill, one that requires practice over the course of the term. Therefore, students will derive much greater benefit from this game if they play it at the end of each course unit (or perhaps even at the end of each week of classes), instead of only once at the end of the term.

My students clearly enjoyed playing; they were visibly excited (perhaps nervously so) that they might be called on to actively recognize a previously unstated connection (for example, comparing the contrarian aspects of Aphex Twin's *Selected Ambient Works, Vol. II* and J Dilla's *Donuts*), rather than simply parrot something from the textbook or a lecture. They also seemed liberated by knowing there was not one true answer they had to divine; sometimes a team would advance an answer half in jest, thinking it insufficiently substantial to merit points, only for me to affirm that yes, it is a perfectly valid connection. This sort of positive energy would build over the course of the game, in contrast to the brief flash of anticipation and dread when students would first see the board and imagine that I might actually make them play Twister, with the physical contact that entails, followed by both relief and disappointment when they learned that they would be only metaphorically stretching across the game "mat."

Next Moves

The above examples illustrate a fraction of the possibilities for game-based learning in the popular music classroom. My own background as a composer and songwriter led me to devise games that largely focus on musical details, but any pedagogic goal can be supported through appropriate gameplay. For basic recall of information, the gameplay need not be complex; a simple game of "Bingo" with course information in place of numbers can activate prior knowledge (Weisskirch, 2009). Games can also supply a means of limited role-playing to dramatize aspects of the course material and promote critical thinking (Crocco, 2011).

The backward design model (introduced near the beginning of this essay) provides a systematic method for devising new games for learning, but ideas can also occur fortuitously. That is, in a non-academic social setting, one may encounter an enjoyable game, recognize an aspect of its gameplay that reflects an aspect of some course material, and then custom-tailor an adaptation to that material. The Ordering game described above derives from the commercial game *Chronology* (Buffalo Games, 1997), which I received as a gift years before teaching my first popular music history course. When I discovered the need to sharpen my students' focus on what happened when, the game immediately sprang to mind. Conversely, I only recently discovered the chaotic card game *Fluxx* (Looney Laboratory, 1996); its continual, sudden, drastic changes in the rules of play (including the conditions by which to win the game!) immediately put me in mind of the historic impact of new technologies on markets for popular music (including, but not limited to, the advent of radio, electric microphones, long-playing records, 45 rpm singles, cassette tapes, compact discs, peer-to-peer online sharing, and portable MP3 players—remember those?), as well as the dramatic shifts in popular taste that have periodically redefined the hit parade.

A parodic frame of mind can find possibilities everywhere: A game simulating a zombie invasion, such as *Zombicide* (Guillotine Games, 2012), could be adapted to teach the 1960s "British Invasion"; a game such as Klaus Teuber's *Settlers of Catan* (Mayfair Games, 1996), which simulates building a settlement by acquiring and utilizing a variety of material resources (grain, wood, livestock), could be adapted to simulate building a record label by signing a variety of human resources (producers, songwriters, performers). Ultimately, the broader the spectrum of games familiar to instructors, the more types of gameplay we can apply in our classrooms.

For deep student engagement with the course material, popular music courses still await a month-long role-immersion game on the Reacting to the Past model I mentioned at the start of this essay (Carnes, M.C., 2014). A list of currently published games is available at https://reacting.barnard.edu/curriculum/published-games, and a list of games currently in development is available at https://reacting.barnard.edu/curriculum/games-in-development. As of this writing, none of these games recreates a focal situation in the history of popular music. Nonetheless, interested instructors can view existing materials as models and follow their example in developing a new game, as well as consult the RttP *Game Designer's Handbook* (Proctor, N., 2011) and other guides to better game design (Gunter, Kenny, & Vick, 2008; McCall, 2014; Westera, 2019). One might also consider published suggestions for applying the RttP model to teaching classical music history (Burke, 2014) and then adapt them to popular repertoires.

Whatever the nature of a new game, however modest or grand its scope, instructors must always allow for ample playtesting: no matter how comprehensively you believe you have thought out the possibilities for what could arise during gameplay, in practice your students will find a way to do something else. The need might arise to make the rules stricter, or more relaxed; to frame the game's curricular content more narrowly, or more broadly; to allow student teams more time to formulate a more careful, detailed response, or less time in order to maintain a more active, engaging rhythm of play. Hence another benefit of many short rounds of play over the course of the semester, rather than concentrating all the gameplay in only a few class meetings. Over the course of the term, the game can evolve to suit the needs of both the instructor and that particular cohort of students.

Lastly, I should emphasize the importance of pedagogic transparency. At some point before, or during, or after gameplay (and preferably all three), you should explain to the students exactly why you are playing the game: that is, highlight what the game does that would not be accomplished in a simple lecture. One of my students actually complained in a course evaluation that they thought the class time we spent on games could have been better spent on traditional lectures! In the case of the games presented above, the pedagogic goal of developing mastery requires students to engage in active practice and application; passive listening to a lecture does nothing to advance students' mastery. Likewise, although an instructor could devote a lecture to pointing out connections across units, the students can better organize their knowledge through a rich network of associations by actively seeking such connections, rather than passively receiving them. Most importantly, playing a game several times during the term could inculcate a habit of actively seeking such connections, in all their courses, and thus help students to advance toward the ultimate goal of self-directed learning (Ambrose et al., 2010). Whatever our pedagogical intentions, we need to articulate them explicitly and spell out how the game complements the students' other learning experiences, to counteract the misconception that any break from a traditional lecture format is necessarily a break from learning.

Note: The illustrations that depict student teams around a table are derived from clipart posted by user Piet Luk at www.designdroide.com.

References

Ambrose, S.A., Bridges, M.W., DiPietro, M., Lovett, M.C., & Norman, M.K. (2010). *How learning works: 7 Research-based principles for smart teaching*. San Francisco: Jossey-Bass.

Burke, K.R. (2014). Role-playing music history: Honing general education skills via "Reacting to the Past." *Journal of Music History Pedagogy*, 5(1), 1–21.

Carnes, M.C. (2014). *Minds on Fire: How Role-Immersion Games Transform College*. Cambridge, MA: Harvard U. Press.

Crocco, F. (2011). Critical gaming pedagogy. *The Radical Teacher*, 91, 26–41.

Gareau, S., and Guo, R. (2009). "All work and no play" reconsidered: The use of games to promote motivation and engagement in instruction. *International Journal for the Scholarship of Teaching and Learning*, 3(1). https://doi.org/10.20429/ijsotl.2009.030112

Gunter, G.A., Kenny, R.F., & Vick, E.H. (2008). Taking educational games seriously: Using the RETAIN model to design endogenous fantasy into standalone educational games. *Educational Technology Research & Development*, 56(5/6), 511–537.

McCall, J. (2014). Simulation games and the study of the past: Classroom guidelines. In K.

Kee (Ed.), *Pastplay: Teaching and Learning History with Technology* (pp. 228–253). Ann Arbor: U. of Michigan Press.

Michaelson, L., Knight, A.B., & Fink, L.D. (2004). *Team-based learning: A transformative use of small groups in college teaching.* Sterling, VA: Stylus Publishing.

Popiel, J., Carnes, M.C., & Kates, G. (2015) *Rousseau, Burke, and Revolution in France, 1791* (2nd Ed.). New York: W.W. Norton. Descriptive summary from https://reacting.barnard.edu/node/3166.

Proctor, N. (2011). *Reacting to the past game designer's handbook.* Seattle: Createspace Independent Publishing Platform.

Weisskirch, R.S. (2009). Playing bingo to review fundamental concepts in advanced courses. *International Journal for the Scholarship of Teaching and Learning, 3*(1), article 14. https://doi.org/10.20429/ijsotl.2009.030114.

Westera, W. (2019). Why and how serious games can become far more effective: Accommodating productive learning experiences, learner motivation, and the monitoring of learning games. *International Forum of Educational Technology & Society, 22*(1), 59–69.

Wiggins, G., & McTighe, J. (1998). *Understanding by design.* Alexandria, VA: Association for Supervision & Curriculum Development.

About the Contributors

Raymond **Blanton** (M.Div., Westminster Theological Seminary; Ph.D., University of Nebraska–Lincoln) is an assistant professor of communication arts at the University of the Incarnate Word in San Antonio, Texas.

Ignatius **Calabria** (M.A.T., the University of the Arts–Philadelphia) is a music teacher at Woodland Hill Montessori School in Rensselaer, New York.

Jay Scott **Chipman** (M.A., Louisiana State University–Baton Rouge; Ph.D. University of Pittsburgh) is a professor of communication and theatre arts at Nebraska Wesleyan University in Lincoln, Nebraska.

James L. **Deys** (M.A. and Ph.D., Binghamton University) is an associate professor of English at Nichols College in Dudley, Massachusetts.

Jacob A. **Dickerson** (M.A., University of Colorado; Ph.D., North Carolina State University) is an assistant professor of communication at Berea College in Berea, Kentucky.

Daniel **Guberman** (M.A. and Ph.D., University of North Carolina–Chapel Hill) is a senior instructional developer and musicologist in the Center for Instructional Excellence at Purdue University in West Lafayette, Indiana.

William M. **Knoblauch** (M.A., Northern Arizona University; Ph.D. Ohio University) is an associate professor of history at Finlandia University.

Michael W. **McFarland** (M.A. and Ph.D., Northwestern University) is an associate professor of communication and media studies at Stetson University in DeLand, Florida.

Jeff **Mohr** (M.S.W., University of Kansas) is an associate professor of social work at Nebraska Wesleyan University in Lincoln, Nebraska.

Justin **Patch** (M.M., the Boston Conservatory, M.M. and Ph.D., the University of Texas at Austin) is an assistant professor of music at Vassar College in Poughkeepsie, New York.

Brian **Robison** (D.M.A., Cornell University) is an assistant teaching professor of music at Northeastern University in Boston, Massachusetts.

Eunice **Rojas** (M.A., University of Georgia; Ph.D. University of Virginia) is an associate professor of Spanish and Latin American studies at Furman University in Greenville, South Carolina.

Shawn **Schwaller** (M.A., State University of New York at Buffalo; Ph.D., Claremont Graduate University) is a lecturer in the department of history at California State University, Chico.

Charles R. **Warner** (M.A., Kent State University; Ph.D., Bowling Green State University) is a professor of communication at East Stroudsburg University of Pennsylvania.

David **Whitt** (M.A. and Ph.D., University of Nebraska–Lincoln) is a professor of communication studies at Nebraska Wesleyan University in Lincoln, Nebraska.

Tom **Zlabinger** (M.A., Queens College, CUNY; Ph.D., The Graduate Center, CUNY) is an assistant professor of music at York College, CUNY in Jamaica, New York.

Index

AC/DC 179
activism 21, 137, 146, 147, 149, 152, 156, 158
African diaspora 86, 88, 92
Afro-futurism 92, 97
Alarcón, Rolando 32, 33, 36
Aldean, Jason 209
Allen, Rick 182; see also Def Leppard
Allende, Salvador 32, 33
Altamont Speedway Free Festival (1969) 42–43, 55, 63–64, 68, 69; see also The Rolling Stones
Amnesty International 154; A Conspiracy of Hope Concert 156, 159
Amr, Cherine 188, 189
Analogies (game) 235
The Animals 66, 68, 69
Anthem 187
Apatow, Judd 215
Aphex Twin [Richard D. James] 238
Aspinall, Neil 121
Aung San Suu Kyi 154
authenticity 172–175

Baby Boomers 40, 44, 50, 137
Babylon 75, 79, 82, 96
Backstreet Boys 235
Baez, Joan 18, 20, 42, 57, 68, 69, 137
Bag, Alice 50
Bakersfield Sound 42, 237, 238
The Band 68, 69; see also Dylan, Bob
Band of Gypsys 138; see also Hendrix, Jimi
Batista, Fulgencio 27
Bay of Pigs 110
Bayside Boys 35
The Beach Boys 39, 44, 46, 48, 49, 51, 59, 61, 66, 69
Beat Generation 40, 110
The Beatles 54, 55, 56, 57, 58–59, 62, 63, 66, 69, 78, 107, 116, 135, 136, 226, 233
The Bee Gees 66
Belafante, Harry 77
Bellver, Catherine 24
Benitez, Conrado 28

Bentley, Dierks 211, 220
Berlin, Irving 202; see also Smith, Kate
Berry, Chuck 2, 136
Best, Pete 121; see also The Beatles
Bieber, Justin 35
Big Brother and the Holding Company 40, 61, 66; see also Joplin, Janice
Bikini Kill 170
Bingo (game) 238
Black Lives Matter 93, 203
Black Panthers 41
Black Sabbath 181, 184, 187, 190
Blakey, Art 200–201
Blondie 74, 82, 83
The Blues Project featuring Al Kooper 66
Bon Jovi 179
Bono [Paul Hewson] 4, 146, 148, 149, 150, 152, 154, 156; see also U2
Bonsall, Byron vi
Booker, Cedella 78
Booker T. and the M.G.'s 41, 68
Bowie, David 66, 148, 153, 170, 187
Brenston, Jackie 77
bricolage 154–155
Brown, James 89, 91, 135, 227
Bryan, Luke 209, 211
Buckley, Tim 66
Buffalo Springfield 41, 48, 66
Burke, Kenneth 9
Burnham, Bo 174
Buster, Prince 77, 81
The Byrds 48, 66, 68

Cabuli, Marcelo 183; see also Nightwish
Canned Heat 66, 68, 69
Cannibal Corpse 190
Captain Beefheart 66
Carter, James 14–15
Cash, Johnny 165, 168, 212
Castro, Fidel 27, 28, 31
CBGB (club) 80, 82
Cerebral Bore 185–187, 192
Chandler, Chas 135

245

Chapman, Tracy 133
Chesney, Kenny 211
Chess Records 110
The Chiffons 233
Chirino, Willy 31, 36
Chitlin' Circuit 134, 141
Church, Eric 211
Cinderella 179, 182
Civil Rights Movement (US) 8, 17, 18, 32, 41, 97, 110, 130, 226, 232, 235
Clapton, Eric 69, 79, 136
The Clash 74, 80, 81, 83, 153, 201
Clayton, Adam 146, 150, 156; see also U2
Cliff, Jimmy 79
Clover, Joshua 209, 214, 216
Cobain, Kurt 143–144; see also Nirvana
Cohen, Leonard 66, 68
Cold War 110
Collins, Judy 69
Columbus Day Riot 233
Cooke, Sam 96, 201
Copeland, Stewart 78; see also The Police
Costello, Elvis 82
counterculture 40, 41–43, 46, 48, 49, 59 130, 138, 232
Country Joe and the Fish 42, 66, 68
Countrypolitan 209, 236, 237
Cox, Bill(y) 138; see also Hendrix, Jimi
Cream 66, 69
critical pedagogy 180
Crosby, David 69; see also Crosby, Stills, Nash and Young
Crosby, Stills, Nash and Young 68, 69, 198
The Crystals 233
Cuban Nueva Trova 32
Cuban Revolution 26, 27–29; see also Castro, Fidel
Cusic, Don 212

Daddy Yankee 35
Davis, Angela 94, 95
Davis, Miles 94, 68, 142
The Dead Kennedys 50
Dead Prez 45
Death (band) 190
Def Leppard 182
Dekker, Desmond 77, 79
Dilla, J. [James Dewitt Yancey] 238
Dion and the Belmonts 78
Disco 82, 93, 233
Dr. Dre 50, 51, 95
Donovan 61, 66, 68, 69
Douglas, Alan 144
The Drifters 78
Dylan, Bob 2, 18, 25, 54, 55, 56–57, 59, 64, 66, 69, 135, 137, 198, 201; see also The Band

The Eagles 49, 172
Earthshaker 187

The Ed Sullivan Show 57, 105, 122, 233
Edge [David Evans] 145, 146; see also U2
Egyptian Brotherhood 188
El Chicano 47
Epica 184
Epstein, Brian 121; see also The Beatles
Evans, Mal 121

Fender Stratocaster 131, 138
Ferrer, Pedro Luis 29–30, 32, 36
Figueroa, Joaquín 33, 36
Fluxx (game) 239
Fonsi, Luis 35
Foster, Stephen 165, 168, 169
Franklin, Aretha 91, 97, 227
Free Speech Movement 41
Freire, Paulo 20, 180
Friedan, Betty 232
Funk music 89, 91, 93, 98, 235, 237, 238

game-based learning 222–223, 225
Gangsta rap 50, 236
GarageBand 113, 204
Garcia, Jerry 69; see also The Grateful Dead
Garry, Len 120
Garvey, Marcus 74, 75
Gaye, Marvin 137, 199, 201
gender studies 47, 236
Girlschool 184, 185
The Grateful Dead 40, 43, 54, 58, 61, 63, 66, 68, 69
The Great Kat [Katherine Thomas] 185
Great Migration 135
Green Day 201
Greenfield, Susan 24
Greenwich Village 57, 135
Guerrero, Lalo 46, 48
Guevara, Ernesto "Che" 28
Guns N' Roses 182
Guthrie, Arlo 66, 68
Guthrie, Woody 18, 201–202

Haight-Ashbury 42, 43
Halford, Rob 186–187; see also Judas Priest
Hall, Stuart 87
Harlem 134–135, 139
Harrison, George 116, 120, 121, 123; see also The Beatles
Hart, Mickey 69; see also The Grateful Dead
Harvey, P[olly] J[ean] 233
Hatebeak 180
Havens, Richie 68, 69
Hawkins, Screamin' Jay 170
Hayes, Isaac 45
Heavy metal (genres): black 180, 191; death 180, 191; doom 179; Finnish 183; glam 179, 182; Japanese (Visual kei) 182, 187, 189; sludge 179; symphonic 183
Hendrix, Jimi 41, 42, 54, 61, 62, 63, 66, 68, 69, 70, 89, 91, 93, 129

Hietala, Marco 183; see also Nightwish
Holiday, Billie 200, 201
Holopainen, Tuomas 183, 184; see also Nightwish
Holt, Peter 82
hooks, bell 180
Homer: *The Odyssey* 9, 15
House, Son 17
Howard, Ron 116
Hudson, Jennifer 90, 198
Human Be-In (1967) 40

Ice Cube 50, 51, 95
Iglesias, Enrique 35
Inti-Illimani 32
Iraq War 203, 235
Iron Butterfly 69
Isbell, Jason 165, 166
Isle of Wight (England) 55, 63, 64, 68, 69

Jackson, Michael 83, 90, 132
Jagger, Mick 43, 61, 136; see also The Rolling Stones
Jah 75
Jan and Dean 44
Jara, Victor 32, 33, 34, 36
Jazz music 19, 46, 76, 77, 86, 87, 90, 91, 98, 130, 133, 137, 172, 195, 200, 201
Jefferson Airplane 40, 53, 58, 61, 62, 63, 66, 68, 69
Jeter, Lucille 131
John, Elton 163
Johnson, Robert 12, 140
Jones, Gordon vi
Joplin, Janice 40, 41, 42, 61, 63, 66, 68; see also Big Brother and the Holding Company
Jubilee 2000 152
Judas Priest 181, 182, 185, 186–187; see also Halford, Rob

K-Pop 192
Kaye, Lenny 79
Kent State University 198, see also Crosby, Stills, Nash and Young
Kerouac, Jack 57
Kesey, Ken 54, 57, 58, 62, 63
King, Albert 45
King, B.B. 110
King, Ben E. 78
King, Carole 48, 233
King, Martin Luther, Jr. 18, 46, 57, 197
The Kingsmen 79
The Kinks 67, 70
Kirchner, Astrid 121; see also The Beatles
Kirk, Rahsaan Roland 135
Klein, Naomi 232
Kooper, Al 66, 68, 70; see also The Blues Project
Krupa, Gene 76

Lady Gaga [Stefani Germanotta] 233
Lamar, Kendrick 21, 86, 173
Lanz, Therese 191
La Santa Cecilia 47
Latin American New Song Movement 26
Leary, Timothy 55, 60
Led Zeppelin 79, 172, 179, 182
leitourgia 153–155
Lennon, John 55, 63, 69, 116, 131, 186; see also The Beatles
Lesh, Phil 65, 69; see also The Grateful Dead
Lester, Richard 119; see also The Beatles
Letts, Don 80–81
Lincoln, Abraham 33, 36
Lipsitz, George 38, 40, 50
Little Richard 2, 91, 94, 97, 107, 110
Live Aid (1985) 151–152, 156, 159
Los Aldeanos 31, 36
Los Del Rio 35
Los Lobos 47
Loudness 187
Love, Robert 75
The Lovin' Spoonful 66
LSD (lysergic acid diethylamide) 40, 54, 55, 56, 57, 58, 60; see also Psychedelia/Psychedelic

Madness (band) 81
Madonna [Ciccone] 139, 233
The Mamas and the Papas 39, 43, 44, 45, 46, 49, 67, 137
Mandela, Nelson 153
Manns, Patricio 32, 36
March for Our Lives 198
Mares of Thrace 191
Marley, Bob 77, 78, 81, 82, 83, 93, 97; see also The Wailers
Martin, George 57, 58, 121, 122, 124; see also The Beatles
Martin, Ricky 35
Masakela, Hugh 61, 62
Massive Scar Era 188
Mau Mau Uprising 201
Maytals 79
McCarthyism 110
McCartney, Paul 61, 69, 116, 120, 136, 137; see also The Beatles
McGraw, Tim 211
McGuire, Barry 201
McKenzie, Scott 61, 66, 68
McLaren, Malcolm 80, 83; see also The Sex Pistols
Megadeath 186
melisma 226–228
The Melodians 79
Mento 73, 75, 76, 77
Metallica 181, 190
M.I.A. [Mathangi "Maya" Arulpragasam] 200
Mickichan, Stefani 191

248 Index

Milanés, Pablo 28, 36
Miles, Buddy 138
The Milton Berle Show 105
Minaj, Nikki 170
Mitchell, John "Mitch" 70, 138, 139, 141; *see also* Hendrix, Jimi
Mitchell, Joni 48, 64, 68, 69, 70
Moby 19
Moby Grape 61, 66
The Modern Jazz Quartet 201
Monae, Janelle 87, 88–90
The Monkees 2, 67, 70
Monterey International Pop Festival (1967) 39, 41, 43, 55, 61, 62, 63, 65, 68, 69, 130, 136, 137, 138
The Moody Blues 67
Morrison, Van 67
Motörhead 185, 187
Motown 61, 93, 135, 199
Mullen, Larry, Jr. 146, 150; *see also* U2
Murvin, Junior 81
Musgraves, Kasey 209
Music Rising 152
Music Television (MTV) 2, 50, 73, 81, 82, 83, 146, 150
MusiCares 156

Nash, Graham 69; *see also* Crosby, Stills, Nash and Young
Nash, Johnny 77
Neruda, Pablo 33
Nevalainen, Jukka 183; *see also* Nightwish
New Wave music 72, 73, 81, 82, 83
New York Dolls 80
Newport Folk Festival 57, 59
Nico 67; *see also* The Velvet Underground
Nightwish 183, 184, 185
Nirvana 170, 172, 231, 235
Notorious B.I.G. [Christopher Wallace] 19
*NSYNC 235
Nugent, Ted 163
N.W.A. 39, 50–51, 137, 173

O Brother, Where Art Thou? (film) 15
Obsesión 31–32, 36
Ochs, Phil 199
Olzon, Anette 183, 184; *see also* Nightwish
ONE Campaign 154
Ono, Yoko 118
Orishas 30, 36
Osbourne, Ozzy 184; *see also* Black Sabbath
Ozomatli 47

Parra, Angel 33, 36
Parra, Isabel 32, 36
Parra, Violeta 32, 36
Parton, Dolly 168
Paul, Les 142, 231
The Paul Butterfield Blues Band 66, 68
Pearlman, Lou 235

Penderecki, Krystof 192
A Perfect Circle 186
Perkins, Carl 91, 107
Perry, Katy 209
Perry, Lee "Scratch" 170
Peter, Paul and Mary 67, 70
Pickett, Wilson 135
Pink Floyd 54, 67, 70, 79
The Platters 78
Po' Lazarus 14, 15
Poison (band) 179
The Police 78, 82, 83, 146; *see also* Copeland, Stewart; Sting
Presley, Elvis 2, 91, 103, 170
The Pretenders 82
Primera Base 31, 36
Procol Harum 67
Progressive rock 79, 82, 236, 237
Psychedelia/Psychedelic 40, 53, 91, 217; *see also* LSD
Public Enemy 45, 201
Puebla, Carlos 27, 36
Punk music 26, 49, 50, 73, 79, 80–83, 171, 201, 222, 230

The Quarrymen 120; *see also* The Beatles
Queen 231
Quetzal 47
Quilapayún 32

The Ramones 80, 82, 148, 153
Rap music 167, 173
Rastafarianism 75, 79
Red Rocks Amphitheatre 150, 152, 159, 160; *see also* U2
Redding, Noel 70, 139, 141; *see also* Hendrix, Jimi
Redding, Otis 41, 61, 68
rhetorical criticism 196
Rhumba box 76
Rice, Chase 220
Rich, Buddy 76
Richman, Jonathan 80
Robertson, Robbie 69; *see also* The Band; Dylan, Bob
Rodriguez, Silvio 28, 36
The Rolling Stones 42, 43, 61, 63, 67, 70, 78, 107, 135, 136, 139
The Ronettes 233
The Roxy (club) 80
Rush 82

Saborit, Eduardo 28, 36
Santana, Carlos 40, 68, 70
Saturday Night Fever (film) 233
Saxon 187
Scott-Heron, Gil 201
Seeger, Pete 201
Selassie, Haile 75
Settlers of Catan (game) 239

The Sex Pistols 80, 83, 201
Shakira 35
Shakur, Tupac 172, 173
Shankar, Ravi 61, 68
Shaw, Caroline 192
Shelton, Blake 209
Sigh 189
Simeon, Paul 80; *see also* The Clash
Simon and Garfunkel 62, 68, 69
Simone, Nina 91, 97, 201
Simpson, Jessica 186
Simpson, Sturgill 217
Sinatra, Frank 2, 42, 150, 233
Sinatra, Nancy 45
Ska music 51, 73, 75, 76, 77, 81, 82, 83
Skehill, Michael 211
Slayer 179
Sly and the Family Stone 45, 66, 68
Smith, Kate 202
Snoop Dogg 51
Som [Simone Pluijmers] 185–186; *see also* Cerebral Bore
Southern, Eileen 85
The Specials 81, 83
Spector, Phil 233
Springsteen, Bruce 137, 194–195
The Staple Singers 45
Starr, Ringo [Richard Starkey] 120, 125; *see also* The Beatles
Stax Records 45
The Steve Allen Show 105
Steve Miller Band 40
Sting [Gordon Sumner] 82; *see also* The Police
Strawberry Alarm Clock 67
Subverso 33, 34, 36
"Summer of Love" (1967) 40, 57, 61, 64, 65, 130, 138
Sun Records 105

Talking Heads 82
The Temptations 135
Ten Years After 67, 68
Theatre of Tragedy 184
The 13th Floor Elevators 66, 79
Thomas, Rufus 45
Thornton, Willie Mae "Big Mama" 110
Tierra 47
Tijoux, Ana 34, 36

Tosh, Peter 78
Tosti, Don 46, 47
Traffic 67
Turunen, Tarja 183–184; *see also* Nightwish
12-bar blues 132, 133, 140, 143
Twisted Sister 187
Twitter 189

U2 137, 139, 145, 146
UB40 81
Urban, Keith 212

Valens, Ritchie 46–47
Van Halen 145
Vanilla Fudge 67
Vaughan, Stevie Ray 142, 143
The Velvet Underground 67
Versailles (band) 187
Vietnam War 40, 137, 142, 199, 232, 235
Vixen 184

The Wailers 74, 78; *see also* Marley, Bob
Walker, T-Bone 132
Warren G. 51
Waters, Muddy 12, 13, 132, 136, 143
Wattstax 45
Weston, Kim 45
Whitman, Walt 11
The Who 41, 61, 62, 67, 68, 70, 136,
Williams, Hank 210, 212
Within Temptation 184
Wolf, Howlin' 136, 140, 181
Wolfe, Tom 56; *see also* Kesey, Ken
Woodstock Festival (1969) 2, 42, 63, 68, 69, 130, 138, 144, 233
Woolf, Virginia 232
Work, John 12

X (band) 50
X Japan 187

The Yardbirds 67, 136
Young, Neil 21, 48–49, 69, 198, 199; *see also* Crosby, Stills, Nash and Young
Yupanqui, Atahualpa 33

Zappa, Frank 59, 67, 70, 172
Zion 75, 79, 82
Zombicide (game) 239

Index 247

Hietala, Marco 183; *see also* Nightwish
Holiday, Billie 200, 201
Holopainen, Tuomas 183, 184; *see also* Nightwish
Holt, Peter 82
hooks, bell 180
Homer: *The Odyssey* 9, 15
House, Son 17
Howard, Ron 116
Hudson, Jennifer 90, 198
Human Be-In (1967) 40

Ice Cube 50, 51, 95
Iglesias, Enrique 35
Inti-Illimani 32
Iraq War 203, 235
Iron Butterfly 69
Isbell, Jason 165, 166
Isle of Wight (England) 55, 63, 64, 68, 69

Jackson, Michael 83, 90, 132
Jagger, Mick 43, 61, 136; *see also* The Rolling Stones
Jah 75
Jan and Dean 44
Jara, Victor 32, 33, 34, 36
Jazz music 19, 46, 76, 77, 86, 87, 90, 91, 98, 130, 133, 137, 172, 195, 200, 201
Jefferson Airplane 40, 53, 58, 61, 62, 63, 66, 68, 69
Jeter, Lucille 131
John, Elton 163
Johnson, Robert 12, 140
Jones, Gordon vi
Joplin, Janice 40, 41, 42, 61, 63, 66, 68; *see also* Big Brother and the Holding Company
Jubilee 2000 152
Judas Priest 181, 182, 185, 186–187; *see also* Halford, Rob

K-Pop 192
Kaye, Lenny 79
Kent State University 198, *see also* Crosby, Stills, Nash and Young
Kerouac, Jack 57
Kesey, Ken 54, 57, 58, 62, 63
King, Albert 45
King, B.B. 110
King, Ben E. 78
King, Carole 48, 233
King, Martin Luther, Jr. 18, 46, 57, 197
The Kingsmen 79
The Kinks 67, 70
Kirchner, Astrid 121; *see also* The Beatles
Kirk, Rahsaan Roland 135
Klein, Naomi 232
Kooper, Al 66, 68, 70; *see also* The Blues Project
Krupa, Gene 76

Lady Gaga [Stefani Germanotta] 233
Lamar, Kendrick 21, 86, 173
Lanz, Therese 191
La Santa Cecilia 47
Latin American New Song Movement 26
Leary, Timothy 55, 60
Led Zeppelin 79, 172, 179, 182
leitourgia 153–155
Lennon, John 55, 63, 69, 116, 131, 186; *see also* The Beatles
Lesh, Phil 65, 69; *see also* The Grateful Dead
Lester, Richard 119; *see also* The Beatles
Letts, Don 80–81
Lincoln, Abraham 33, 36
Lipsitz, George 38, 40, 50
Little Richard 2, 91, 94, 97, 107, 110
Live Aid (1985) 151–152, 156, 159
Los Aldeanos 31, 36
Los Del Rio 35
Los Lobos 47
Loudness 187
Love, Robert 75
The Lovin' Spoonful 66
LSD (lysergic acid diethylamide) 40, 54, 55, 56, 57, 58, 60; *see also* Psychedelia/Psychedelic

Madness (band) 81
Madonna [Ciccone] 139, 233
The Mamas and the Papas 39, 43, 44, 45, 46, 49, 67, 137
Mandela, Nelson 153
Manns, Patricio 32, 36
March for Our Lives 198
Mares of Thrace 191
Marley, Bob 77, 78, 81, 82, 83, 93, 97; *see also* The Wailers
Martin, George 57, 58, 121, 122, 124; *see also* The Beatles
Martin, Ricky 35
Masakela, Hugh 61, 62
Massive Scar Era 188
Mau Mau Uprising 201
Maytals 79
McCarthyism 110
McCartney, Paul 61, 69, 116, 120, 136, 137; *see also* The Beatles
McGraw, Tim 211
McGuire, Barry 201
McKenzie, Scott 61, 66, 68
McLaren, Malcolm 80, 83; *see also* The Sex Pistols
Megadeath 186
melisma 226–228
The Melodians 79
Mento 73, 75, 76, 77
Metallica 181, 190
M.I.A. [Mathangi "Maya" Arulpragasam] 200
Mickichan, Stefani 191

Milanés, Pablo 28, 36
Miles, Buddy 138
The Milton Berle Show 105
Minaj, Nikki 170
Mitchell, John "Mitch" 70, 138, 139, 141; *see also* Hendrix, Jimi
Mitchell, Joni 48, 64, 68, 69, 70
Moby 19
Moby Grape 61, 66
The Modern Jazz Quartet 201
Monae, Janelle 87, 88–90
The Monkees 2, 67, 70
Monterey International Pop Festival (1967) 39, 41, 43, 55, 61, 62, 63, 65, 68, 69, 130, 136, 137, 138
The Moody Blues 67
Morrison, Van 67
Motörhead 185, 187
Motown 61, 93, 135, 199
Mullen, Larry, Jr. 146, 150; *see also* U2
Murvin, Junior 81
Musgraves, Kasey 209
Music Rising 152
Music Television (MTV) 2, 50, 73, 81, 82, 83, 146, 150
MusiCares 156

Nash, Graham 69; *see also* Crosby, Stills, Nash and Young
Nash, Johnny 77
Neruda, Pablo 33
Nevalainen, Jukka 183; *see also* Nightwish
New Wave music 72, 73, 81, 82, 83
New York Dolls 80
Newport Folk Festival 57, 59
Nico 67; *see also* The Velvet Underground
Nightwish 183, 184, 185
Nirvana 170, 172, 231, 235
Notorious B.I.G. [Christopher Wallace] 19
*NSYNC 235
Nugent, Ted 163
N.W.A. 39, 50–51, 137, 173

O Brother, Where Art Thou? (film) 15
Obsesión 31–32, 36
Ochs, Phil 199
Olzon, Anette 183, 184; *see also* Nightwish
ONE Campaign 154
Ono, Yoko 118
Orishas 30, 36
Osbourne, Ozzy 184; *see also* Black Sabbath
Ozomatli 47

Parra, Angel 33, 36
Parra, Isabel 32, 36
Parra, Violeta 32, 36
Parton, Dolly 168
Paul, Les 142, 231
The Paul Butterfield Blues Band 66, 68
Pearlman, Lou 235

Penderecki, Krystof 192
A Perfect Circle 186
Perkins, Carl 91, 107
Perry, Katy 209
Perry, Lee "Scratch" 170
Peter, Paul and Mary 67, 70
Pickett, Wilson 135
Pink Floyd 54, 67, 70, 79
The Platters 78
Po' Lazarus 14, 15
Poison (band) 179
The Police 78, 82, 83, 146; *see also* Copeland, Stewart; Sting
Presley, Elvis 2, 91, 103, 170
The Pretenders 82
Primera Base 31, 36
Procol Harum 67
Progressive rock 79, 82, 236, 237
Psychedelia/Psychedelic 40, 53, 91, 217; *see also* LSD
Public Enemy 45, 201
Puebla, Carlos 27, 36
Punk music 26, 49, 50, 73, 79, 80–83, 171, 201, 222, 230

The Quarrymen 120; *see also* The Beatles
Queen 231
Quetzal 47
Quilapayún 32

The Ramones 80, 82, 148, 153
Rap music 167, 173
Rastafarianism 75, 79
Red Rocks Amphitheatre 150, 152, 159, 160; *see also* U2
Redding, Noel 70, 139, 141; *see also* Hendrix, Jimi
Redding, Otis 41, 61, 68
rhetorical criticism 196
Rhumba box 76
Rice, Chase 220
Rich, Buddy 76
Richman, Jonathan 80
Robertson, Robbie 69; *see also* The Band; Dylan, Bob
Rodriguez, Silvio 28, 36
The Rolling Stones 42, 43, 61, 63, 67, 70, 78, 107, 135, 136, 139
The Ronettes 233
The Roxy (club) 80
Rush 82

Saborit, Eduardo 28, 36
Santana, Carlos 40, 68, 70
Saturday Night Fever (film) 233
Saxon 187
Scott-Heron, Gil 201
Seeger, Pete 201
Selassie, Haile 75
Settlers of Catan (game) 239

Index

The Sex Pistols 80, 83, 201
Shakira 35
Shakur, Tupac 172, 173
Shankar, Ravi 61, 68
Shaw, Caroline 192
Shelton, Blake 209
Sigh 189
Simeon, Paul 80; *see also* The Clash
Simon and Garfunkel 62, 68, 69
Simone, Nina 91, 97, 201
Simpson, Jessica 186
Simpson, Sturgill 217
Sinatra, Frank 2, 42, 150, 233
Sinatra, Nancy 186
Ska music 51, 73, 75, 76, 77, 81, 82, 83
Skehill, Michael 211
Slayer 179
Sly and the Family Stone 45, 66, 68
Smith, Kate 202
Snoop Dogg 51
Som [Simone Pluijmers] 185–186; *see also* Cerebral Bore
Southern, Eileen 85
The Specials 81, 83
Spector, Phil 233
Springsteen, Bruce 137, 194–195
The Staple Singers 45
Starr, Ringo [Richard Starkey] 120, 125; *see also* The Beatles
Stax Records 45
The Steve Allen Show 105
Steve Miller Band 40
Sting [Gordon Sumner] 82; *see also* The Police
Strawberry Alarm Clock 67
Subverso 33, 34, 36
"Summer of Love" (1967) 40, 57, 61, 64, 65, 130, 138
Sun Records 105

Talking Heads 82
The Temptations 135
Ten Years After 67, 68
Theatre of Tragedy 184
The 13th Floor Elevators 66, 79
Thomas, Rufus 45
Thornton, Willie Mae "Big Mama" 110
Tierra 47
Tijoux, Ana 34, 36

Tosh, Peter 78
Tosti, Don 46, 47
Traffic 67
Turunen, Tarja 183–184; *see also* Nightwish
12-bar blues 132, 133, 140, 143
Twisted Sister 187
Twitter 189

U2 137, 139, 145, 146
UB40 81
Urban, Keith 212

Valens, Ritchie 46–47
Van Halen 145
Vanilla Fudge 67
Vaughan, Stevie Ray 142, 143
The Velvet Underground 67
Versailles (band) 187
Vietnam War 40, 137, 142, 199, 232, 235
Vixen 184

The Wailers 74, 78; *see also* Marley, Bob
Walker, T-Bone 132
Warren G. 51
Waters, Muddy 12, 13, 132, 136, 143
Wattstax 45
Weston, Kim 45
Whitman, Walt 11
The Who 41, 61, 62, 67, 68, 70, 136,
Williams, Hank 210, 212
Within Temptation 184
Wolf, Howlin' 136, 140, 181
Wolfe, Tom 56; *see also* Kesey, Ken
Woodstock Festival (1969) 2, 42, 63, 68, 69, 130, 138, 144, 233
Woolf, Virginia 232
Work, John 12

X (band) 50
X Japan 187

The Yardbirds 67, 136
Young, Neil 21, 48–49, 69, 198, 199; *see also* Crosby, Stills, Nash and Young
Yupanqui, Atahualpa 33

Zappa, Frank 59, 67, 70, 172
Zion 75, 79, 82
Zombicide (game) 239